C000165530

ORGANIZING AND
ORGANIZATIONS

ORGANIZING AND ORGANIZATIONS

AN INTRODUCTION

DAVID SIMS ▪ **STEPHEN FINEMAN** ▪ **YIANNIS GABRIEL**

SAGE Publications
London • Newbury Park •New Delhi

© David Sims, Stephen Fineman and Yiannis Gabriel,
1993

First published 1993

All rights reserved. No part of this publication may be
reproduced, stored in a retrieval system, transmitted or
utilized in any form or by any means, electronic,
mechanical, photocopying, recording or otherwise,
without permission in writing from the Publishers.

SAGE Publications Ltd
6 Bonhill Street
London EC2A 4PU

SAGE Publications Inc
2455 Teller Road
Newbury Park, California 91320

SAGE Publications India Pvt Ltd
32, M-Block Market
Greater Kailash–I
New Delhi 110 048

British Library Cataloguing in Publication data

Sims, David
  Organizing and Organizations: Introduction
  I. Title
  302.3

ISBN 0–8039–8702–1
ISBN 0–8039–8703–X (pbk)

Library of Congress catalog card number 93–084578

Typeset by Photoprint, Torquay, Devon
Printed in Great Britain by The Cromwell Press Ltd,
Broughton Gifford, Melksham, Wiltshire

CONTENTS

PREFACE

Over the years we have tried to convey to our students something of the excitement and mystery of life in organizations – with the aid of one or more textbooks. But often the neat (and usually similar) topic headings have left us feeling dissatisfied. Typical of our students' comments are:

– 'Yes, but when I worked in my uncle's shop it was nothing like that.'

– 'These books don't tell you what working really *feels* like.'

– 'It all reads so rationally – can it really be like that?'

– 'They don't say much about the life you bring with you into the organization – like that row, or busting up with your boyfriend.'

There is a gulf between the lived experience of organizing and being organized by others, with its uncertainty and confusion, and the tidy, rather sanitized, texts on organizational behaviour. In this book we attempt to bridge this gulf.

We have done this in three ways. Firstly, we have written chapters which reflect live issues and activities of organizational life. We could have added many more if we had the space. After the introductory chapter, you can start reading any chapter that catches your interest; they are not sequenced or divided according to conventional textbook topics.

Secondly, our narrative is often based on stories told by, or about, organizational members. This includes the work experiences of our students and ourselves, our research in organizations, and what managers and working people of all sorts have related to us. These are knitted together with plain-speaking accounts of some of the key concepts in the study of organizations.

Finally, to enhance the accessibility of the book, we have avoided the usual reference formats and extensive citations of research studies. However, research underpins all of our endeavours, and references to many studies may be found, in user-friendly form, in the thesaurus at the end of the book.

This book is the product of a truly co-operative effort – so much so that we had to toss a coin to decide the order of authors on the front cover. Initially, we divided the chapters equally between us, but thereafter it was a group activity. We discussed and argued each chapter, and shared re-writes. A valuable part of this process was a consumer test on our own undergraduate students – who spotted things we missed and relished 'marking' the work of their lecturers. We are grateful to our colleague Ian Colville, nearly a fourth author. Ian played a key role in the inception of this work, but unfortunately had to withdraw because of other commitments. We also want to thank Sue Jones, of Sage Publications, whose exceptional drive, encouragement and critical feedback were a valuable source of support. And finally, the fine-tuning of the book was enhanced by the very helpful comments of Craig Lundberg, Barbara Czarniawska-Joerges and Barry Turner.

Any book reflects the backgrounds and partialities of its authors, and this one is no exception. We have taught courses on organizations and organizational behaviour for many years, and share the joys and tribulations of teaching both undergraduates and postgraduates at several universities. Together, we bring teaching, research and consultancy backgrounds in psychology, sociology and management to our courses – and to this book.

Yiannis Gabriel
Stephen Fineman
David Sims

Bath, 1993

HOW TO USE THIS BOOK

Unlike most books on organizations, which are structured in a sequence (the individual, the group, the organization), you may think of this book as a wheel. The introduction and conclusion is the centre, Chapters 2–17 are the spokes, and the Thesaurus is the rim. We invite you to move from section to section as your fancy takes you – but please read the introduction, Chapter 1, first. We also offer a table of common organizational topics and our chapter headings (on p. x–xi). With this you can locate directly which chapters to turn to if you want information on a more conventional organizational behaviour topic (perhaps 'change', 'motivation', 'personality').

Theories provide and clarify many of the concepts used in discussing the experiences of organizing. Such concepts are flagged in the text through the use of **bold** print and can be studied in the Thesaurus, which covers much of the material you will find in other textbooks. Thesaurus entries are listed at the end of each chapter, and are cross-referenced in the Thesaurus itself to enable you to study whole clusters of inter-related concepts. The match between a bold word in a chapter and an entry in the Thesaurus is not always perfect. For example, 'bureaucratic' and 'unemployed' are not in the thesaurus, but 'bureaucracy' and 'unemployment' are.

We would regard our effort as successful if, as you read this book, you begin to see organizations in a different light; things which might have escaped your attention in the past may suddenly become full of meaning; things which you may have taken for granted in the past may begin to look rather less solid. In doing so, you can share some of the pleasure and excitement which we experienced in planning and writing this book.

TRADITIONAL TOPICS: WHERE TO FIND THEM

In the following table, we cross-reference some of the chapter headings found in many textbooks with the chapter headings we have used. We give two ticks where there is a strong connexion between the topic and our chapter, and one where there is a noticeable but less strong connexion.

For example, if you are looking for something on motivation, you will see that some of our chapters have two ticks on motivation, and so these are the most promising places to start, after the Thesaurus, of course. Depending on the aspect of motivation that you wish to know about, you may alternatively find what you need in one of the chapters with only one tick.

The table may also be used in the other direction. If you have read our chapter on, for example, 'Working and living', you might want to read more. You can find out where else to go partly by following up Thesaurus entries, but also the table will show you the most likely headings under which to find more on the same topic in other textbooks.

Chapter headings in this book ◊

Traditional topics →

Traditional topics	2 Entering and Leaving	3 Rules are Rules	4 Dealing and Double-Dealing	5 Morals	6 It's Not My Problem	7 Knowing the Ropes	8 Machines and Mechanizing	9 Leading and Following	10 Judging Others	11 Feelings	12 Sex	13 Serious Joking	14 Us and Them	15 Looking Outward	16 Career-ing	17 Working and Living
Change	√√					√√	√√						√√	√√		
Communication		√√			√	√	√						√	√		
Conflict	√	√√	√	√	√	√	√	√		√	√	√			√	
Control	√	√√	√		√√	√√	√	√	√	√√	√	√				
Culture (Organizational)	√	√		√√	√√	√√	√	√	√		√√	√√		√		
Decision-Making	√	√	√√	√			√√						√√	√√		
Environment	√												√√		√	
Ethics		√√				√	√	√	√	√√			√			
Gender	√		√					√√	√√	√√	√		√	√		
Group			√	√	√	√	√	√	√√	√	√√	√√				
Leadership				√	√√	√√	√	√	√		√	√	√	√		
Learning	√√	√	√	√	√√	√	√		√	√		√				
Motivation	√√								√						√√	√√
Organizational Structure	√√					√		√					√			
Perception (Social)	√			√√	√		√√	√√	√				√	√		
Personality	√						√√	√√	√	√					√	
Power and Politics	√	√√				√	√	√		√				√	√	
Technology	√	√					√√						√	√		

1

ORGANIZATION AND ORGANIZING

What is an organization? Everyone knows: universities, airlines, chemical plants, supermarkets, government departments. These are all organizations. Some have been around for a long time, employing numerous people across many continents – Shell, IBM, McDonald's, Toyota. Others are smaller, locally based – a school, a family-owned restaurant, a small law firm, a pottery.

Organizations enter our lives in different ways: we work for them, we consume their products, we see buildings which house their offices, we read about them in the newspapers and absorb their advertisements. When we look at organizations, especially the larger, older, famous ones, they seem *solid*, they seem *permanent*, they seem *orderly*. This is, after all, why we call them organizations. Images of organizations as solid, permanent, orderly entities run through many textbooks. But, in our view, they only tell half the story. They obscure the other half: the chaos which looms behind the order, surfacing from time to time, such as when computer systems break down, when products are sent to the wrong destinations or when bookings are made for the wrong dates. They also obscure the immense human efforts and energies which go into keeping organizations solid and orderly.

In this book, we shift the focus from 'organization' to 'organizing'; from the product to the processes which make the product possible. We do not take organization for granted; after all, many large and well-known organizations have faded or died for one reason or another. Instead we focus on the *processes* of organizing and being organized. We highlight the *activities* which go on in organizations. We look at our emotions, the stories and gossip which we trade, the deals we strike, the games we play and the moral dilemmas we face when in organizations.

Organizations get likened to many things – machines, armies, rubbish bins, theatrical plays, the human body, and so on – there is even a 'garbage can' model. We find the analogy of a river helpful. Like a river, an organization may appear static, especially if viewed on a map or from a helicopter. But this says little about those who are actually in the *moving* river, whether swimming, drowning or safely ensconced in boats. Our aim in this book is to highlight the experiences of those people who actually know and understand the river well, to present their stories and learn from their adventures. We are hoping that the images of organization which we generate have more in common with the moving, changing, living river than the tidy lines of a map.

ORGANIZING – WORKING AGAINST DISORDER

Whether we plan our summer holidays, tidy up our desks or think of launching a new business, we organize. In this book, organizing is treated as a continuous set of activities. We often sense that to relax on the organizing will quickly result in chaos. In our homes, as soon as we stop tidying up, things start to go missing. At our desks, as soon as we stop filing our papers, they spread all over the place and work life becomes that much more difficult. Not all of us find organizing easy or agreeable. This is how one of the authors described his 'typical day':

> Getting organized is something that I don't find easy. While some have a natural flair for organizing, some of us do not. I have in front of me a book called *Get Yourself Organized* offered by a friend, who was perhaps trying to give me a hint. It looks appealing; it looks sensible. It is written in clear type, with a bold 'key message' printed on every other page:
>
> – DECIDE ON YOUR MAJOR PRIORITIES.
> – PUT A TIME-SCALE AND DEADLINE ON EACH PRIORITY.
> – IF YOU CAN DO IT TODAY, DO IT!
> – WHO DO YOU NEED TO CONTACT TO MAKE THINGS HAPPEN?
> – INTERRUPTIONS – AVOID THEM!
> – AT THE END OF THE DAY LEAVE YOUR DESK CLEAR.
>
> Well. . . . let me tell you how things worked out the other day:
>   I arrived at work and was faced with a formidable pile of papers. I began to sort them. The phone rang – a student was unable to keep an

appointment with me – could I give him another date? Just as I put the phone down, it rang again. The internal auditor wanted to see my new portable tape recorder, of all things. I think he suspects I have sold it, or something. I went for a quick cup of coffee and then had another crack at the three 'very urgent' things on my desk.

One hour later and things were looking a bit better; I was getting on top of the day at last. Anna, a colleague, knocked on my door; she was 'just passing', she said. Well, I like Anna, so we had a bit of a chat and sorted out a teaching schedule – while moaning about the incompetence of the University administration.

I had twelve identical letters to send – with different addresses on them. I wanted Helen, our Departmental secretary, to do them for me. When she is busy I have to go carefully, not to upset her. I did a quick reconnoitre of her office before taking the plunge.

I wrote a whole page of a new article. Not much, but **real** progress at last! I felt I was doing some substantial work – what I really wanted to do at 9.00 a.m.; it was then about 11.45. I felt good, and then . . . another knock on the door. A sort of shy knock. I felt irritated at the interruption, and barked sharply at the visitor.

Estelle, a quiet second-year student, entered looking pale, with barely concealed tears in her eyes. I immediately felt guilty for my brusque reaction. I asked her to sit down and began to ease my way into her world. An hour and a half later she was still with me, and the room was filled with her distress. She was having chronic difficulties with her studies, and her private life. She left looking a little brighter, and I made sure I was available to see her again the next day. I was exhausted – but never mind my article, Estelle's well-being is more important.

At 4 o'clock we had a Departmental meeting – chaired as usual by Joe (Head of Department). It was about the appointment of a new professor, in 'international management'. Joe outlined the case, and his personal enthusiasm for the appointment. He then opened up the meeting for general discussion. Silence. I have never quite under-stood why this particular appointment should suddenly be more important than others we have been pressing for years. I sensed the unease in the room. Shared glances seem to reinforce a kind of solidarity against the move. Alan, my neighbour, scribbled a note and passed it to me. It read, 'Does it really matter what we think?' Joe tried again. 'Do I take it that there are no strong objections?' Of course there were, but what was the point? A fairly muted discussion followed and each objection raised was met with long response from Joe pointing out how misguided we were. It was management by attrition.

The meeting broke up at 5.15; people looked sullen. I went back to my office, collecting my mail en route. One nice letter from a colleague in Manchester, and a flattering letter from a student in California. They brought some sunshine to the end of the day. The three internal memos looked boring; two of them I ignored.

AT THE END OF THE DAY LEAVE YOUR DESK CLEAR, says the book.

They must be joking!

Most people in organizations have a lively sense of the chaos or potential chaos that surrounds them. Almost everyone can give you a story of the disorder in their organization. They tell of the company that ordered 100 times as much paper as was needed, the computer error that paid everyone the wrong salary, the boss who promoted the wrong person, the meeting which never happened, the expensive marble staircase that was built when the organization was running short of cash, and the new set of office furniture which arrived in head office the week one hundred people were made redundant. When you hear of these things you get a sense of what is meant by 'organizing'. Whatever it is, in these cases it has not been done, or at least not properly.

ON STAGE AND BEHIND THE SCENES

The process of organizing defies tidy, universal, categories. Most of the time, we take it for granted that things will get done. Lectures, meetings, examinations, happen. Individual and group effort come together to create the hard product – the car, hi fi, vacuum cleaner, pen, paper; or the service – delivering a meal, cutting hair, preaching a sermon, policing a city, running a train. We hardly bother with the organizing processes behind these events. The struggles, politics, negotiations, anguish and joys of actual organizing remain, for the most part, invisible to the 'consumer'; they are back stage. When they are inadvertently revealed, showing how precarious organization can be, it can come as something of a shock – as the following tale from of one us reveals:

Once I was booking tickets for a European rail holiday at a local, family-run, travel agent. They were busy, and I queued for a long time. Eventually I was served by an elderly gentleman who fumbled with a weighty European Rail Timetable. He got very confused. The queues behind me were growing ever longer. The staff were getting hopelessly overloaded and stressed. The tension was growing, but, like good British customers, no-one in the queue complained. The breaking point came with a loud, sharp, whisper from a younger member of staff to the man who was serving me: 'For Christ's sake, give it up, Dad! He only wants a rail reservation; it's not worth our trouble.'

The man turned on her immediately and retorted, through clenched teeth: 'How dare you! A customer is a customer; that's what we're here for!' He then proceeded to tell me that 'they only tolerated him in the shop at weekends now' and they had their 'differences of opinion'.

Some of the entrails of the organization had suddenly been revealed. I had seen something I should not have seen, and I was uncomfortable. I did not want to witness a row or receive a confession – I wanted a ticket! I now mistrusted the service. I could not play my customer **role** properly if they did not play out their role as 'travel agents'.

I decided to go elsewhere.

ORGANIZING AS A MEANING-CREATING PROCESS

When we get close to the experience of people organizing, there is the impression of a lot of personal and inter-personal **work** going on. In the above exchange, the protagonists were not just observing or responding to each other's **actions**; they were also busily interpreting each other's behaviour.

Seen through the eyes of different individuals, what happened may have seemed very different. Each may have told a different story about what 'really' happened. For example:

- the elderly gentleman's story: 'Customers were happy to queue for personal, caring service'
- his daughter's: 'Customers were in a hurry, dear old Dad all at sea'
- the story-teller's: 'Customer pressure reveals cracks in the organization'
- other customers': 'Incompetent travel agents', 'rude young people'

The **meaning** of the incident is not obvious. Even the meaning of particular words or sentences may be ambiguous. 'It's not worth our trouble' could be interpreted as a personal insult, or as an expression of frustration with dad – or with customers in general.

'A customer is a customer' could be taken as a brave assertion of good old-fashioned service. But in this case, what about all the customers waiting? Does their inconvenience count for nothing? Alternatively, it may have been a dig at the way young people conducted business, just for the money.

While most of us in organizations seem to be 'doing a job', attending lectures, tapping keyboards, talking into telephones or soldering electronic components, we are also making and exchanging meanings. Life and work without meaning are unbearable. Consider, for example, convicts forced to carry rocks from point A to point B one day, and from point B to point A the next; or children obliged to fill pages with 'lines' which will then be ritually torn to pieces and thrown away by the teacher. Organizing, as we are presenting it in this book, is intimately concerned with the way that people create meaning for themselves, with others, during their working lives. As we interact with others at work, we bring our personal histories and our past experiences with us – finding common ground, compromising, disagreeing, negotiating, coercing. This is a vibrant, mobile process, often full of tensions, frustrations and possibilities.

Some portraits of organization give a bleak picture of the isolation of the individual, lost in an impersonal **bureaucracy**, engaged in socially and psychologically impoverishing work. We shall not pretend that all or even most work is enjoyable or fulfilling. But a contrasting picture of organizations reveals the ever-rich **symbolic** life that we create to give us a sense of who we are and where we belong. We can share some of our day-dreams and **fantasies**, others we just keep to ourselves. So, in addition to business-like encounters with different people, we swap rumours, stories, gossip, **jokes** and laughter. We pick up and contribute to the chat about the organization's heroes, villains and fools. In this way 'the organization' takes on a special, personal **meaning**. It is not a surrogate for the 'real' organization; it is what informs our daily **actions**; daily organizing. It is the organization.

ORGANIZING AS A SOCIAL PROCESS

For much of the time organizing is also a social process, involving **groups** working together – part of the raw material of meaning-making. This is well illustrated when organizing something from scratch. We invite you to imagine doing this with some colleagues – such as organizing a welcoming event for new students on your course.

You must first agree on what it is that you are meant to organize, and then on a *plan*. In order to plan, you must *interpret* your brief and your constraints. What is the *real* purpose of the function? What kind of function is it going to be. 'Serious'? 'Light-hearted'? A mixture of both? What is your budget? What are the possible dates and venues for the event? What events may compete or clash with yours? How are you going to publicize it?

Initially different members of your group will have different ideas, preferences and interests. Conflicts may arise, compromises may be struck, but decisions cannot be made until differences have been discussed and negotiated. Agreeing on a plan involves a lot of **talk**, some of which is done in meetings, some in offices or over the telephone. To be sure, some people talk with louder or more persuasive voices than others; they may end up having a greater say in the event. Some may be so disenchanted that they drop out. Some may go along resentfully. Others are won over by the strength of the plan.

Once you and your group agree on a plan, things begin to fall into place. Different individuals may undertake different tasks, each having a distinct set of responsibilities. Their activities must be co-ordinated and harmonized, to ensure that they are all working within the same plan. The plan itself may be re-negotiated, as problems arise or as new ideas crop up. It then becomes imperative for everyone to be aware of changes.

Throughout this period **communication** and co-ordination are essential, as is **control** – of resources, information, and above all, of people. Control is part of the experience of being organized. At times we willingly relinquish control to someone else. At other times, we control ourselves – we do 'what we are supposed to do' without having to be told. Finally, there are times when we experience control as oppressive, but we resentfully do what is expected of us because we are unwilling to suffer the consequences.

ORGANIZING AND IMPROVISING

Things never go entirely according to plan; even the best-laid plans occasionally come to grief. On the day of the event you may face something unforeseen: guest speakers may send their apologies, cooks may burn the food, cars may break down, accidents happen. All these may threaten to throw your plans off course. You and your fellow organizers may have to fall back on contingency plans or you may have to improvise.

Successful organizing may depend on a sound plan but planning alone is no guarantee of success. When crisis strikes, your group may fall apart. Those who had expressed reservations about the plan may say 'We told you so, you insisted on doing things *your way*, now *you* sort out this mess.' Being able to work effectively as a team, thinking on your feet, maintaining your cool and the goodwill of those involved under pressure – these are all important in ensuring the success of your project.

Some people are quite happy improvising and managing crises. They can live with uncertainty and chaos, placing their faith in 'muddling through'. They believe that 'it will be all right on the night', and they are frequently proved right – to the intense annoyance of others. These others seek to **control** uncertainty. They are serious, methodical people; they like order, plan and routine and do not generally like 'fooling around'. They mistrust improvisation, chance and spontaneity; but what they really abhor is unpredictability.

SUCCESS OR FAILURE?

Some of the causes of success and failure in organizing are common, no matter what the specific organizing at hand seeks to achieve. Placing excessive reliance on a machine, an animal, a person or the weather, on anything over which you have limited control, may undermine your plan. Poor communication, inadequate budgets, irreconcilable differences, personality clashes, unanticipated events, low motivation can frustrate any organizing.

However, even if things run smoothly, an event may not be a success. In fact, success and failure are themselves meanings which we attribute to events, meanings which we usually develop as we talk, joke and gossip with others. Imagine if, a few days after the function which you organized and which everyone enjoyed, your group comes under criticism from the head of your department for 'mis-spending' the organization's money on 'irrelevant' activities, like that 'farce of a drunken party organized recently'.

You may be surprised at such an **attitude**. Instead of thanks for organizing what seemed like a splendid event, you come in for criticism. This may be one of the best lessons that the example teaches us: just when we think that we are free to organize others, we may ourselves be part of someone else's organizing activities. Your event may have been a success in terms of *your* plan but a resounding failure in terms of *theirs*.

Under such circumstances, it may be helpful to present to the departmental head some arguments and evidence, showing that most of those participating in the function found the event not just enjoyable but also extremely useful. This type of evaluating and assessing is itself an important aspect of organizing. What have you learned from the way that things happened? Would you do things differently, if you were organizing the same function all over again? Are there any shortcuts that you have learned? Might you have opted for a different event? Would you like to work with the same people again?

Some major events are organized on a one-off basis, as in the example above. A military campaign, the staging of the Olympic Games, a business takeover, a wedding: such events seem to call for their own unique organization. Most events, however, are not organized like this. They are part of on-going processes of organizing. Admitting a new class of undergraduates to a degree, preparing a company's accounts, taking in new stock, recruiting new staff, purchasing new equipment and many other activities are like painting the Golden Gate Bridge in San Francisco: by the time you have finished, it is time to start all over again.

IN SUM . . .

We have argued for a shift from the notion of *organization* to *organizing*. Organizing is to be seen as a social, meaning-making process where order and disorder are in constant tension with one another, and where unpredictability is shaped and 'managed'. The raw materials of organizing – people, their beliefs, actions and shared meanings – are in constant motion, like the waters of a river. In the chapters that follow we attempt to communicate the feel of this flow; to portray something of the richness, variety and surprise of life in organizations.

THESAURUS ENTRIES

actions	meaning
attitudes	organization
bureaucracy	real
communication	role
control	symbolism
fantasies	talk
group	work
jokes	

2

ENTERING AND LEAVING

Joining a new organization is usually a memorable experience, because of its mix of emotions – apprehension, excitement, tension, confusion. Each new encounter, each new person introduced, adds to the impression of what the place is like. It is the first of many steps through which we become simultaneously part of, and apart from, something called 'the organization'. It sets the initial psychological and physical boundaries to the space which we call **work**. We cautiously experiment with what we say or do. What is the reaction? Is it acceptable? We are **learning** the ropes, finding where we fit in. In social science terminology, we are seeking clues to the **culture**, norms and values of the community we are entering. None of this appears in the organization's recruitment literature. No-one told us about it. There may be a hint of things to come in unofficial prospectuses, as can be found in some colleges and universities where existing students tell something of what things are really like. But mostly we have to find out as we go along.

Leaving the organization changes the scene. It may occur smoothly and comfortably at the statutory end of the working life-time, celebrated by the presentation of the proverbial gold watch – for 'long, loyal service'. We witness similar **rituals** when people leave for another job, for marriage, to have a baby, or simply to retire early. The usual warmth of such occasions contrasts strikingly with the 'letting go', 're-structuring', 'retrenchment', 'laying off' or 'redundancy' which are now commonplace in our times of boom or bust. These actions mark a pragmatic approach by companies: when times are tough people will lose their jobs. Dismissal, for whatever reason, is a harsh way of separating a person from an organization. Like most separations or drastic **changes**, it quickly exposes the raw elements of the relationship.

FIRST IMPRESSIONS

Each year many companies undertake a tour of higher educational institutions. They set up their stalls and hand students glossy brochures containing colourful descriptions and photographs of corporate life. The exercise is designed to extol the benefits, and delights, of joining the organizations. Collectors of recruitment brochures will detect common images – implicit messages – which are not difficult to decode. For example:

– On the inside cover: a head-and-shoulders colour picture of a smartly dressed, serious-looking man (usually). The Managing Director gives a message of welcome and reassurance:
   Implicit message: 'Do not think that this is a fly-by-night company. We mean business; we know what we are doing, and someone important is in charge.'

– Pictures of people working at computer consoles:
   Implicit message: 'There is nothing old fashioned about us. We are an up-to-date, high technology company.'

– Pictures of men and woman, black and white, looking earnest, discussing things, making important decisions:
   Implicit message: 'There is equal opportunity here. Anyone can get on if they work hard. It's ability and performance that counts.'

– Pictures of people in a classroom; a tutor heads the group:
   Implicit message: 'You will not vegetate here. We believe in training. We will give you opportunities to improve your skills and qualifications; we will look after you.'

– Pictures of people playing sport:
   Implicit message: 'It is not just work, work, work. We have places for you to relax.'

– Picture of someone getting off a plane in an obviously foreign land:
   Implicit message: 'We are not just a local firm. We have international interests and there are opportunities for you to travel.'

In this way the **organization** parades its best costume, tailored carefully by its public relations department. The business of **self-presentation** has begun. Wooing new, desirable-looking, employees means presenting an attractive organizational image. Blemishes are heavily camouflaged, or simply omitted from the picture. It is assumed, not unreasonably, that when people have to make a difficult decision on what job to choose, relatively unambiguous information is helpful. Given that the organization wants your skills, it gains little by revealing that, actually, very few black people or women get to the top, that international travel is reserved for senior managers, that the computer system is in desperate need of renewal, or that the training budget has just been substantially cut. Moreover, it is likely that many potential applicants will *want* to believe the organization is glamorous, international, aggressive, or whatever, because that represents some ideal image they hold of themselves. They are therefore content to collude in the myth of the exemplary organization – especially if jobs are in short supply. The business of selection has begun – both parties, candidate and organization, are sounding each other out.

Typically, interested job candidates will groom themselves for the part. 'Respectable' suits and shirts replace the usual jeans and T-shirts – for males and females alike. To deviate too far from conservative dress risks being labelled as 'unreliable', 'radical', or 'will not fit in.' First appearances are notoriously poor guides to character, nevertheless we use them all the time in our inter-personal judgements. Street-wise job applicants know this, and learn to adjust their CVs or résumés to the apparent requirements of the job – accentuating some features, playing down others. They also research the company in advance to demonstrate the seriousness of their intent to an interviewer. Some will have topped-off their armoury of **skills** with special training on being an effective interviewee to create the right **impression** or **perception** (countered, ironically, by interviewers trained to see beneath a feigned presentation).

RITUALS – TO REDUCE UNCERTAINTY

The initial coming together of company and candidate involves careful make-up and posturing. At first sight this may appear irritatingly trivial – 'What's it got to do with the real me, and the actual job?' But the way we *present* ourselves to others, through a rich array of social protocols – **language**, dress, gestures, **rhetoric** – constitutes an essential part of social reality. We inherit certain social conventions through which we can interact – with a fair amount of shared **meaning**. As some customs seem increasingly daft, or inappropriate, they die because of non-usage – such as the wigs worn by barristers and judges. At a given point in time, though, getting our **performance**, appearance or act right – doing what is socially correct within extant conventions – is vitally important. That is the social currency, whether we like it or not. If we fail in our judgement or act, we risk rejection. This sometimes means a strange double bluff, of the sort: 'I need to give that person interviewing me a strong impression of my strengths and enthusiasm for the job. But I'm sure he knows I'm doing that, so will he believe what I say?' If we extend this analysis, it is possible to view life as a stream of public performances accompanied by private, in-the-head, commentaries.

THE SELECTION

The time and effort a company wishes to devote to selecting its personnel can vary enormously. A selection decision could be made on the basis of a letter of application and a short **interview**. On the other hand, it is not uncommon for large companies to expose candidates for managerial and professional jobs to a sequence of interviews, **psychological tests**, group discussions, and exercises. Assessors will record their observations, and candidates will be judged against a set of previously agreed criteria of competence. This is the questionable science of selection – questionable because there are many studies which reveal that devices such as selection interviews and **personality** tests have modest to poor reliability and predictability. Judging people's competence in areas such as leadership, interpersonal relationships, working under pressure and so forth, is notoriously difficult, not least because, as hinted above, a candidate's performance in a selection procedure can reveal more about that procedure than the candidate's actual work behaviour. But an elaborate selection process offers the *apparent* reassurance that a poor decision will be unlikely, and it will be possible to **control** entry to the organization. It is also a **ritual** through which impossibly difficult decisions can be made to appear possible. With tools that promise 'objectivity', selector and candidate alike can feel that a thorough and fair job is being done (see Chapter 10, Judging others).

The ritual of selection can border on the absurd when some of the common methods are omitted – such as face-to-face interviews. For example, United Kingdom applicants for academic jobs in Australia can expect to be accepted or rejected after a telephone interview (considerably cheaper than a flight plus expenses). This normally means that they receive a pre-arranged conference telephone call at their home in the early hours of the morning. They then have to respond intelligibly to serious questions from a group of disembodied voices, many miles away. People on the receiving end of this process report a sense of surrealism, only slightly reduced by changing from their pyjamas to a smart suit.

. . . AND POLITICS

It is likely that the final selection for a job results more from **politics** than from the elegance of the entry structure. Politics focuses attention on the personal interests and idiosyncrasies of the selectors, and their power to make their own particular judgements prevail.

An associate of ours recently failed to win a top appointment with a London-based publishing company. She was one of two shortlisted candidates, and she had attended four separate interviews, the last one being with a panel of directors in the company. To all outward intents and purposes the job should have been hers. She had a fine reputation in her field – she outshone the other candidate. Furthermore, the night before the final interview she heard, from an 'inside source', that the job was hers. So what went wrong?

It was hard to find out – details of the proceedings were secret. But the insider, now much embarrassed, was determined to uncover the reason. It transpired that, in the final interview, our colleague had mentioned that if she were offered the job, she would have to commute to work for a time. Her family were well settled in their home town out of London where her children went to school. She would consider setting up a second home if necessary, but first she would like to take the commuting route. The point was well taken, with apparent sympathy, during the interview. Her honesty, however, proved to be a tactical error. After the interview the Managing Director, who was chairing the selection panel, declared firmly that this was not his idea of commitment or loyalty to the job; it was not what he would do if he were in the applicant's position. He would not permit the appointment of someone who did not move to the job right away.

This is a clear example of 'homosocial reproduction', a rather inelegant shorthand for the phenomenon of hiring people who are similar to those already in place. Put another way, people feel less anxious about working with others who are similar to them, so they will consciously, or unconsciously, veer toward people who seem, on first impressions, like them in social **values**, **gender**, **attitudes**, educational background and age. This is the psychological explanation for the 'old school tie' phenomenon. It also explains why certain organizational cultures perpetuate themselves – that 'Shell' 'Proctor and Gamble', 'IBM', or 'Marks and Spencer' feeling. And it is a reason why fairly drastic changes in key personnel have to take place if strong organizational values are to shift significantly – a frequent tactic of new chief executives who wish to make their mark.

Job applicants who dutifully respond to advertised vacancies can unwittingly fall foul of invisible political structures. Personal contacts and friendship networks bring some people, and not others, to the special attention of employers. In close communities, informal channels (rumour, casual chat) can keep many available jobs filled – especially in times when work is scarce. It is not unknown for an applicant to be processed right through a selection procedure, ignorant of the fact that the job has already been offered to someone else – secretly. The pretence of a fair selection procedure is maintained to save face.

SETTLING IN

The period of settling in can be a confusing time. Ways that were taken for granted no longer fit; the familiar customs and practices of the previous job or role are inappropriate. Things begin to happen which remind newcomers that they are indeed part of a new **environment**, but which also point the way to what they have to do, or be, to become part of the social group. For example:

– John, straight from secondary school at 19, joined a prestigious retailing chain as a management trainee. After a couple of days feeling lost, he was approached by a departmental manager: 'I suppose you are used to getting long holidays, eh? Well, you can forget that here. It's 8 till 6.30 six days a week.

That's what it takes to get on here.' John was stunned at what sounded like a prison sentence. A week later he was called to see the Store Manager, who asked him to recite the names of the staff in the store. John stumbled though most of their first names. The manager was furious: 'How can you ever expect to be taken seriously as a manager if you call people by their first names!?'

–   'OK then, young upstart lady, get a hold of this and put it in the car,' said an assembly line worker, handing Helen, a young management trainee, a windscreen. Eventually he helped her fit it. All the men gathered around to witness the incident. After some tense moments: 'She's all right lads, nearly one of us now.'

–   Hassan discovered he had made a mistake and mentioned it to his boss. 'Listen,' retorted the boss, *you* haven't made a mistake. The *system* has. Whenever something is wrong you must come and tell me the accounts system has screwed up. Then we can look at the problem and try to improve the system. The system will lose prestige, whereas you have gained recognition because you spotted the error. You see, this company likes winners.'

Anthropologists refer to events such as these as **'rites of passage'**: ways by which established organizational members induct new people into the actual working customs of the organization. Some inductions are gentle; others are harsh, even humiliating. Groups as diverse as military personnel, prisoners and public school children will use degradation as a way of initiating the newcomer.

Rites of passage are part of the unwritten procedures of organizational life; they are not to be found neatly listed in a job description. They are akin to a second selection system, but every bit as important as the first one. Rites of passage reveal themselves most clearly and consistently in 'strong' culture companies – those that have the same clear beliefs and values throughout all aspects of their business. For example, the IBMs and Proctor and Gambles of the world present new recruits with a series of specific hurdles to jump – surviving punishing working hours; performing very basic work to remind them of their humble status in the face of all they will have to learn; complete immersion in one part of the company's core business, until they have full mastery of it; sacrificing domestic and leisure time for the company.

McDonald's, the pervasive hamburger chain, is meticulous in ceremonially rewarding its staff with badges and certificates as they move from one hurdle to the next. In this way one's progress is visibly delayed until one conforms to the company's expectations. Such is the potency of this form of conditioning that it can take a remarkably short time for people to fall into line. They soon speak the corporate language and perform according to the rules. Those who do not will be delayed in their progress, or dismissed. Some will leave voluntarily because they cannot stand it any more.

. . . AND LEAVING

The farewell party is perhaps the most common organizational ritual, or final rite of passage, for the leaver (who has not been dismissed, or resigned in anger or disaffection). There are the complimentary farewell speeches tinged with nostalgia and humour, and the presentation of a gift. A mix of alcohol and bonhomie helps transcend political frictions which may have existed, and the leaver should feel able to quit gracefully, with a sense of completion to his or her endeavours. A brief period of mourning may follow, with people talking about how things used to be when the leaver was around. If the person strongly influenced the direction of the organization (for good or ill) his or her memory may be enshrined in stories which are passed on to future employees.

As well as marking an end to someone's organizational efforts, the farewell celebration legitimates vacating the job for someone else. It is problematic if this point is misread, or misunderstood. To illustrate: many a leaver will exit to the sentiment, 'It will be great to see you around here any time.' Those who respond literally to such an invitation may be disappointed, as the following tale from a personnel manager reveals:

Brian was a production executive. He loved his work with us; I guess he was a workaholic. He's been retired about a year now. We gave him a lavish send-off, a huge party. He was a popular man, you see. About a month after he left he popped in to see us. Of course it was great to see him and to exchange stories. I got the feeling then that he wasn't adjusting too well to retirement. He said he'd keep in touch with us, and that he did! It seemed like every week he'd be in – trying, really, to be where he thought he belonged. Eventually one of his old colleagues came to see me, in despair. 'He's driving us mad,' he said. 'He's a nice guy, but we don't want him any more. He wants to do our job for us; he can't let go'.

The emotional bonds of organizing are very real, but often temporary, and heavily entwined with daily work routines. The leaving ritual effectively marks an end to a person's organizational membership, and disenfranchisement can be rapid. Only special friendships survive. Without the everyday sharing of work, old interpersonal feelings are left without roots, or a proper context for expression. This can come as quite a shock to people who quickly find their old school, college or workmates relative strangers once they have left the organization. More cynically, one can regard many organizational relationships as a means to an end. We try to get on with people because we have to – to get the job done, to get through the day.

There is another image of leaving, which is far removed from the canapés and congratulations. This is the world of redundancy and re-structuring. People have to leave because their jobs no longer exist. The vagaries of the market economy can, sometimes overnight, turn a 'caring, family' organization into a beast which consumes its own children – in order to survive. 'Our most important asset, people' rarely survives a severe downturn in trade, or new mechanization; other interests take precedence. When people invest fair parts of themselves and their security in their employing organizations, job loss comes as a very worrying event. Those who have been made redundant more than once tread warily through the world of work, cautious about their commitment to any one company. For the first-time **unemployed**, the loss of income, **status**, and routine activity can feel like a collapse of meaning at the centre of their lives.

The anxiety and threat which surround job loss are also reflected in the ways organizations manage the process. The closest one finds to a supportive ritual are attempts to soften the blow through generous redundancy payments and 'out placement' support – to help people find new jobs or other activity. Otherwise, there is a mish mash of responses. Some senior managers cannot face the task of announcing redundancies themselves, so they delegate it to an internal, or external, 'hatchet person'. Then there are people who find out about their own redundancy from what they read in their local newspaper. Others hear by letter, or return from a break to find that their job, and office, has disappeared – perhaps the ultimate symbol of redundancy and rejection. Deceit and camouflage seem to flourish in the emotional confusion of redundancy.

We cannot but wonder at the apparent courtesy and charm which can bring a person into an organization, and the acrimony and disarray which, sometimes, can mark the leaving. Perhaps, most of all, it reminds us of the curious fragility of social orders and of organizing.

- Entering and leaving organizations are critical transitions in our work lives.
- Entering and leaving are marked by both formal and informal social rituals.
- The rational procedures of recruitment and selection are often overlaid with political interests – which may not give the candidate a 'fair' hearing or decision.
- Most organizations wish to present a glossy image to the outside world; but once inside an organization you get a different picture.
- There is a gradual process of getting to know one's place in an organization – learning its customs and practices. This is crucial to survival, and can sometimes be very testing.
- An organization can soon become part of our self-image and identity.
- Sudden unemployment or retirement can leave people confused; they are often unprepared for a life without paid employment.

THESAURUS ENTRIES

attitudes	language
change	learning
control	meaning
culture	norms
environment	organization
gender	perception
impression management	performance
interview	personality

politics
psychological testing
rhetoric
rites of passage
ritual
self-presentation

skills
status
unemployment
values
work

3

RULES ARE RULES

'PASSWORD!' – MIKE'S STORY

I applied to Securecops on the off chance. I attended an interview in their fortress-like headquarters on the Thames Embankment. It lasted all of five minutes. I would get my first job the following week. What I had to remember, at all times, was SECURITY, they said. I would be given a secret password, which would be changed each night. All communications with HQ, and with any caller to the place I was guarding, had to use the password.

I left HQ with my free kit under my arm: an ill-fitting blue uniform, a peaked cap, a whistle, a torch and a truncheon.

A week later I turned up to my first job. It was a US Navy stores depot in an isolated spot in North London. As far I could tell it contained things like Coke, soap and paper towels. I could not figure out why the US Navy should have such a place in London. I felt self-conscious – a bit of a nerd in my new uniform. A Securecops supervisor met me to show me around. The rules the supervisor told me were these:

- Keep everything locked.
- Patrol the building and the perimeter wire once an hour.
- Ring in and report to HQ after each patrol. They'll chase you if you don't call.
- Get the password from HQ at the start of each shift, and use it in all calls.
- *Don't* smoke on patrol.
- *Don't* let anyone in unless they give the password.
- *Don't* fall asleep on the job, or you will be sacked.

The supervisor left. The guard I was replacing packed up his stuff. As he was leaving he winked at me and said: 'Listen. Skip a patrol or two and get all the sleep you can.' I was puzzled.

I got through the first night, exhausted. It was really scary going around the dark buildings. The very thought of *using* my truncheon on a human being filled me with horror. I decided the best thing to do was to run it against the wire fence and along doors as I patrolled. It made a hell of a racket but that should deter an intruder – I hoped.

Night two. I realized that I could easily skip a few patrols – as long as I rang HQ on time. Also, I found myself plotting other ways of bucking the system. Surely, you could do a deal with another guard, elsewhere, to ring HQ on your behalf? You'd then get more sleep some nights, and he could sleep while you're doing it for him. I later learned that such a dodge was well-known, but no-one had prevented it.

I found myself falling asleep between patrols, so I kept an alarm clock to wake me on time to report to HQ. In the middle of such a slumber, at about 4 in the morning, I was jolted awake by the loud, persistent hooting of a car horn. I scrambled for my uniform jacket, and grabbed my truncheon. I dashed outside, my heart racing.

I was facing the headlights of a van, shining through the wire mesh of the locked main gate. In front of the lights was the silhouette of a tall man. 'Christ, where the hell have you been? Let me in!'

I got a bit closer and saw the guy was wearing a Securecops uniform. I plucked up courage and shone my torch in his face. I recognized the supervisor. What a relief! I fumbled for my keys – and then hesitated. Hell, this could be a trick, I thought. To test me out. I'd better watch it. 'Oh hi,' I said, 'Could you tell me the password please?'

The man looked confused. Then he shouted at me: 'Like hell I can! Open these bloody doors and let me in. Just stop fooling around!'

I fingered the keys nervously. What on earth should I do? I was sure he was OK, but I was breaking a cardinal rule if I let him in. And he still might be tricking me. I tried very hard to sound authoritative: 'I can't let you in unless you tell me the password. *Rules are rules.*'

'I don't know the bloody password for tonight,' he retorted, getting more and more wound up.

Fearing for my physical safety, I eventually phoned HQ, who were not the slightest bit interested in the man's identification. I should let him in. He marched past me, saying not a word. He left the same way – after a very cursory check.

RULES IN ORGANIZATIONS

Mike did not last long in this job. But the incident raises important issues. Entering the organization is entering a world of formal **rules** and procedures. They govern every aspect of work, leaving little room for discussion. 'No smoking' means precisely 'No smoking', no matter who you are, how badly you wish to smoke or what you would choose to smoke. Yet, after a few days at Securecops, Mike **learned** that rules were sometimes disregarded, broken or bent, occasionally with the consent of **management**.

Train drivers found out long ago that if every rule and every procedure of starting their locomotives were followed, the trains would never leave the stations or reach their destinations on time. 'Work to rule', sticking to every small rule and regulation in the book, was recognized as a very effective way of paralysing organizational performance. Sometimes, it takes a major accident before it is realized that official procedures have been flouted for so long.

Organizational rules can be usefully distinguished from social **norms**. Norms are the 'unwritten rules'. IBM employees, for example, wear white shirts, even though this is not enshrined in any formal rule. Nor is it a rule of the road that truck drivers should flash their headlights to indicate to an overtaking truck that it is safe to pull in again, or that the overtaking driver should flash their indicator, as a sign of appreciation. Social norms guide many of our **actions**, both inside and outside organizations. Some of the other chapters highlight their importance and implications. This chapter focuses on the formal written rules and regulations which seem to set modern organizations apart from other types of human **groups**, like families, or truck drivers on highways.

Rules and factory despotism

Formal rules and regulations are not a new phenomenon. Medieval monasteries had detailed penalties for different offences. For instance, a monk guilty of sexual intercourse with an unmarried person was required to fast for one year on bread and water, a nun guilty of the same offence between three and seven years (depending on the circumstances), a bishop for twelve years.[1] However, the proliferation of rules at the workplace coincides with the rise of the factory system and especially of large **bureaucratic organizations**. Consider the following extracts from the rules of a 19th-century mill in Lancashire.

RULES
TO BE OBSERVED AND KEPT BY THE PEOPLE
EMPLOYED IN THIS FACTORY

1. Each person employed in this factory engages to serve THOMAS AINSWORTH AND SONS, and to give one month's notice, in writing, previous to leaving his or her employment, such notice to be given in on a Saturday, and on no other day. But the Masters have full power to discharge any person employed therein without any previous notice whatsoever.

2. The hours of attendance are from Six o'clock in the morning until half-past Seven at Night, excepting Saturday when work shall cease at half-past Four. . . .

5. Each spinner shall keep his or her wheels and wheelhouse clean swept and fluked, or in default thereof, shall forfeit One Shilling. . . .

10. Any person smoking tobacco, or having a pipe for that purpose, in any part of the Factory, shall forfeit Five Shillings.

12. Any person introducing a Stranger into the Factory without leave of one of the Proprietors, shall forfeit Two Shillings and Sixpence. . . .

17. Any Workman coming into the Factory, or any other part of these Premises, drunk, shall pay Five Shillings.

18. Any Person employed in this Factory, engages not to be a member of, or directly or indirectly a subscriber to, or a supporter of, any Trades Union, or other Association whatsoever.

19. Any Person destroying or damaging this Paper, shall pay Five Shillings.

Such rules may shock us, as being unfair and one-sided. Imposed unilaterally by the employer, they make no secret of whose interest they seek to protect. Their aim is **control**. Like political dictators, Messrs Ainsworth and Sons and other early capitalists sought to bolster their **power**. They made little pretence that the rules served anyone's welfare other than their own.

Rules and modern organizations

Most Western organizations today would shy away from brutal rules like those above, especially those which emphasize the potential for **conflict** between employers and employees.

Nevertheless, when we join an organization, we usually undertake, through a written contract, to obey its rules and procedures. These are *impersonal*, they apply to all, and are laid down in company manuals and ordinances, dictating, sometimes in minuscule detail, what we can and what we cannot do, our rights and our obligations.

What has changed since the days of Messrs Ainsworth and Sons is not the nature of the rules but our perception of their rationale. Instead of 'Do A, B and C because I say so', rules in modern organizations proclaim 'Do A, B and C because it is sensible to do so'. Unlike the exploitative rules of the illustration, the rules of modern organizations appear **rational**. In this sense, they resemble the rules of the road. Most of us will stop at a red traffic light not because we are afraid of the policeman or because of our sense of moral duty, but because we recognize that stopping at red lights is a rational means of regulating traffic. At times a red light will cause us great frustration, especially if we are in a great hurry, it is late at night and there is no other traffic on the road. Nevertheless this does not make us argue that stopping at red lights is silly, senseless or unfair.

In a similar way, we recognize most of the organizational rules we obey as rational. To appreciate the exact sense of 'rational', consider a rational rule next to a patently irrational one. Most colleges and universities have formal rules requesting students to write essays when asked by lecturers. They have no rules requiring students to wash their lecturers' cars, much as some lecturers might appreciate it. Is this accidental? Hardly. What formal *educational* or *organizational* purpose could possibly be served by rules authorizing superiors to order their subordinates to carry out personal favours? Such rules would not merely be immoral, but also irrational. Of course, the fact that there is no car-washing rule does not imply that no personal favours are ever requested. Favours, bribes, backhanders can all be part and parcel of doing business, embedded in the **norms** of some organizations. But they are not in any of the rulebooks (see Chapter 4, Dealing and double-dealing and Chapter 5, Morals). Organizational rules are rational in as much as they are seen to be means enhancing the achievement of organizational ends. This type of **rationality** is often referred to as instrumental or means–end rationality. Information regarding alternatives and technical **knowledge** are indispensable ingredients of this type of rationality. Ideally, rational rules would be the result of a methodical comparison and analysis of alternatives and the choice of those alternatives which are best suited to the **organization's goals**. In practice, as we shall see, this is not always the case.

Formal technical rules underpin the single-minded pursuit of efficiency that characterizes many organizations. The frying and serving of potatoes becomes the object of extensive 'scientific' study for a fast food organization. This determines specific types of potatoes, fat and fryers, the design of a new wide-mouthed scoop and other hardware and the drafting of 26 different rules on 'how to fry French fries'. All this is aimed to ensure that even a person who has never cooked at home could produce, after a minimum of training, a standardized 'market-winning product', without accidents or waste.

BUREAUCRACY

Formal rules do not only affect employees of an organization. Next time you visit a park, have a look at the 'bye-laws' stating what you are and what you are not allowed to do. Or consider the regulations governing behaviour in a swimming pool:

No eating	No bombing	No swearing	No verrucas
No drinking	No kissing	No singing	No pushing
No running	No shouting	No ducking	No diving
No smoking	No spitting	No jewellery	No petting

During a conference in Copenhagen, someone brought to the attention of the delegates a set of regulations issued by the Fire Brigade:

In the event of a fire:

1 Stay calm.
2 Locate the fire.
3 Call the Fire Brigade.
4 Close windows and doors.
5 When the Fire Brigade arrives, introduce yourself.
6 If possible, put out the fire.

We all had a good laugh at these regulations. Fortunately no fire disrupted the proceedings. Had there been one, however, it is unlikely that anyone would have remembered the regulations or acted according to them, as people would hurry to the nearest fire escapes.

Seen through the eyes of delegates, rules like those above are the products of bureaucrats, who have little sense of the chaos and confusion that a fire would cause (see Chapter 1, Organization and organizing). They treat an event like a fire as something which can be controlled or at least contained through neat and orderly procedures. Their concern for organizing, order and plan blinds them to the forces of disorder that a fire would unleash. Seen through the eyes of those who devised them, both the fire regulations and the swimming-pool regulations are not daft at all. They are quite rational, seeking to minimize damage, injuries and insurance liabilities and to contain the disorder.

Managers and administrators spend a lot of time fine-tuning rules and procedures; they are always on the look-out for new rules which will do what old rules did, only better. They believe that this is very important. What they sometimes fail to do is to question the objectives served by these rules and procedures. Are the objectives themselves rational? Are all different objectives in harmony? Are there any other objectives which should be served? Whose interests do these objectives serve? Is it realistic to expect people to follow rules like those above?

Organizations vary in their emphasis on rules. Some offer a considerable margin of freedom to their members, allowing them to use their judgement and discretion in making **decisions**. Here is 'the rulebook' of Nordstrom, one such company.

WELCOME TO
NORDSTROM

We are glad to have you with our company.
Our number one goal is to provide
outstanding customer service.
Set both personal and professional goals
high. We have great confidence in your
ability to achieve them.
Nordstrom Rules:
Rule 1: *Use your good judgement in all
situations.*
There will be no additional rules.
Please feel free to ask your department
manager any question at any time.

Other organizations, like Securecops in our opening example, appear to be strict and regimented, but insiders soon realize that their bark is worse than their bite. Most of their rules are routinely side-stepped. Yet other organizations seek to **control** everything through precise prescriptions and procedures. Employees are expected to 'do everything by the book', without asking questions. In such organizations, the rules become ends in themselves, rather than means of achieving organizational objectives. In a French hospital, a rule stipulated that receptionists in the Accident and Emergency Unit were to admit only patients arriving by ambulance. The aim of the rule was to ensure that only genuine emergencies were given priority. Once, a patient brought to the Unit by taxi was refused admission and sent to the Outpatients' Department; he died while waiting to be admitted.

Organizations in which rules are inflexibly applied, with no regard for the particulars of each individual case, are frequently referred to as **bureaucracies**. Such organizations remind us of machines. Order, predictability, reliability are the qualities towards which they strive. Judgement, improvisation and fun are dismissed as the enemies of order. Standardization, **hierarchy** and **structure** are of the essence. By contrast, the term 'adhocracy' is sometimes applied to organizations which treat each case on its individual merits, and have few general rules and procedures to guide behaviour. Such organizations must rely on training, trust and strong shared **values** to ensure co-ordination and control. Adhocracies are never particularly orderly or predictable. But they appeal to individuals with artistic or anarchic temperaments.

How rational are bureaucratic rules?

What is important is that you should *understand* why your work has to be done in a certain way and that you do it properly, to the best of your ability. *Not because you have to, but because you want to. In the end this is the BEST WAY.*

(Handbook of fast food company)

But is 'the book's way' always the best way? Most of the time, we assume that if a rule is there it is there for a reason. The rules governing behaviour in the swimming pool may displease us, but most of us would not really question whether they are rational or not. We take on trust that 'experts', who have studied the situation, have enacted these rules for everybody's benefit. We assume, for example, 'no running' is there to stop people from slipping and injuring themselves, 'no bombing' to stop people intimidating or injuring others, and so on. We take the rationality of organizational rules and procedures for granted and do not question their legitimacy. We rarely complain about them and tend to disregard the inconvenience in which they result. Some of these rules eventually are observed mechanically, they become part of ourselves. Life without them becomes inconceivable.

Yet, no rule can anticipate all contingencies. The ambulance rule at the hospital was rational *until* the arrival of the fated patient; until then it had served what most would regard a useful purpose. However, one would have to suffer from bureaucratic blindness to argue that it was still rational when it led to loss of life. Whether a rule is rational or not depends largely on circumstances. No rule can be rational at all times. There comes a time, usually under exceptional or unforeseen circumstances, when it is rational *not* to apply a particular rule. Some organizations recognize the constitutional inability of rules to be rational at all times. They also trust their employees. They allow them to use their discretion.

This, however, may lead to a different kind of difficulties. Imagine if the hospital allowed receptionists to exercise 'discretion' as to whom to admit directly and whom to refer to the Outpatients' Department. This is likely to put great pressure on the receptionists; how can they judge who is an 'emergency' and who is not? Besides, patients may complain that they are not treated fairly; why should a drunkard with a broken jaw-bone be admitted and the child with a fever referred?

Dependence on rules and impersonality

Officials become dependent on rules to guide and justify their **actions**. They sometimes feel that any rule, *even a non-rational one*, is better than no rule. Rules save one the trouble of having to make awkward **decisions** and then having to explain and defend them. **Impersonality** means that each decision is unaffected by the specific circumstances of individuals. No amount of begging, pleading or arguing will alter the decision. Some of the decisions people make in organizations are very unpleasant. Sacking an employee, putting a patient on a long waiting list, failing a student, are not easy or agreeable decisions. Impersonality cushions us from the suffering and misery of others. 'It was nothing personal, Mrs Jameson, but rules are rules!' But impersonality can also have advantages for those affected by decisions. If everyone is treated according to the rule, everyone is treated the same; there is no cause for complaints.

Rules can become the opium of bureaucratic officials. Without the rules, they are lost, paralysed. With the support of the rules, they are persons with **authority**. Without rules, chaos. With rules, order and organization. Unlike the authority of the father or the mother in a family or of the founder of a movement, the officials' authority is legal, it rests on the rules which define their rights and responsibilities. Their authority lies not in who they are but in the hats they wear, that is, in the positions they occupy.

Impersonality underwritten by rules seeks to ensure that a task will be performed in a uniform way, no matter who is performing it. Officials will discharge their duties unaffected by erratic factors like their mood, their passions and their idiosyncrasies. Finally, it means that staff in organizations are replaceable, since they are appointed not for who they are but for what they can do.

Impersonality, its costs and 'personal service'

As the size and power of organizations has increased throughout the 20th century, impersonality has become a dominant feature of Western societies. Constrained by countless rules, stripped of initiative and discretion, increasingly the players of **roles**, we frequently relate to others not as full human beings but as names on forms, numbers on computer terminals, voices at the end of telephone lines or distorted faces behind counters. A mastectomy may be a life-shattering ordeal for a woman and her family, but for the hospital administrator it is an extra demand on hospital beds, for the medical secretary a mere tick in box 6B.

We are all aware of the frustrations that impersonality causes. Generally we do not like being treated as numbers and many organizations will try hard to create the impression of a personal service. The air stewardess will address business class passengers with their names and the waiter in certain restaurants may introduce himself saying 'Hello, I am Pierre, your host for the evening.' Some of us feel uncomfortable or embarrassed about such personal touches, which smack of premeditation and artifice. We may also suspect that they will increase the figure at the end of our bill. A fast food employee said:

> It's all artificial. Pretending to offer personal service with a smile when in reality no one means it. We know this, management know this, even the customers know this, but we keep pretending. All they want to do is take the customer's money as soon as possible. This is what it's all designed to achieve.

The irony, of course, lies in the fact that the 'personal service' is itself the result of carefully planned rules. As if offering an efficient service were not enough, the rulebooks of some organizations seek to **control** our **emotions** and our thoughts (see Chapter 11, Feelings).

Faced with mock personal service many prefer the no-nonsense anonymity of the machine. When cash dispensing machines were first introduced by banks, it was thought that people would prefer the personal touch of the cashier to the fully impersonal transaction with the machine. It didn't take long to find that most people given a choice prefer the latter. Anonymity and impersonality have advantages not only for the organization but also for the customer. For one thing, they remove the need to reciprocate false smiles and other unfelt pleasantries.

RULES AS CONTESTED TERRAIN

We have seen that the rigidity with which organizations enforce their rules varies. The more bureaucratic organizations are fastidious in the application of rules while others take a more relaxed attitude and allow their members a measure of discretion. We sometimes laugh at bureaucracies and their ridiculous regulations, like those of the Danish Fire Brigade. Rules which seem to serve no useful purpose are derided as 'red tape'. Bending such rules appears more rational than enforcing them.

But bending rules has its own difficulties. For one thing, it undermines one of the most important functions of rules, their guarantee of equal and consistent treatment. Some may fear that, once a rule has been bent or violated once, a precedent is created for future bigger violations. The rule may then lose all credibility. In most British universities, students must get 40 percent in order to pass a particular course. Student A has obtained 39.5 percent. Should he/she pass or not? Common sense and tolerant judgement may argue for lenience. What should then happen to Student B on 39 percent? Or Student C on 38.5 percent? Bureaucratic rationality would suggest that a line has already been drawn at 40% and should be observed.

Bureaucratic rationality often rules in organizations. The student on 39.5% may be failed. But then, he/she may not. If every organizational rule was rigidly applied, life could grind to a halt. The fear of creating a precedent, frequently referred to in emotive terms like 'opening the floodgates' or 'the thin edge of the wedge', is often imaginary; most precedents are quickly forgotten or brushed aside with suitable excuses. What seems to happen in the majority of organizations is the establishment of a range of permissible deviations from rules. To new recruits all rules and procedures may seem unbreakable. Nevertheless, as our opening example illustrated, individuals quickly realize that not all rules and regulations are equally sacrosanct. Some of them (like stopping at red lights) are fairly inflexible, but most of them contain loopholes or can be dodged in different ways. Many rules are highly circumstantial, applying only in specific situations, for instance during visits by inspectors. Others have fallen into total neglect. Yet others are the topic of constant **conflict** and negotiation, a continuous give and take between different organizational members.

Even in fast food restaurants, rules are routinely bent. At peak times, more than four pieces of fish may be fried simultaneously, or French fries may be kept for more than seven minutes. Such practices are against the regulations but essential in meeting the demand. What is more, managers themselves are seen bending the rules or turning a blind eye when others violate them. Side-stepping a rule is often essential to meet the demands of a job, but equally individual workers may earn exemptions in the form of privileges. A particularly hard-working employee who turns up to work on a busy day wearing an ear-ring or having forgotten to wear his deodorant is unlikely to be disciplined or turned away.

It is important, then, to emphasize that rules are not things, blindly controlling our behaviour in organizations. They permit different interpretations and their enforcement becomes tied in with the **culture** as well as the **power relations** of organizations. The same rule may have very different **meanings** in different organizations or even to different individuals within the same organization. Contesting the meaning, the interpretations and the implications of rules is one of the central activities contributing to the instability, unpredictability and richness of organizational life.

CHANGING FASHIONS IN THINKING ABOUT RULES

In general, where there are rules, people will look for ways of making more elbow room. Even in the strictest organizations they are likely to get some, with or without the collusion of their superiors. It would be as short-sighted then to reduce all behaviour in organizations to the following of rules, as to disregard the profound and far-reaching implications of rules in our lives.

Management thinking about rules and procedures is changing. At one time the fine-tuning of rules and procedures was regarded as the secret of organizational success. Flexibility and initiative, embodied in the Nordstrom rules illustrated earlier, are the current fashion. In the past, the frictionless machine represented the managerial ideal of an organization. The lean, highly responsive organism lies closer to current thinking. It is increasingly argued that rules and procedures, however carefully designed, cannot cope with a highly complex and changing organizational **environment** or with massive **technological changes** (see Chapter 8, Machines and mechanizing).

In the past, some bureaucratic organizations prospered because of their predictability and order. Inflexibility and sluggishness were no problems in a stable, friendly **environment**. After all, dinosaurs ruled the earth for over two hundred million years, inflexible and sluggish though many of them were. No-one knows for sure why dinosaurs died out, but we all assume that it had something to do with their inability to adapt to new environmental conditions, whether these were brought about by a colliding asteroid or some other cause. The same, argue modern management theorists, will be the fate of rigid bureaucratic **structures**. They stifle innovation, discourage new ideas, fail to capitalize on advantages conferred by modern **technologies** and are generally too slow and cumbersome to meet **competition**. Sooner or later, they will give way to quicker, smaller, more adaptable, more enterprising organizations.

Such organizations seek to unleash human potential and

creativity rather than constrain it through rules and regulations. 'Empowerment' has replaced control as a management buzz word. This does not mean that control has faded away or that organizational rules and discipline have been replaced by trust and autonomy. It does mean, however, that many organizations seek to complement bureaucratic regulations with subtler forms of organizational control. Selection procedures aimed at ensuring highly committed staff, organizational values, reward structures and corporate culture are currently much-favoured mechanisms of control; their importance becomes clearer in some of the other chapters in this book.

- Most organizations have formal, impersonal and highly specific rules.
- Rules can be seen as 'rational' if they are carefully chosen to serve generally agreed organizational goals.
- Rules are an important means of achieving control over individuals' behaviour in organizations.
- Organizations differ in their reliance on rules and on the rigidity with which they apply them.
- At times it becomes more rational to bend or disregard a rule than to enforce it.
- Bending rules may lead to ever-increasing violations and eventual anarchy; but in most organizations, a degree of rule-bending is accepted as normal and necessary.
- Officials often become dependent on rules to justify their actions and decisions and to bolster their authority.
- Rules give organizations an impersonal quality; they reduce the influence of emotions on the way people do their job, and control the way emotions are displayed.
- People in organizations frequently contest the meaning of rules and try to interpret them or change them to their advantage.

THESAURUS ENTRIES

action	change
authority	competition
bureaucracy	conflict

control   management
culture   meaning
decision making   norm
emotion   organization
empowerment   power
environment   rationality
goals   role
group   rules
hierarchy   structure
impersonality   technology
knowing   values
learning

4

DEALING AND DOUBLE-DEALING

While interviewing staff at a historic hospital in the centre of London, I was surprised to find that Mick, a porter, came to work by car. Now everyone knows that there is nowhere to park in this part of London, so I asked him where he left his car. He became quite defensive and indicated vaguely that he found a place within the hospital perimeter. I interviewed numerous other catering workers, none of whom drove to work. I was sufficiently intrigued to ask one of his colleagues about Mick's parking. 'Mick's got his own private parking space, with his name on it, right next to the consultants', I was told. 'How come?' I asked, quite perplexed. 'Politics', came the answer.

Later I learned that Mick received his parking space as a reward for strike-breaking. A few years earlier, a tough new manager had imposed a strict roster regime in the kitchen and had clamped down on pilfering and overtime. Most workers went on strike, but were eventually forced back on management's terms. During the strike, the managers had provided a service with the help of a few workers, including Mick, who were smuggled into the hospital in taxis. All of these workers had been rewarded with promotions, benefits or simply by being assigned the most desirable jobs in the kitchen, the 'gravy jobs'. Those who had joined the strike were denied overtime work and were systematically landed with the 'stinkers', those jobs no-one wants to do.

The secret deals, the politicking, fascinate. Rarely coming into full view, **power** games are hidden behind closed doors. Machinations, intrigues, collusions, plotting, above all dealing and double-dealing, are images which readily come to mind. The major business scandals which erupt suggest that deception, cheating and lying are key ingredients of business **politics** (see

Chapter 5, Morals). But this is just one, extreme, view of politics. In many respects politics can be regarded as a very normal feature of organizational life.

It is hard to think of organizing without politics. Differences of opinion, value and interest, clashes of personality, limited resources and personal ambition ensure that **conflict** will be present where there is organizing. And where there is conflict, there is power, whether it appears as influence, persuasion or force. But also, where there is conflict, there is co-operation. No-one can take on the rest of the world by themselves, so alliances are made, deals are struck. Trust and loyalty are as much part of organizational politics as are deception and corruption.

CO-OPERATION, COMPETITION AND CONFLICT

One way of looking at the dealings that people have with each other is as **games**. Referring to dealings as games does not mean that they do not have serious intentions, or that they may not have serious consequences. The game is a metaphor for the postures that people take with one another, and how they attempt to influence, or score 'points'. Indeed, one psychologist, Eric Berne[2] has suggested that some of our most intractable interpersonal conflicts can be unravelled by seeing them in terms of games we play with each other, with rules that are sometimes so taken for granted that we do not see the harm we can inflict. In organizations we have a sense of some of the rules of play, the turns, the refereeing and so on. We learn some of their intricacies, such as that it is OK to criticize John when you are talking to your friend Sue, but not when you are talking to Mary, who is John's boss and yours. If such niceties are misunderstood or ignored there can be a price to pay (maybe personal embarrassment, a lost friendship or working relationship, even your job). Another 'rule' might be that new product ideas must always be taken to the development committee before the production department are asked to comment on them. Organizations abound in such rules of the game (see Chapter 3, Rules are rules).

Many organizational games are of the someone-wins-someone-loses sort. In the appointment and promotion game, if there is only one vacancy, and one person gets it, another does not. However, there are organizational games where one person's gain is not necessarily another person's loss. These are rather like the informal games at a children's party: if one person or group wins too convincingly or too often, the others will not want to play with them any more. So the art is to learn just where to co-operate sufficiently to make sure that your opponents are doing well enough not to quit: a win–win situation. Skilled negotiators in industrial relations conflicts on pay, productivity or working conditions, know this only too well. A complete loser is likely to feel demotivated and refuse to bargain on another occasion. They may find other ways of scoring off an opponent – such as wrecking the efforts of others through poor workmanship, blocking initiative, spreading rumours, **sabotage** or sheer bloody-mindedness.

There are, however, occasions where the principle at stake for both parties is so high that nothing but an all-out win will do; yet that win is unattainable. It is not uncommon to observe the sad and destructive spectre of two-loser games in organizations: a strike which leaves the workers none the richer and a company in ruins; an interdepartmental rivalry in which each department effectively blocks the other's efforts; a price war between two firms driving both of them to bankruptcy.

If some organizational games disintegrate into no-win situations, others generate multiple winners. Situations that appear stubbornly win–lose can suddenly be unlocked through the art of politics and diplomacy. There is the delightful tale of two pharmaceutical companies after the same resource – ugli orange.[3] The oranges were in very short supply so they were both prepared to pay 'any price' to obtain them. The fruit were indispensable for crucial research projects. Two senior executives from the two companies had a meeting to see if they could reach a compromise, but they soon discovered that they were both in an all-or-nothing situation. They were both after the full supply of oranges.

Just as they were preparing to part and declare war on each other, it occurred to one of them to ask the other what they were going to use the oranges for. It quickly emerged that they wanted them for different types of project. Then came the breakthrough:

'Which part of the orange do you need?'

'Why the juice, of course!'

'Good God, let's have another drink. We only need the rind!'

ABOVE AND BELOW THE TABLE

Some of the conflict or competition in organizations is built into the structure. So the board of directors will have members with **roles** which invite them to fight for different interests within the company. The marketing director, the production director and the finance director are appointed to represent different interests. They need to collaborate for the good of the company, but they are also expected to do the best deals they can for their department, and to see their own department's point of view. This is a way of formalizing conflict, containing it by establishing rules and formulae within which it takes place. In many commercial organizations certain types of conflict are legitimized as **competition**, a force for profit, growth and **constructive** contest. Competition has its rules, such as there being an 'even playing field', undistorted by monopoly power or special privileges. Organizations which engage in international trade can often be seen to be in dispute or conflict because the tax, legal or employment conditions in one country give organizations there a competitive edge – a little like a runner in a race starting from a point ahead of all the rest of the field.

Once certain rules and formulae are recognized as the sensible way of doing business, they acquire special significance; they become **institutions**. Institutions shape our expectations and generate a sense of fairness. Consider the democratic institution of general elections, through which much political conflict is channelled. Your party loses the elections; you may not be happy about this, but you accept it. You do not like some of the laws which the government pass, but you observe them. The party in opposition are not pleased, but they do not try to mobilize the army to gain power by force. In this way institutions, rarely perfect, can work.

The same goes on in organizations. You fail to gain promotion. You are not happy about this. But you are able to live with it if (a) it is the result of a clearly stated procedure, and (b) your colleague who was promoted instead of you was noticeably better on the stated criteria. In other words, the decision appears fair and by the rules. This does not mean that people always accept the rules as they find them. In organizations the referees are themselves players. Trying to change the rules, twist them, re-interpret them, is itself an important part of organizational politics. Nevertheless, having some rules which give all sides a 'winning chance' is necessary if people are going to accept the outcomes as fair. This may be seen more clearly in the dealings between management and trade unions. The declining power of trade unions in the UK in the 1980s was widely admired by many. But it was regretted by managers who found that the **institutionalization** of conflict through collective bargaining made their lives easier. They could deal with a clear negotiating partner, and were much less comfortable when it was less obvious who the negotiating partner was, or what rules governed any agreements that were made.

Is it better for conflict to come out into the open? There are no hard and fast answers. Sometimes we feel better if a conflict that has been bubbling away for some time becomes open and acknowledged. A middle manager in a high-volume factory producing biscuits told of his own experiences:

> It's funny. You can be supervising someone who has been cheerful for weeks on end, and then suddenly he turns on you – for no apparent reason. This has happened to me a number of times. I'm always caught unprepared, and I'm always baffled by it. It has worried me a lot. I've now started to talk about it more with the people involved. I've noticed that their anger is nearly always about something that happened weeks ago – maybe at work, maybe outside. They have been sitting on it until it becomes just too much to hold.

A big storm can sometimes clear the air. At other times small quarrels can escalate into major disputes. Sometimes the very act of declaring a conflict creates one. As soon as there are two sides in a dispute it becomes difficult for people not to join up with one side or the other. The theatre of conflict is enlarged, making a resolution tougher to achieve. So unleashing conflict may or may not be a wise thing to do. This creates some dilemmas. For example, the advantages of cohesive, strife-free, workgroups are extolled by many managers. The **groups** instil a positive team spirit in their members, they are pleasant to work in, and they are not split by differences of opinion. The down-side is that, in their desire to remain cohesive, the group members suppress internal conflicts and disagreement which could lead to more creative actions or solutions; and worse, they become blind and deaf to disturbing information. This phenomenon has been called group-think, and it has been used to explain events as calamitous as the unpreparedness of the USA for the invasion of Pearl Harbor in the Second World War and, less dramatically, the failure of an organization to see critical changes in the demand for its product.

The moral, it seems, is to be suspicious of conflict-free zones in organizations.

WHO WILL GET THE RESOURCES?

An oft-cited source of conflict in organizations – where politics, haggling, dealing and double-dealing, flourish – is in the getting and giving of resources. Resources are the people, buildings and equipment that a manager requires to run and develop his or her part of the business. They are funded from a budget allocated from the total monies available to the organization. Given that the cake is rarely large enough to meet the appetites of all managers, its division is almost bound to disappoint someone.

The fact that the vast majority of organizations have to function with less resources than they would ideally like (and considerably less in times of recession) means that there is potential for serious conflict at least once a year, perhaps every quarter, when budgets are decided. Also the legacy of such allocations, with its winners and losers, can rumble on for a long time, setting the tone of working relationships both within and between working groups.

The players in the conflict are already in place. As mentioned, the various directors – marketing, production, finance, sales, personnel, training, quality control, research and development – each have their own interests to fight for and protect, and they are in continuous **communication** with one another. These interests will include their personal **careers** as well as the size, prestige and effectiveness of their particular department or function. Given the centrality of budget-setting in an organization's functioning, one would expect it to be well institutionalized, with clear, rational and fair rules to play by. In practice it is institutionalized, but the rules are not all that apparent or clear. They are much contested and negotiated. We have a glimpse of just how from the Production Director of a medium-sized clothing manufacturer:

> We were about three months off the new financial year, and things had been tough for the company. I knew I could do much better with a special new cutting machine – made only in Germany. The MD knew of the problem, but said that the £75,000 was just too much; it was cheaper to keep repairing the old one. I disagreed, but I couldn't shift him. I knew that Bob from Sales was after a new fleet of trucks,

and Alan was determined to increase his marketing staff, and get them all into a decent office. They each had a strong case, so I had to do something. Firstly, I found an excuse to get the MD down on the shop floor on the next breakdown, to *see* the waste and chaos. It happened three times; some people think I actually fixed the breakdowns! Next, I had a long chat on the phone with the German supplier. I got them to knock 15% off the price and give us one year's interest-free credit, and install the machine. A brilliant deal, I thought. Finally, I got their rep to call by with a sample of the cutter's work at a time when I knew I'd be with the MD. The MD was non-committal – but that was better than a refusal. Then, on April 3rd, I received my new budget – with an allowance for a new machine! Bob and Al didn't get half of what they wanted, and they aren't too happy. Bob says he's now looking for a new job, and Al seems to avoid me and the MD.

We see here the reality of lobbying, politicking, and creating alliances. The MD, for his part, was faced with a number of competing, but plausible, claims for extra resources. He also had to try and make a wise budget distribution for the overall survival, and ultimate success, of the organization. In such difficult and ambiguous conditions he is likely to find it hard to ignore special pleading – particularly if it is handled skilfully and seems to link with his own aims and plans. In this particular case, however, his decision was costly in certain non-financial ways – the disaffection of two of his senior managers. In the longer term that could translate into financial costs from the poorer effectiveness of the managers, and from their possible replacement. There are no simple recipes for **decision making** in these sorts of circumstances. Skilled managers will need to acknowledge the political and emotional features that underlie such resource allocations, and, as shrewdly as possible, steer a path between the various interests involved.

There are a number of variations on the theme of this case. In some organizations groups will fight hard, and bitterly, with each other over available resources. Others will do secret deals with colleagues to their mutual advantage. Less furtively, senior managers may sit around a table in a private room and not emerge until they have thrashed out a budget allocation with which they can all live, accepting that not everyone can get all they want. Many would argue that this is the best way of making the most of a seemingly impossible situation. On the other hand, some executive teams are so divided from the outset that nothing short of a directive from 'above' will sort it out.

AND CRITERIA . . .

Inextricably entwined with resource allocation are the goals and criteria by which individuals and groups are judged (see Chapter 10, Judging others). The likelihood of conflict is high when one **group** regards organizational **goals** as less realistic, or less attainable, than another group. Each group wishes to have organizational criteria adopted that will make them look the best. Universities, for example, are known for such behaviour. As well as for teaching, universities are mandated to produce original research; they are judged, and rewarded, according to their publication record. But how do you compare the impressive number of publications which come out of a department of physics, reporting many small experimental variations on a number of themes, with a modern languages department which produces far fewer publications – but some weighty tomes on linguistics? And when is a publication a publication? What journals count? What is the worth of a long article in a quality newspaper compared with a research note in an obscure academic journal, compared with a chapter in a book?

The contention that surrounds such questions leads to all sorts of anxiety, and much political behaviour – partisan negotiations, lobbying heads of department to have the criteria changed, 'creative' declarations of what one has published, and contesting the research record of a colleague, boss or other department. At worst it produces an air of divisiveness and mistrust. More whimsically, it serves as a challenge for those who wish to send up the system (see Chapter 13, Serious joking). We have a colleague who works in a department of education at a university. By choice, he does precious little research. However, he has a passion for gardening, and writes a weekly column in a popular gardening magazine. He insists that these are bona fide publications, and should be treated as his contribution to his department's efforts. So each year, when his department's publications are collated, amongst the learned articles on topics such as classroom violence, syllabus design, and ethnic differences on attainment tests, there are titles such as 'Geraniums in a Drought', 'Lawn Care without Tears', and 'Weeds to Treasure'.

RESOLVING CONFLICT

The natural flow of conflict and co-operation in organizational life, and its attendant politics, means that the removal of all conflict, were it possible, is an unrealistic ideal. Furthermore, as we have illustrated, there are ways in which conflict can contribute to the richness of organizational life.

It is tempting to extract conflict from its particular organizational context, and seek universal managerial 'fixes' to damaging disputes. Some which are typically promoted are:

- smoothing the differences between conflicting parties by providing them with new information
- voting – the majority wins
- seeking compromise, everyone gets a bit of what they want
- seeking consensus, a solid best solution worked out by those in conflict
- confrontation – encouraging straight talking between opposing parties.

Each technique has its pros and cons. For example, smoothing conflict only works if the information given is trusted; majority rule can be felt as unfair if you are often on the losing side; compromise is fine if people resist the urge to exaggerate their demands in the first place. More important, though, conflict management needs to be sympathetic to, or in tune with, the prevailing political **culture** of the organization. An organization that 'thrives' on deals and double-deals is unlikely to respond well to consensus-seeking. In an organization that prides itself on its strong culture people will be puzzled if asked to vote. And an open confrontational style would be hard to implement in a company predominated by power and **status** divisions.

Resolving conflict, therefore, is partly a matter of appreciating the political **culture** of an organization. One way of describing political cultures is via **metaphors**. Commonly, and casually, metaphor slips into everyday conversation, often without our noticing. So we may say things such as 'The view from the window was a glimpse of heaven', 'I'm tackling a mountain of work', 'When they get drunk they are a pack of wolves'. Heaven, a mountain and wolves are used as devices for embellishing our thinking and seeing, for conveying special meaning in a powerful, yet succinct, manner. So metaphors can offer tidy and evocative analogies for complex social processes. Let us look at some metaphors which describe different political cultures:

The family

This organization emphasizes the **emotional** bonds that tie its members together and seeks to disregard inequalities of power, status and wealth. Authority is assumed to be wholly benevolent and deals are rarely acknowledged as such. Everyone is assumed to share the same interest. Loyalty, respect and commitment are taken for granted. Conflict rarely assumes forms more extreme than argument, criticism or reprimand. Many organizations aspire to be like this, few manage it. Underneath the appearance of harmony, powerful resentments and hostilities may lurk – as in real families. Confrontations, when they do occur, can be explosive, and painful.

The machine

This organization seeks to do away with both love and **power**. Each individual is a cog in the machine, playing his/her part without rancour or enthusiasm, simply following rules. Orders are not questioned, hierarchies are strictly adhered to, command is strictly from the top to the bottom. Criticism, argument and discussion, in general, are absent. The notion of a deal is hardly conceivable. Meticulous attention to the rules and total subordination are valued. The individuals' interests are not so much shared as non-existent. They are there to do a job. If they do not do it, or do not like it, they are out.

The king and his barons

In this organization power rests firmly with a single individual. The original industrial moguls of the steel, newspaper, car, cattle and film businesses were of this sort – and many of their heirs continue to uphold the family tradition. He (or she) makes all the appointments and hands out favours and largesse according to his/her whim. The barons ceaselessly compete for favour through flattery and exaggerated displays of loyalty and affection. Loyalty is of the utmost importance. Unlike in the family model, corruption, crimes and wrongdoing are all accepted, as long as they please the king. Occasionally the barons will gang together into cliques, conspiring against each other or against the king, looking for an opportunity to stab him in the back. He, for his part, endeavours to keep them constantly on their guard, playing them off against each other. The control and manipulation of information is of paramount importance for the king, who may employ spies and informants to keep him in touch with the moves of his barons, while at the same time spreading rumours which unsettle them and keep them guessing.

The civil service

Like the previous organization, this one too is characterized by machinations, conspiracies and double-dealing. There are, however, some important differences. First, power is not concentrated in the hands of one man/woman. Second, the whole process is covered by a veneer of democracy, accountability and responsibility and there is very rare recourse to violence or force. Third, there are many different interests, 'plurality', competing for prevalence, the final result often being a compromise resulting from all kinds of more or less vicious horse-trading. Alliances, sometimes of the unholiest kind, are commonplace; yesterday's hated adversary becomes today's trusted friend if the circumstances demand it. Information is essential here, but equally important are subtle psychological skills of manipulation and persuasion. The specific analogy, often lampooned, refers to senior government departments where experienced and skilled civil servants seek to serve their frequently changing political masters in ways which also serve their own personal interests, especially survival. Dealing and double-dealing is their way of life; actual consensus is not.

Nest of vipers

Here each person stands for him/herself. Subterfuge, back-stabbing and bad-mouthing are commonplace. At all times people strive to keep their backs covered, to take credit for every success and distance themselves from every failure, to undermine the credibility of others and to generate an aura of power, competence and charisma for themselves. Cliques and alliances may emerge but they tend to be short-lived, as each member seeks to gain personal advantage of them. At times in organizations like this, politics degenerates into something akin to the law of the jungle. Information and disinformation are crucial in gaining advantage over one's adversaries. Innuendo, slander and rumour abound. What then holds such organizations together? Very frequently, the stakes of the game are so high that people are willing to put up with it. Alternatively, the cost of dropping out of the nest are so extreme that the effect is the same, people stick together with people they loathe and fear. Secret intelligence organizations, police departments and some military groups sometimes look like vipers' nests. But so also do some advertising agencies, television and film companies and departments in academia.

Warring camps

In these organizations a number of different camps can be distinguished. Each camp has its own politics, whether it be that of a family, an alliance or any of the others. The camps are distinguished from each other in terms of a powerful difference, the origin of which may lie inside the organization (say, management vs. workers, sales vs. production) or outside (say, religion, ethnicity, gender). People have some loyalty to their camp, but in most cases each camp is an alliance. Nevertheless, there are strong forces preventing the merging of the camps, the crossing of lines. Politics often takes the form of continuous contest over territory, with now one side prevailing and now another. Hostilities fluctuate, as does the extent to which the parties choose to abide by mutually agreed rules and procedures. With warring camps, who have a vested interest in maintaining their differences, conflict resolution usually amounts to a temporary lull in hostilities – through compromise. This is most evident in the annual pay wrangle between some employers and their employees' unions. Both 'sides' are firmly committed to their own, very different, views of each other's worth and intentions.

The battle simply continues from where it left off the previous year. The perspective is neatly illustrated by the following brief, and actual, exchange between the managing director of a pharmaceuticals firm and a management consultant. They were taking a drink together during a break in a management training course:

> *MD*: You know, we're in dispute again, just like last year. They are demanding more money and are doing even less work. They want more perks – and for what? And I know for a fact that many of them are moonlighting, so they are getting cash on the side. How can we deal with people like that?
> *Consultant*: Yes. But the funny thing is that they are saying exactly the same things about you.

In practice organizations can be a mix of political types. Even those which appear locked into a particular pattern may suddenly shift into a different one. This is most radically illustrated by the fundamental transformation in the economies of Eastern Europe in the 1990s. Organizations that yesterday were managed by a combination of central edict and worker committees, today face the broader political range of the market economies. In other words, people have their first taste of the best and worst of a new industrial relations – especially the warring, family, and machine type.

TO SUMMARIZE . . .

In this chapter we have presented organizations as a 'natural' reflection of the people who comprise them. In other words, it should come as no surprise that, in some way or another, people will bring their interests, attitudes, prejudices and allegiances into the making of organizational life. Who they meet, who they work with, and who they are controlled by, will influence how people 'present' themselves, and what they choose to do. This is organizational politics. So 'dealing', tacitly or openly, nicely or nastily, with or without open conflict, is part of organizational life. How much, though, and in what form, depends on the issues faced and the political culture of the organization – and we have offered a framework to indicate the range of possibilities.

- Politics are a normal feature of organizational life.
- Politics are as much about trust and loyalty as about deception and corruption.
- Organizational politics do not have to be conducted in a destructive way.
- Conflict in organizations is often regarded as acceptable and even good if it is kept within bounds.
- Many of the deals within organizations are about resource allocation.
- The criteria by which departments and proposals are evaluated are a key issue in organizational politics.
- Different ways of handling conflict may be appropriate in different organizational cultures.
- The metaphors used to describe conflict and deals in organizations say a lot about how they work and how things may be influenced.

THESAURUS ENTRIES

career	group
communication	institution
competition	institutionalization
conflict	metaphors
culture	politics
decision making	power
emotion	roles
games	sabotage
goals	status

5

MORALS

In the Summer of 1991 the Bank of England took a sudden and extraordinary step: it shut down the London base of a major international bank (the Bank of Credit and Commerce International). This bank served considerable financial interests in Arab countries and Asia, as well as in the UK and America. It was known for its philanthropic use of funds, inspired by the religious beliefs of its founder. It provided banking facilities for individuals as well as major corporations, including the accounts of a number of British charities. It also laundered drug money, supported shady arms deals, bolstered military dictatorships, underpinned a secret nuclear bomb project involving Libya, Argentina and Pakistan, was party to a CIA deal on the prosecution of General Noriega, ex-dictator of Panama, and consistently falsified its records. How could this happen? How could the principles of a respectable and cautious part of the business community become so corrupted?

Elsewhere, completely out of the news, a manager at a prestigious British firm of Chartered Accountants confidently adds an administration charge to a client's account, based on an invented item of 'work done'. And, in the forecasting department of a multinational cigarette company a clerk wryly alters the sales forecasts for a fourth time – because top management 'still don't like them'. The clerk has learned that she needs to produce work which will back up management's objectives for end-of-year sales.

These are actual events. How are we to understand them, both great and small? Are they all part of the **game** of business and organizing? (See Chapter 4, Dealing and double-dealing.) Does it not matter what you do, as long as you are not found out? Is it power that determines what has to be done – who wields the biggest stick? What unites the incidents are questions of **value** and morality; the distinctions between what is right or wrong in organizational behaviour, and whether, and how, such distinctions are made and acted upon.

KNOWING RIGHT FROM WRONG

We can add further examples which, in their different ways, go to the heart of moral beliefs:

- police officers who fabricate a confession
- the 'charity' organizer who takes our money, and then vanishes
- the Exxon oil company's reluctance to take responsibility after one of its tankers massively pollutes the Alaskan shoreline.

When we look closely at such incidents there is a cluster of 'dubious' behaviours – lying, deceit, fraud, evasion, negligence. In most cultures such behaviours have a hard edge to them, and sometimes strong moral implications. We may argue that no organization should be run that way. But many are, and organizational members invent terms which help them to do so – such as 'creative accounting', 'being economical with the truth', 'tidying the books', 'not rocking the boat', and 'safeguarding the interests of the shareholders', symbols of a sub-morality – to which we shall return.

But when are issues really *moral* ones? And who makes such judgements? This is problematic. At a psychological level the distinction has been drawn between actions which produce feelings of guilt in the actor, and those which produce embarrassment. The former relate to morality. So, if a fitter knowingly fails to properly service a valve on a gas-line which then leaks and kills a colleague, the guilt he feels relates to his feeling of culpability in harming another human being. The principle of not harming somebody through one's actions, directly or indirectly, lies at the heart of moral concepts. The person who lets down colleagues by not turning up for a key meeting, which leads to the loss of a client, may feel deeply embarrassed. She has transgressed the expectation of her work **group**, but it is not felt as a moral issue. The harm is neither as devastating nor as irreversible as that which followed the fitter's actions. The roots of the harm principle go deep into society's codes of conduct, but it is expressed in different ways according to the cultural and religious history of a country.

Institutional processes can subvert, even obliterate, moral judgement, producing their own counter-morality or amorality. Police officers have knowingly falsified confessions which have sent innocent people to jail – or to their execution. Any feelings of guilt are rationalized away in terms such as 'well, that sort of person deserves what they get', or that 'it was important to get a conviction at all costs'. Many organizations so strongly inculcate their members with their own values that people become blind to individual moral issues. In effect, the organization's values come to stand for what is moral and what is not. This was most horrifically demonstrated in Nazi Germany. The defence offered by German officers who systematically brutalized and annihilated millions of human beings was, 'I was only obeying my orders.' Indeed, the response to organizational 'orders' says much for the frailty of human moral conduct when it is subjected to a strong organizational mould. The Nazi doctrine had an additional feature to help crush conventional moral thought: Jews, gypsies, the mentally ill and others were to be considered as amongst the sub-humans of mankind, so they merited their fate.

When morality is replaced by organizational **norms**, or by a professional code of practice, people can defer to those as the arbiters of the rightness or wrongness of their action. They provide a short cut to moral **decision making**, relieving people of much of the burden of having to make up their own mind. This can, step by step, move people into self-justifying positions, rationalizations, which, by any other criteria, would be immoral. So it's 'just tough', or part of the 'realities of doing business', that Joe's job will be removed when he is away on holiday and he will not know until he gets back. And 'we'd lose the contract' if community representatives were told the true noise levels of the new factory that is going to be built near their village. 'If we don't harvest that old forest, someone else will.' Robert Maxwell, perhaps the king of do-it-yourself business morals, owned a vast international commercial empire before his death by drowning in 1991. It transpired that he had happily bent and broken just about every rule of 'proper' business practice in the pursuit of a vast personal fortune and power. The harm he did to thousands of pensioners (he appropriated and spent their funds) was incalculable. 'Doing business', it seemed, whatever and however, served as a self-sustaining objective.

WORKING MORALITY

Some medical and research organizations have 'ethics committees' to consider the morality of adopting new programmes or procedures in their work. However, decisions in most organizations are rarely subjected to such scrutiny. Most just happen, a product of the personal beliefs of the actors involved, their **roles** and professional expectations, and the **politics** and **culture** of the organization. All these come into play when, for instance, a board of directors is deciding on which bit of their company to close down, whether to continue promoting a product with a poor safety record, or the extent of their own pay rises compared with those of their employees.

Do the men and women who run organizations make sound moral judgements? Are their personal and commercial interests served by doing so? While there are many companies which profess caring corporate policies, 'business with a human face', the law of the jungle, each to his or her own, has a habit of re-emerging. In the early 1990s the directors of many large British corporations decided to award themselves massive pay increases (ranging from 50 to 300 per cent) while insisting that their staff receive no more than 6 per cent – 'in order to survive the recession'. 'It makes good economic sense', asserted the directors, 'to pay the market rate for leadership talent'. 'It is greedy, unfair and extraordinarily insensitive', cried the workers.

Moral logic is fluid when it comes to protecting vested interests. It is not uncommon for one group to challenge another in morally toned language, while the defenders offer an 'obviously reasonable and practical' explanation for their actions, disclaiming the relevance of moral considerations. Moral accusations make powerful **rhetoric**, and it is sometimes seen as wiser to disengage from such **discourse** and fight on other terms.

Many organizations will claim that their prime obligation is to serve their shareholders, to give them as good a return on their investment as possible. Then, they say, as long they operate within the law (although some will fight it or bend it), issues of moral culpability are not really relevant to their actions. Such pragmatism has justified the commercial exploitation of the seas, rivers and forests, despite the devastating harm that has been wreaked upon the Earth – its animals, plants and human communities. Only recently has there been a slight convergence between these patently moral concerns and the amoral logic of economics. The latter can begin to incorporate the former if the Earth itself is not considered as akin to income – something that can be spent and used because there will always be more of it.

PERSONALIZING AND DEPERSONALIZING

We are most likely to **feel** issues as moral ones when they touch us personally: the disquiet or guilt from feeling party to a possible injustice or harm. There are decisions which some people find hard not to experience as morally problematic, such as sacking, takeovers, not promoting, demoting. The anguish can be seen in the following comments from a senior computer analyst:

> There are parts of my job that I hate. Today I've written a report where I've almost suggested that there ought to be redundancies in certain areas. I've felt dreadful about it. It's the first time I've done anything like that, and I'm really not sure what I'm doing. I'm talking about people I know. It would be a new computer system which would replace two people with one part-timer. I never thought I'd be in a position where I would be making these recommendations. But it's just a recommendation, not a decision.

Advice on how to handle these situations is usually aimed at damage limitation, not at confronting the moral dilemma. So we find instructions to the carriers of bad tidings to 'offer help and constructive criticism along with the bad news'; 'present the broader organizational and economic picture', or 'hire an external expert to do the job'. A crisp and soothing organizational language exists to help decision makers depersonalize and rationalize their anxieties and put them into the *organization's* 'moral' framework – where it is just part of the job: the rules of the game. For example:

- On dismissing someone:
    'Sometimes you have to be cruel to be kind; it's in their ultimate interests to work for someone more suitable.'
    'It's your job or theirs.'

'The organization's efficiency is at stake.'
- On promising an unlikely delivery date:
    'Well, we must win the contract first. We'll worry about delivery later.'
- On selling an environmentally damaging product:
    'It's our job to make profits. It's the government's job to protect the environment.'
    'It's not illegal yet. If we don't sell them, someone else will.'
- On selling weapon-potential chemicals to an unreliable military regime:
    'As far as we are concerned they are for agricultural purposes, and the government has not opposed an export licence.'

In the world of economic rationalizations winning a contract, staying in business, satisfying shareholders, are 'what it is about'. Lies are not lies; they are 'part truths' which 'make good economic sense'. Someone has to get hurt in market place competition and **conflict**, goes the argument; there 'must be winners and losers'. Additionally there is the concern that **motivates** people to protect the security and income that, in our culture, is obtainable only through a job; fine altruistic values cannot survive the cut-and-thrust world of business. In these various ways tough, and potentially harmful, decisions are transformed to the status of an organizational procedure, or control device – and a seemingly enduring feature of organizational functioning (see Chapter 3, Rules are rules).

BETWEEN THE CRACKS

Not all morally questionable actions are easy to hide or neutralize within the organization. **Harassment** is a case in point. Verbal, sexual or physical harassment is usually felt as a moral violation. The perpetrator, however, might talk about it as 'simply a bit of fun' or 'a game', 'all part of everyday working'. Individuals are often alone with their moral conscience when they experience, or witness, harassment. Should they complain? If it is happening to them, will anyone be sympathetic? Helen, one of our students, recalls her first week in a major corporation:

We were in this boardroom, three male managers and me. One pointed to the large table in the middle of the room, and said to me:

'Go on, lie out on that. We'll all have a go then.' I felt dizzy, sick and horrified. I wanted to run out, but I held on. They thought it was a great joke.

Joanne, another student, describes the constant sexual taunts, disguised as joking, from male managers in the oil company in which she worked. It went on so long that she eventually summoned up the courage to turn on the men responsible. They immediately chided her for her 'over-reaction'. She ended up feeling embarrassed and humiliated.

With Helen and Joanne we enter the realm of the sexual politics of organizations (see Chapter 12, Sex). In many companies codes of sexual conduct and 'acceptable' sexual attitudes are dominantly male, and male-dominated. This can be powerfully oppressive, leaving women vulnerable and unsupported. The male-centred ideology can also contribute to a devaluation of the worth of women when it comes to decisions on selection and promotion. The 'gender logic' of the organization, like the commercial logic, is influenced by the values of the dominant coalition of people who hold the **power**.

Other social and interpersonal matters are also affected in this manner – from AIDS, gays, blacks and the disabled, to policies on maternity leave, paternity leave, job sharing and creches. The tension is between decisions which, at one level, may be regarded as about morally significant issues, but at another level as a matter of **conformity** to the values, or convenience, of the organization.

POWER, AND THE ORGANIZATIONAL IMPERATIVE

People will act with apparent moral integrity in one situation, but then with little moral concern elsewhere. The key to this paradox lies, as already hinted, in the power that different organizations (the 'church', the 'office', the 'business') can have over what we do. One social psychological experiment forcefully illustrates the point. Forty seminary students, who expressed particularly high standards of moral behaviour, were told to prepare a lecture on one of two topics – the parable of the Good Samaritan or job opportunities for graduates. Half the students in each group were told they had a very tight time schedule; the rest were told they had plenty of time. Then, sneakily, the experimenters made it impossible for the students not to pass an obviously 'distressed man' on their way to the lecture room. Only sixteen stopped to help him, most of them from the group that thought they had plenty of time to get to the lecture. Those who were going to give a Good Samaritan lecture were just as likely to walk past the man as those who were not.

So here we have morally aware people acting in ways quite contrary to their expressed values – in order 'to get the job done.' An even more alarming, and famous, experiment, was conducted by social psychologist Stanley Milgram in the 1960s.[4] Forty males, of various ages, volunteered for paid participation in an experiment on 'the effects of punishment on learning'. They were instructed to administer electric shocks to a 'learner' who was strapped to a chair in an adjoining room. Each time the learner gave a wrong answer, or no answer, the shock had to be increased. The volunteers operated their own control switch which was marked from 'slight shock' through to 'danger: severe shock', ending with an ominous 'XXX' marking. As the shocks increased the volunteers would hear cries from the learner, and pounding on the adjoining wall. Any hesitation to go on was met with a cool instruction from the experimenter to the effect that they had to continue in order to complete the experiment. Milgram found all the volunteers were prepared to administer 300 volts to the learners, and 26 of them went to the end of the shock series, despite the fact that the learner had gone silent by then. The experiment (itself criticized as morally dubious) was rigged so that the learner would deliberately give wrong answers and feign distress. There were no actual electric shocks.

There are two important messages that we can take from these studies. Firstly, we may firmly *espouse* a moral stance to help, or not to injure others, but organizational life is a severe testing ground where the best of us can fail to support our belief with moral *action*. Secondly, obedience to commands from a superior is a strong force in our society, even if it means we will hurt another human being.

CHEATING – INSTITUTIONALIZED 'IMMORALITY'

The revelation of massive fraud and criminality of organizations such as the Bank of Credit and Commerce International and those of Robert Maxwell leave most people with a mixed response. On the one hand there is the sense of moral indignation that such empires can cheat and exploit in the way that they have done. On the other hand there is the growing expectation that all businesses have their seamy side and some are simply more seamy, and more hypocritical, than others.

It is likely that few organizations operate without some form of hidden economy, individual profits made from **fiddling** – bending the rules, pilfering, short-changing or overcharging. Our moral appraisal of fiddling depends on where we stand. If we do the fiddling ourselves we can view it as a 'fair perk', or a 'necessary action'. If we are the victims of fiddling we become morally indignant. Also *who* we fiddle from comes into the moral equation. We might regard the wealthy, and well-insured, superstore as fair game for a little pilfering. The same action towards the small corner shop could inflict unacceptable injury on its owners.

Fiddling has a long history. There are ancient records of theft from Egyptian storehouses which reveal a remarkably similar recipe to today's thefts.[5] An insider supplied grain and fabrics from the storehouse to an outside ship's captain (the 'fence') who in turn bribed the temple scribes to alter the stock records so no-one would notice the shortfall. Fiddling can take various forms – from organized theft to unauthorized phone calls, and 'borrowed' pens, paper and computer discs. The persistence of fiddling suggests it is intrinsic to the social organization of work, acting as a necessary adjunct to other financial and psychological rewards. Fiddling offers some people the opportunity to rectify, or compensate for, felt injustices in their working arrangements. It can offer an escape from stifling **bureaucracy** and arbitrary **control**. For a minority, fiddling can make the difference between a job they can financially survive on, and one they cannot. Such was the rationale presented for fiddling time sheets in a building-repairs organization where one of us once worked:

> Every Friday we had to fill in our time-sheets for work done that week. Bert, the tradesman I worked with, called them 'fiddle sheets'. It was soon apparent why. At the bottom of the sheet was a space for hours overtime worked. Every week Bert put in 15 hours, and told me to do the same. The first time this happened I was astonished. We hadn't worked 15 hours overtime; in fact we hadn't worked any overtime. We hadn't even worked our required 42 hours! Bert reassured me: 'Listen. You do exactly what I do. Our pay is lousy and

this bumps it up a bit, helps us get by. As you work with me we both put down the same hours, OK? It will be all right'. And it was all right. The foreman received our time-sheets and immediately signed them – without a blink. It soon became apparent that he was in the same game. I felt really torn to start with, as it was so plainly dishonest. Soon, though, I saw their point. Their take-home pay was amongst the lowest in the country.

Here we see a guilty conscience transformed with a rationalization of the sort: 'Well, it's fair to lie in these particular circumstances.' Usually, fiddles have a complex set of internal rules and checks – small fiddlers do not automatically turn into big ones; lone fiddlers do not necessarily progress to gang fiddlers. How much is taken, and by whom, is usually fairly well worked out within the group. For example, restaurant workers on the fiddle will work out a hierarchy of reward – the food, alcohol and other products – which each person can take. There are shop assistants in clothing stores who have bought similar clothing, on discount outside the shop, to re-sell it – just one or two items a month – at a personal profit in the shop. Fiddling is taken for granted in some big corporations, by fiddlers and fiddled alike. It is built into the overall running costs, and is tacitly accepted as part of the informal organization of work. Often preventive policing simply gives rise to more cunning fiddling, and the costs of heavy surveillance may soon outweigh the company's losses.

BLOWING THE WHISTLE

There are, as we have shown, social processes within organizations which create their own particular brands of morality. They permit, and often encourage, conduct which is self-serving: conduct dislocated from the values the organization might publicly profess, and from the principles by which, privately, organizational members try to live. Sometimes, the uneasy balance between these different forces is dramatically upset: someone blows the whistle. The whistle blower may reside within the corporate ranks, or be an outsider. Either way, the motive is the same: a deep disquiet about something that is going on in the organization that they regard as very wrong, so wrong that they are prepared to take on the organization in order to ensure that the 'malpractice' is brought to public attention, and prevented from recurring. Typically, whistle blowers will act from an overriding sense of moral conscience, whatever the personal consequences. Because the personal risks are high, there are not many whistle blowers. The Mafia is an example, albeit extreme, of an organization which has a distinctive way of dealing with members who blow the whistle on them.

Some external whistle blowers have strengthened and protected themselves by becoming organized as pressure groups. They act as watch dogs, sniffing out dubious or immoral organizational practice. In the 1960s Ralph Nader started a consumer-watch after he publicly exposed the American Ford Motor Company, who were, it seemed, deliberately continuing production of a car they knew was liable to explode on impact. His style of work is reflected in some of the activities of consumer associations across the world. Certain whistle blowers focus their work in particular areas, such as Friends of the Earth and Greenpeace, who make it their business to expose companies whose actions are harming the natural environment.

The status of whistle blowers in broader society is usually high. Some are elevated to the level of hero or heroine, depending on the cause they espouse and the risks they take. Not surprisingly, they are seen rather differently by the enterprises they attack. If they are employees they can be branded as traitors, disloyal. Complaints based on moral grounds are often met by a wall of organizational defensiveness. The organization is keen to demonstrate its moral integrity.

Big pressure groups, such as trade unions and consumer organizations, may be a reasonable match for large corporations in the hassle which usually follows whistle blowing. On their own, though, individual employees are far more vulnerable. Their intimate knowledge of the organization and its secrets poses an enormous threat to those who have profited from irregular practices, negligence, or law breaking. Whistle blowers are to be feared, and some corporations will go to extraordinary lengths to disable them. Robert Jackall,[6] an American anthropologist, tells the tale of a large food-processing company which amply illustrates the point. We paraphrase:

> Brady, a conscientious financial officer (trained as a chartered accountant) noticed that a peer of his in Marketing had overshot his budget, and had faked $75,000 of invoices to cover the discrepancy. He submitted a report on the matter to the CEO, but was dismayed to find the report blocked before it got to him. Brady was asked, several times, to drop the matter.

Gradually, he was frozen out of key decisions and his authority cut back. Nevertheless, he stumbled across further, even larger, financial irregularities – the manipulation of pension funds which guaranteed large personal bonuses for top managers. Brady was deeply troubled and, for want of some access to the CEO, informed a friend in the company who had the CEO's ear. The information reached the CEO, without mentioning Brady's name. Immediately following a meeting between the CEO and his top aides Brady's friend was fired and escorted from the building by armed guards.

Brady then realized that the CEO was part of the conspiracy, and took the matter to the corporation's chief lawyer – who 'did not want to touch it with a barge pole'. Brady was advised by a senior manager to accept it as 'part of the game in business today'. He could not. He was summarily fired and was ejected from the company building by a security guard.

This story poignantly characterizes the way an organization can evolve a 'working' morality to suit parts of itself. Using power and fear, certain members can twist the professional conventions of business to serve their positions and greed. As fear and secrecy take hold, moral concerns give way to the pragmatics of 'keeping your nose clean', 'doing what you are told', and 'obeying orders'. As one manager in Jackall's study pithily asserts:

> What is right in the corporation is not what is right in a man's home or in his church. What is right in the corporation is what the guy above wants from you. That's what morality is in the corporation.[7]

It would be wrong to conclude that organizations inevitably sap the moral energy of those who work in them. However, what we do need to appreciate is that in organizations as various as food processing, churches, steel manufacturing and schools, the most moral of human beings can gradually find themselves doing things that they never would have imagined they could – or should.

- Caring, upright, moral citizens can change dramatically when they arrive at work, breaking their personal moral codes.
- People's personal morality can be subverted by strong organizational norms.
- Organizations can invent their own brand of morality which may be in conflict with more conventional moral behaviour.

- Self-interest, drive for profit, and fear can induce individuals and corporations to harm others and the environment.
- Organizational humour can disguise acts such as harassment and abuse.
- Cheating, to some degree, is a part of most enterprises; it can be organizationally helpful as well as destructive.
- Whistle blowers act as the organization's conscience – and are often treated roughly for being so.

THESAURUS ENTRIES

bureaucracy	institution
conflict	jokes
conformity	motivation
control	norm
culture	politics
decision making	power
discourse	rhetoric
ethics	role
fiddling	sexual harassment
games	values
group	

6

IT'S NOT MY PROBLEM

> One of my problems, Helen, is that whenever I have a problem to face, I always have another problem concurrent with it, which seems to take precedence. So bear with me if I seem abstracted. I cannot give my full attention to anything, because too many things require my full attention. My life has chosen to arrange itself on ramshackle lines, like a badly wrapped parcel about to burst open; I can secure one corner of it only by disturbing the others, which then must be secured in turn.
>
> (Keith Waterhouse, *Billy Liar on the Moon*)

An important part of what people are employed to do in organizations is to solve **problems**. Or is it? In this chapter, we are going to suggest that people may do other much more important things with problems than solve them. Like create them. And that people may like having problems, and may organize their lives so as to keep themselves supplied with problems. It can be important to know who owns problems; also, at any particular time, there are some problems which are the fashionable ones to be associated with.

To save confusion, we need to make a clear distinction. We are going to say that someone has a *problem* when something is not as they would like it to be, they feel unsure about what to do about it, and some anxiety about whether they can do anything. We would distinguish it from a *difficulty*, where something is not as someone would like it to be but they feel reasonably confident that they will be able to deal with it. For example, if someone is lost in a strange town, that could be a difficulty. They will probably have confidence that they will eventually find their way. They have procedures that they can adopt (asking a policeman, buying a map, telephoning the person they are going to see) which mean that they are sure they will get there. If, on the other hand, they are trying to persuade a team to adopt a project, this may be a problem; they want the team to adopt it, but they may not be sure how to go about persuading them or whether they will be able to exercise such **leadership**.

THE REAL PROBLEM IS . . .

What do we mean when we say that the *real* problem is something rather than something else? Often in organizations, it means that we think our way of looking at the situation is correct, and should prevail over other people's views. We describe our view as 'real' to imply that other views are not, and that everyone should accept our view.

We know that different specialists have different **perceptions** of the same situation. If a person takes the same problem to a friend, to a counsellor, to a doctor, to a tutor or to a priest, each of those people will hear different problems in what that person says. In the same way, in a company, if the same data are given to the marketing director, the finance director and the production director, they will see different problems in them. They have different backgrounds, training and responsibilities, different ways of **learning** and **knowing**, and they are looking for different things. Which of these people is seeing the *real* problem? In the view of organizing on which this book is based, the whole idea of a 'real' problem is misleading. Problems are neither real nor unreal; they are a view of a situation, just as a landscape painting represents one person's interpretation of a landscape. Complete **objectivity** is not available.

It may be that some people see a situation as a problem while others do not. Some people seem to take the most horrendous series of personal tragedies calmly. Many other people would like to be able to do that, but find it an unattainable ideal. Other people might be given a lunch menu, and become bogged down in the **decision-making** problem which this offers them. Such people may attract great sympathy except from their work-mates, who tend to find them very irritating.

Yet other people seem to have a set of personal **constructs** making some of their problems insoluble. Consider the problem for a middle-aged man who finds that his hair is steadily becoming thinner. Many people will not take this as a problem. It is 'just one of those things', all part of ageing, which in itself is outside their control, and so taken as not a problem. Other people of the same age will not accept either hair loss or ageing as inevitable, but will instead take them as problems; they then begin to look for solutions in hair transplants, health farms and so on. These examples illustrate why people might prefer not to do anything about some things which other people might take as problems. The potential solutions are likely to be costly, and they might well prefer to turn their attention to something else.

ALTERNATIVE PROBLEM CONSTRUCTIONS

Suppose you pass a car showroom, and see a car that you want. You do not have enough money for it. So you could construct the situation as follows: 'Successive governments have run the economy so badly that I do not get enough money to buy that car.' That could be a very convenient way of constructing the issue from your point of view, because you cannot do anything about it; it is not a problem in the sense that we have been using the word. It could also be a very comforting way of constructing it in terms of **cognitive** dissonance; it does not require you to adjust your thinking in any way. Alternatively, you could construct the problem that you spent too much on your holiday last year. It is still too late to do anything about that, but it does have some implications for action – for example, when considering how much to spend on your holiday next year. Or you could construct the problem that you are not deeply enough involved in your work, and that is why you are wasting time and energy looking at car showrooms, and day-dreaming about the cars afterwards. This problem definition leaves you looking in a different direction for solutions, a direction over which you have more control.

There is a general principle about problem construction here which is shown in Figure 6.1. In this diagram, the nearer one is to the origin, 'me, this, now', the more chance there is that one can do something with the problem that one has defined. Problems that are defined in terms of *me*, *now* and *this* can be worked on, while problems that are to do with *someone*, *some time* and *something* cannot. Not that we want to define all problems in such a way that we can do something about them. There might be

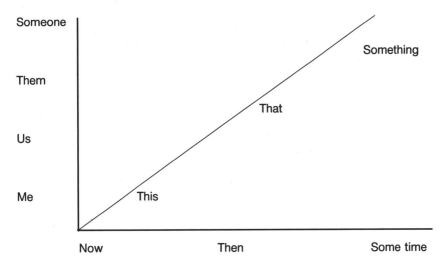

Figure 6.1   *Domains of problem definition*

other things that we would prefer to do with our resources, or we might prefer to do nothing. It is a favourite pastime in organizations to complain about company policy, but without any real intention to do anything, and if anyone does start suggesting that something should be done, they are spoiling a popular leisure activity – having a good whinge. The same is true for conversations about governments or football managers in pubs; the problems defined are not meant to be acted on. The conversation is being held to make people feel better, and for the fun of talking about what fools the powerful people are. The fun is spoiled if you go away feeling you have to do something about it.

The point is illustrated by a true story from one of the authors:

When I was drafting this section for the first time, the door bell rang. As my wife was downstairs and I was upstairs I ignored it. A few minutes later the screen of my word processor went blank and the fan fell silent. The electrician had come to check the earthing of our mains, and he had done what electricians do – turned the power off. Several paragraphs of precious prose had been for ever lost to mankind. But what was the real problem? Here are some possible constructions of it:

1   My wife should have remembered that I was upstairs working, and that a disruption of the power supply was likely to cause a disruption both to my work and to family life.

2   I should have learned to use the 'autosave' facility in the software better, to ensure that not too much was lost if the power went off.
3   I should have known what I was saying well enough to be able to say it all again without trouble.
4   I should have a device for ensuring continuity of power supply to my PC.
5   I should re-learn handwriting, rather than depending on fragile technology.

The first of these definitions of the problem is of a common sort – blame another person. But, in terms of Figure 6.1, the 'she' and 'then' qualities of the definition show that it is likely to be frustrating. The second definition implies an equally unrealistic expectation that a person can stop being lazy in learning software packages; of course everyone should know how the autosave works, but they equally should know that they cut corners to save time, and are likely to continue to do so. The third definition is another way of producing self-punishing but impossible solutions. The fourth is technically possible, but very expensive, and is rather like building a concrete wall behind the stable door through which the horse has just bolted. The fifth definition, to learn handwriting again, is sensible but too boring to use; what we find interesting or boring may be an important part of our problem construction.

The reader can see how the problem construction was eventually handled; it was turned into an example of how different problems can be constructed from the same circumstances. In this case, it did not have to be a problem at all. We do not mean to imply that we all have a free choice in our problem construction. It is often more emotional and involving than that. When we are angry it is less easy to see alternative problem constructions. But even then it may be possible.

AS IF I DIDN'T HAVE ENOUGH PROBLEMS

Problems do not always get solved, nor do we always want them to be. There can be situations that are problematic according to the definition at the beginning of this chapter; the person with the problem is not sure what to do, and they feel anxious as to whether they will be able to deal with the situation at all. But at the same time they may not really want to lose the problem. A problem can be a way of giving **meaning** to our situation.

For example, one of us had a boss whose holidays were a miracle of complexity. On the way to his holiday, he would swap cars with friends, often twice in different countries; he would pick up materials from several different suppliers on the way to the port, make sure that he had persuaded the shipping company to load a case of his favourite holiday wine for him to buy duty free on the ferry, fix a range of meetings to tie in with parts of the holiday, and so on. Then one year everything was going wrong in his job. He was being threatened with losing most of his responsibility, and was working hard to save a department that he had built up. That year he and his family simply went on holiday. He did not need any more problems.

To say he did not 'need' any more problems is not meant ironically. We need problems. Some of us need more than others. But if we did not have problems, we would probably have to invent them. If we have no problems we can get bored, or feel that we are underperforming. And if we do not have any problems in one part of our life, we may look for some in another area of our life. So if your relationships outside work are nicely settled, you may find yourself stirring things up at work. We may seek adventure as a means of causing extra problems, whether at the career, holiday, hobby or marital levels.

This sounds very neat. If that were the whole story, we could all be content generating just the number of problems that we need and can cope with, and then working on them. Most of us do not experience as high a degree of control over the supply of problems as this would imply, for two reasons.

Firstly, each person's world consists of more than just themselves, and different people will have different problems that they like to deal with, and different sources of problems. At the time when someone is experiencing all the problems they need at work, their partner may be bored and needing a family problem to work on. That is when one gets the Billy Liar feeling, from the beginning of the chapter, of a badly wrapped parcel about to burst open.

Secondly, everybody has vulnerable points where they do not feel in control. The death of someone they love; being in a new and frightening organization; having a cold; feelings of despair and meaninglessness; all of these leave a person in a state where they may have no sense of control over their problem supply.

FASHIONABLE PROBLEMS

Problems can be an important part of how we see ourselves. One writer said that if you solve someone else's problem for them, that is robbery.[8] They had something which they had taken some time making, and you go charging in and solve it for them. A participant on a course was talking about a problem he wanted to work on.

> *Participant*: The trouble is, I am not sure that I am any good at my job.
>
> *Tutor*: I see, the trouble is that you are not sure that you are any good at your job.
>
> *Participant*: No, you have not heard me right. The trouble is that I went straight into this job after university, and I think maybe I should have stayed on and done a master's degree first.
>
> *Tutor*: I see, you think you should have stayed on and done a master's degree first.
>
> *Participant*: No, that's not it. The thing is, really, that I got married last year, and in some ways it is very rewarding, but in other ways I find it restricts my freedom a lot.
>
> *Tutor*: I see, your marriage restricts your freedom.
>
> *Participant*: Well no, it's not really that. It's more that I am not sure if I am any good at my job . . .

This conversation continued for an hour and a half. The two parties resumed discussion the following day, and concluded that safely wrapped up in the circle of reasoning was a favourite problem. If you have a problem that you do not want to lose, you may make it like the soap in the bath, so that every time someone thinks they have got hold of it, it slips away somewhere else. This is because it can be an important part of how you see yourself, your **identity**. 'I am the sort of person who has this sort of problem.'

Some favourite problems go in fashions. For example, in the case above, if the participant had not had a marriage problem he might have been regarded, in his **culture,** as 'inadequate'. In many large companies, **stress** is currently the problem to be seen with. People know that stress is bad for them, and stress is a problem because they do not like taking health risks, feeling tired, being bad-tempered, and its various other symptoms. But do they want to lose this problem? If they are *not* stressed, what is wrong with them? Are they not important? Don't they care about the organization? Are they not committed? Thus stress can easily become a favourite problem.

When problems are part of a **communication**, you may use those problems as part of a statement to others and to yourself about who you are, and you will try and make sure that your problems are big ones. 'Mine is bigger than yours' is as important a boast (and as awkward to prove) with problems as with anything else, even if it is not likely to be stated in so many words.

OFFICIAL AND UNOFFICIAL PROBLEMS

There is often an 'official', or 'organizational', problem that you are supposed to be working on, which may have little to do with what you are really working on.

People at work spend a lot of time on illegitimate activities – things that play no part in their formal contract of employment. For example, it is not unknown for people to think about sex. But the boss who asks someone what they are working on rarely gets the answer, 'I was just thinking about sex, and about how I could either get more of it or stop thinking about it so much.' Instead, a much more 'proper' answer will be given. If a person has an official problem to work on, and also one that they are interested in for themselves, it will be the latter which will get most energy. **Motivation** issues may often be traced to just such a conflict of problems.

In organizational life, people do actually work on problems of how to get promoted, how to avoid having to work late on Tuesday, how to avoid working with someone they dislike, how to build their **informal network**, or how to have more dealings with someone to whom they are attracted. A clue to the difference between official problems and the ones the person is interested in can be found in the **language** which is used. If it is full of Business-speak, with lots of macho words like 'strategy', 'business plan', 'walking about', 'the bottom line', 'the end of the day', and other phrases that are current in television soap opera business meetings or trendy management books, then it is at least possible that we are hearing about a problem that they feel they ought to be working on rather than one with which they are actually engaged.

Job titles quite often imply that the occupant of the job should be focusing on a particular problem. In a university department, two people were appointed as 'placement officers'. Their appointments took place at a time when the department was having trouble finding enough good-quality industrial placements for their students, and the placement officers' titles associated them clearly with an attempt to solve this problem. The staff who were appointed were well organized and effective, and have produced an ever-increasing supply of placements, without compromising quality. This then leads other people to suggest that the problem does not exist (which is true – these two are continuously preventing it from becoming a problem), that they have an easy job, and that there are too many resources being put into that activity. People are often employed to solve an official problem, and being too successful in preventing that problem from arising may make other people think that there is no problem there.

A PROBLEM SHARED IS A PROBLEM HALVED

When we tell someone about a problem, we know that it is impossible to tell them everything, so we make more or less conscious choices about the **communication**. Sometimes we forget some details; when we are in the middle of a problem, it is often hard to see any one detail as more salient than all the others. We can never tell the other person the *whole* of a problem; problems are only problems because of the context of things around them, and life is too short to give a full account of that.

The aspects of our problems that we choose to share with others, and the way we present them, depends on the **impression formation** that we are engaged in with the other person. We may not wish to come over as incompetent, or soft, or hard, or whatever. We do not usually have a set of words ready as a description of our problem; more often, we make the description up as we go along, and quite often we are surprised by what we hear ourselves saying. People sometimes say, 'It helps just to talk it over', or 'Thank you – what I needed was a sounding board.' We may be influenced by wanting the other person to be interested in our problem, so we give them what we think they want. You may not trust the other person; for example, you may think that they will tell other people about what you have told them.

You may be trying to protect someone or something else. You

may not want people to think badly of your profession, or of your racial group, or of your class, or of your family. One of us was recently working with a student who was experiencing major problems with her course and her life. For a long time she did not want to talk about her problems. This turned out to be because she thought it would reflect badly on her parents.

From our point of view it looked very different; we shall probably never meet her parents, we would not be likely to make strong judgements about them, and we could not see why her parents should care what we felt about them. None the less, within her moral code, she should not do anything which could reflect badly on them – even if the personal cost of that was to fail her degree.

Similarly, people may fear that to tell someone about a problem may hurt the person they are talking to; that it will damage the listener's grip on reason and meaning, or that they will be shocked by what they hear. If you are seen as a pillar of the community, you may try to protect the community from seeing how wobbly you feel.

Perhaps it is best to acknowledge that problems are never fully shared. In an organization, the different parties to a person's problem each have their own problems, but they may still be able to help each other. It is often possible to find issues that will prove helpful to work on for two or more parties to a situation, even though none of them is working directly on the problem that they had to start off with. Think of the different people involved in the example in Chapter 1, Organization and organizing, who were organizing a party for new students. The new students wanted something to do; the member of staff wanted to be seen to be doing something for them; the older students wanted something to do a project on. They all had quite different problems, but the actions that resolved the problem for one group also helped resolve the different problem experienced by another group.

DON'T BRING ME PROBLEMS; BRING ME SOLUTIONS

This was a favourite phrase of Margaret Thatcher's (Prime Minister of Britain 1979–90), and is a classic statement of what we might call the 'planned irresponsibility' school of management thinking. It has been around in books of 'tips for managers' for a while, with notions like 'get the monkey off your back on to someone else's back': that is, when a person feels that they have a problem in their organization, the first thing to do is to see whether they can 'pass the monkey on' – make the problem someone else's. There may be some problems that are worth keeping, because they are fashionable, or because they fit the person's role. For example, in the early 1990s, many reputations were being made in health care by those who had addressed the problem of caring for patients with HIV and AIDS, and made this problem their own. This has been a fashionable problem.

It may be possible to delegate aspects of the work on a problem, while retaining its ownership and overall control. In some organizations, problem solution and construction are related to seniority. If a senior person needs a problem solved, they may use the bright young minds of junior staff. For problem construction, however, they may want to use all their own experience as a senior manager, and all their background knowledge.

But what of the person who, like Mrs Thatcher and the readers of those books about 'getting the monkey off your back', just wants to be brought solutions? If one is concerned with the survival of the organization this may seem worrying; what if no-one picks problems up? But perhaps the individuals concerned have learned something important for individual survival in organizations, which is that you need personal boundaries, areas in which you do not hold yourself responsible. If someone tries to take responsibility for too much, they may not be able to handle any of it effectively. We came across one manager who lacked such boundaries. He was a charming, caring man. He had time for his employees, and was a mine of information about what was going on and why. To our surprise, some of his subordinates found him very irritating. One of them explained that:

> Whenever he comes across anything, whatever it is, he thinks it is his problem. If we are lucky he forgets about it, and someone who has time will pick it up instead. If we are not lucky, it gets bundled up with all the other problems that he knows about, and popped into the problem soup that's inside his head.

The person who tries to take responsibility for everything – to take all the organization's monkeys on to his or her back – is likely to drop them. Overresponsibility can have consequences just as serious as irresponsibility. In voluntary organizations, it is often possible to see a few people who are taking responsibility for defining and working with too many problems. In so doing, they often feel that they are being heroic supporters of whatever cause the organization is devoted to; other people may just see them as clinging on to too much activity.

SUMMARY

Problems are not things. They are constructions in the minds of people. Different people construct different problems. When people talk about 'the real problem', they are often trying to influence others' views of **reality**. People often feel that they are judged by the problems they are seen with, and may wish to have big enough problems for others to take them seriously, and to be up with the fashion in their problems. Problems are not necessarily solved; they may be forgotten, or die of boredom, or be overtaken by events. People may nurture favourite problems. The problems that people actually care about and work on are not necessarily the ones that they are officially supposed to work on. It is difficult or perhaps impossible to tell another person all about a problem, but quite possible to negotiate with another person a new problem to work on together. There are strategies to stop oneself getting overloaded with problems; if someone is clearly underloaded or overloaded, other people may find this very irritating!

- Problems depend on the view that people take of a situation.
- There is no one 'real' or right way of seeing a problem.
- Some problems may be defined in such a way that the definer does not have to do anything about them.
- We need to have some problems, and people may have favourite problems that they would not want to lose.
- The problems that people care about are not necessarily the 'official' problems in the organization.
- When someone tells someone else about a problem, they always have to make choices about what aspects to disclose.

- People have different problems, but may be able to act together in ways which help several people or groups with their different problems.
- People can become overloaded with problems.

THESAURUS ENTRIES

cognitive
communication
construct
culture
decision making
identity
impression formation
informal networks
knowing
language

leadership
learning
meaning
motivation
objectivity
perception
problems
reality
stress

7

KNOWING THE ROPES

There is an enormous amount that you need to know to survive in an **organization**. You need to know your job, and where the toilets are, and your boss, and when people are joking, and your professional specialism, and how to get a letter typed, and who to take your problems to, and the terms and conditions of your employment. Can these all really be examples of the same activity – '**knowing**'? The answer has to be 'no'. We talk about several quite different activities or states as 'knowing'. We also talk about knowing in many different spheres of life. We know enough economics to pass an exam, and enough driving to pass a test; we also know our neighbours well enough to greet them when we pass them in the street. 'Knowing' goes much wider than the usual sense of **cognition.**

In this chapter, we shall start by considering three different types of knowing that are important in organizing – *professional knowing*, *managerial knowing* and *organizational knowing*. We will then go on to look at different ways of knowing: *knowing that* as opposed to *knowing how*, and *knowing by acquaintance* as opposed to *knowing by description*. Finally, we will examine the old cliché that *knowing is power*, and consider it alongside the idea that sometimes ignorance may be even more powerful.

DIFFERENT TYPES OF KNOWING

We shall discuss three types of knowing that are important in organizing. There is *professional knowing*, which is the kind of knowing that someone doing a similar professional job in a different organization would share with you. An accountant in an engineering company knows many of the same things as an accountant in an airline or a charity, because it comes from their professional and educational background. There is *managerial knowing*, which is the kind of knowing that could be common to managers in different functions and different organizations. This is the knowing that is required to get things done by or with other people, regardless of the function or the organization that the manager is working in. Finally, there is *organizational knowing*, which is knowing one's way around in one's own organization, knowing who links with whom and how. This is the knowing that a person gains from having been around for a while in an organization, and having understood how it works.

Professional knowing

Most people who end up managing and organizing are recruited into organizations for some professional knowing, and it is the use of such knowledge which earns them the right and the opportunity to manage (see Chapter 2, Entering and leaving). Although the new graduate may be described as a 'manager' and be put on a 'management training course', they are then usually given a professional task which gives them plenty to do, but nothing and no-one to manage. What they make use of at this stage of their careers is professional knowing. They will be judged and promoted (or not) according to their use of such knowledge.

So where does professional knowing come from? Most of it is brought into the organization by the person who has it. At the extreme, if someone applies for a job as a brain surgeon or a nuclear physicist, it is generally taken that they will have acquired their professional expertise before they start work; they will be expected to show qualifications to prove this. This is not the whole story; in most **professions**, knowledge goes out of date, and people who value their professional competence are likely to want to develop it continually. In the software industry, employees often look for jobs on the basis of the type of experience they can expect to gain in those jobs; this is at least as important as the pay or the location of the job.

Professional knowing is founded on a body of core knowledge which a person is expected to gain from formal education and **training** before they can enter a profession. It is then built upon by experience, as the professional learns more about putting that knowledge into practice, as well as keeping the knowledge up to date.

Professional knowing entails a number of **skills** that are not merely a matter of technical ability to do the job. One of the authors of this book recommended a builder to a friend. This builder delivered excellent value in terms of craft skills and efficiency, but he could not resist teasing the friend's wife, who worked from home and ran business meetings there, saying, 'Cor – it's all right for some, sitting round drinking coffee and chatting all day.' His **communication** skills were not good enough to enable him to go on delivering the technical part of his professional knowing. Similarly, we knew a hospital physician who, when he was nervous, would emit high-pitched giggles. It made him nervous to give patients bad news about their health, so such news was always accompanied by gales of giggles. He received far fewer referrals from general practitioners than his level of technical competence deserved.

These two examples suggest that social skills are not distinct from professional knowing, but an integral part of what the professional needs in order to practise competently. Interestingly, some professions include the social side of professional knowing in their training (social workers and teachers) while others do not (builders and doctors).

There is an ironic feature to the exercise of professional knowing. For example, a really good engineer may get promoted, with the result that he or she is not allowed to go on doing what they have shown themselves to be good at. If they are still performing well at the level to which they have been promoted, they get promoted again; this goes on till they are no good at what they are doing, and has been described as 'being promoted to your level of incompetence' (see Chapter 16, Career-ing). If organizations are full of people who have been promoted to their levels of incompetence, we can expect a few incompetent actions to result.

Managerial knowing

Management is sometimes described as 'getting things done through others'. While the professional acts according to his or her own professional judgement, the manager relies on managerial knowing to get other people to act. So what kinds of knowing are necessary for this managerial activity? Two kinds, we will suggest: knowing about people and knowing how to act on this knowledge.

Firstly, the manager needs to know about people and **groups**. But what does this mean? There are some people who say that they 'really understand people', or that they are 'very interested in people', but who then show few signs of such understanding or interest. Knowing about people often means having an effective and well-tested **implicit personality theory** about others. Some managers are more aware of other people's **personalities**, and the way that these people are likely to respond to situations. Such interpersonal sensitivity is crucial in a variety of situations, including assigning tasks to people and chairing meetings. Managerial knowing is not only important for the most senior member of a team; it can also be exercised by other members of a team, and has been recognized as one of the main contributors to a team functioning well.[9] People with this sort of knowledge are mostly recognized as important when they are absent; suddenly the whole team becomes much less effective.

Managerial knowing is not just about **perceiving** and understanding others and being sensitive to their needs, but also about knowing how to work with this knowledge. There may be times when a manager knows the needs of a subordinate, and decides to act against those needs, at least in the short term. The manager cannot always afford to be seen to understand. Organizing is not always a matter of people working together as if they were all 'one big happy family'. Genuine **conflicts** of interest arise, and managers have to take **decisions** which will conflict with the interests of some of their colleagues. Managerial knowing sometimes sounds as if it is a matter of being nice to people. However, it may be more important for the manager to know what effect his or her **actions** are having, and to decide when to be sensitive. For example, at the stage when ideas are being developed for a project, it may be important for the team *not* to be distracted from the content of what they are doing.

Managerial knowing is focused more on action than on understanding. Knowing how to get things done through others means knowing something about what makes people want to do things (also known as **motivation**), knowing what leads people to conclusions (also known as **decision making**), and what leads people to want to co-operate with each other (also known as **team work**). Sometimes it means all these together: knowing how to get people to set off in some particular direction together (also known as **leadership**).

Organizational knowing

A person may have good professional knowing, and they may have proved themselves in a previous setting to be a good and effective member of an organization, but they may not be able to achieve much when they join a new organization. This is because they lack organizational knowing.

Many organizational members have told stories about their first few weeks in a new job, in which, so far as they could tell, they were not expected to do anything at all. Someone we know was appointed as a director in a chemical company. He spent a few days reading all the company material that he could get his hands on, and looking at his predecessor's in-tray. Nothing seemed to need doing. After a few days he was getting confused, and was spending an increasing amount of time wandering around the city centre, avoiding doing nothing in his office. As a director, he was probably presumed to know what he was meant to be doing; he did not feel he could ask his secretary what his job was! One afternoon, while browsing in a bookshop, he met another new director from the same company. When they talked they found they were both in the same position. Each of them had previously thought that it was their own personal inadequacy that they could not work out what to do; now they knew it was true for both of them, they realized that it was the structure of their new jobs coupled with the **culture** of their new company. They went back to their offices, and started creating a role for themselves.

A person goes from one organization to another, and does not know how to look for the issues that need dealing with. For new recruits who do not get their own secretary, finding out how to get a letter typed can be one of the most important pieces of organizational knowing to be gained in the first few weeks.

Organizational knowing ranges from very mundane things like getting a letter typed to much bigger things, like knowing how to go about changing the system by which letters get typed. It also includes knowing enough about the current climate in the organization to know whether the time is ripe to attempt to **change** such a system. It also means knowing who to talk to, which may be someone who is well versed in organizational knowing rather than someone who is powerful in their own right. Gaining such knowledge can be daunting in a large organization, and to know the network of connexions between people is a source of **power** for the person who has spent a long time there. Not having this kind of organizational knowing is one of the things that makes entering an organization difficult (see Chapter 2, Entering and leaving).

Also, there is knowing the 'right' people. **Informal networks** are crucial in making an organization work. One of our students was on placement and needed his computer fixed. He telephoned the maintenance department in the company, and was told that they would do it as soon as possible, but that there were forty people in the queue to have computers fixed. He was having lunch with a secretary and told her about this. It struck her as ridiculous, so she phoned her friend Bill in the computer department, and he came round and fixed it straight away after lunch. For another example, one of us used to contribute to an in-company training course. The Personnel Director of the company said that, if we could give useful input to their staff, that would be a very welcome extra. But the main point of running training courses was to get managers from all over the company away from their departments and away from their homes, and let them get to know each other. This would then give them two different kinds of organizational knowing; they would know the different perspectives of other departments, and they would know someone in those other departments whom they could telephone when they needed help or action quickly. The course was really about this organizational knowing, not the professional knowing that appeared on the blurb.

DIFFERENT WAYS OF KNOWING

So far in this chapter, we have looked at different objects of knowledge. Now let us consider some of the different things that can be entailed in the activity of knowing.

The world taken for granted

How do people know things? Sometimes you are aware that you know something. Sometimes it seems so obvious that you do not even think of it as knowing. This is referred to as your *world taken for granted*. For a long time, it was taken for granted that the world was flat. It was so obvious that it was not even seen as knowing – it was just how things were. Similarly, thirty years ago it was taken for granted that there would always be work for shoe repairers. There was no need to say that this would apply 'so long as . . .'. Now the technology has changed, and there is no longer work for many shoe repairers. It was also assumed for a long time that the earth's resources were effectively limitless, and that new sources of minerals and power would become available. Environmental pressure groups campaign for that aspect of the world taken for granted to be no longer taken for granted.

We are bound to take some things for granted. We cannot be checking everything the whole time. Organizations are complicated, and people in them take actions on the basis of hunches and feelings; not everything can be calculated. This is related to *latent* knowing, the things that a person can get access to, but that they are not yet aware of knowing. It is said that Einstein's problem with earlier physics was that 'it did not feel right'. At that stage he had latent knowing that things worked differently, and this was eventually formalized and made explicit in his theory of relativity. Such gut feelings, or 'intuitive' knowing, have been highlighted by several top executives in their autobiographies.[4]

People as scientists

Another view of knowing suggests that we should look at people as if they were scientists – developing theories, anticipating events, and trying to understand the world they are living in. Everybody builds up their own theories of how they get other people (and themselves) to do things, without having labelled this **motivation**. We all have ideas about who does what when people work together, even if we have never thought of describing it as a formal 'theory of **roles**'. We have all developed our own theories about how power operates, even if we have never thought of them as such; if we have ideas about how to respond when someone is trying to exercise power over us, that can be considered a theory of power. One of our friends believes strongly in trying to confuse other people before they confuse him; this is part of his theory of power.

So we have our own 'theories' about how things happen around us, and we go on developing these theories throughout our lives. Some of these theories are about people, and are discussed in Chapter 10, Judging others, as **implicit personality theories**. As children, we may have influenced people by throwing a tantrum when we did not get our own way. This does not necessarily work in later life, although one hears of plenty of people in boardrooms who seem to assume that it will.

When a theory like 'if I throw a tantrum, they will let me do what I want' does not work, we may revise our theory. That is what is meant by 'learning from experience'. But experience is not the same as colliding with events; some people do not seem to learn much from the things that happen to them. Some senior managers have 35 years' experience, while others seem to have one year's bad experience repeated 35 times. Some people are more open to learning from experience, while others are more prone to think that anything which does not fit their existing theories is simply an exceptional case.

Some people gain knowledge from experience. But that still begs the question of what 'know' means. Questions about what we know and how we know that we know it go back at least as far as Plato. People know things in very different ways. A painter and a policeman would look at a riot in quite different ways and could be expected to draw different kinds of knowing from their observations. A poet and a botanist bring different kinds of knowing to the observation of a flower, and they take different kinds of knowing from it.

Acquaintance and description

One distinction that has been made is between 'knowing by acquaintance' and 'knowing by description'.[10] The way a dog lover knows his or her dog is by acquaintance; the way a scientist knows his or her organized scientific theories is by description. I know my friend Ermintrude by acquaintance, and I know about nuclear fission by description.

Knowing by acquaintance can be difficult to talk about. Louis Armstrong said about jazz, 'Man, if you gotta ask what it is, you ain't never gonna get to know'. It may also be difficult to confirm or disconfirm, while knowing by description is more open to traditional forms of testing and proof. However, even knowing by acquaintance can be disproved, as when a close and trusted friend betrays you. Both kinds of knowledge are testable, but the tests for knowing by description are themselves more describable.

The knowledge that people have of their organizations is largely knowing by acquaintance. When we join a new organization, we may be given a description of it. This is unlikely to take us very far (see Chapter 2, Entering and leaving). As we become used to the place, we gain knowing by acquaintance, and we act with more confidence. The knowledge that we use in organizing is overwhelmingly knowing by acquaintance. This book is (inevitably) offering knowing by description; that is all a book can do. It is our belief that the knowing by description that this book offers should enable the reader to learn more rapidly from acquaintance with organizations. The two kinds of knowing are not totally distinct; a really good autobiography is a description, but the reader may come away from it feeling almost acquainted with the subject of the book. Knowing by description can be a help in gaining knowing by acquaintance. If you have not taken the trouble to find out all you can in descriptions of an organization, you may not get the opportunity to become acquainted with it.

Knowing that/how

Another helpful distinction is between 'knowing that' and 'knowing how'.[11] This distinction is related to knowing by description and knowing by acquaintance, but in this case there is more of an action implication. Here is the example given by the originator of this distinction:

> knowing that for a given angle of unbalance, the curvature of each winding is inversely proportional to the square of the speed

versus

> knowing how to balance on a bicycle.

I may know that there are a lot of theories of **interpersonal attraction**, but I may still not know how to make people like me.

Knowledge as it affects organizational members, and as it is used in organizing, is very often knowing by acquaintance and knowing how. Most of the other subjects that students study, and most of the vocational subjects that are studied in gaining professional knowing, are more a matter of *knowing by description* and *knowing that*.

A learning cycle

Figure 7.1 shows a useful model known as the 'Kolb learning cycle', after its originator.[12] For example, I walk into a wall (concrete experience). I cannot fail to notice this, and it occurs to me that it has been happening a lot recently (observation and reflection). I decide that I may need my eyes tested (formation of abstract concepts and generalizations), and then go walking with my new lenses (testing implications of concepts in new situations). This leads me back to more concrete experience, where I do or do not find that I am still walking into walls, and so on.

We tend to associate **learning** with something done in a lecture room. The old 'mugs and jugs' model of learning (teachers, the jugs, pour out learning into students, the mugs) is still going strong. Lecture rooms symbolize the idea that learning is cut off from the rest of everyday life. Textbooks symbolize the idea that learning is about understanding and remembering knowledge by description. Learning is a preparation for living, not part of living.

In Kolb's view, learning can start from any point of the cycle, but must involve all four points. Concrete experience means being open to what happens, and being able to respond to events without distorting them to fit pre-existing ideas. Reflective observation means being able to reflect on these concrete experi-

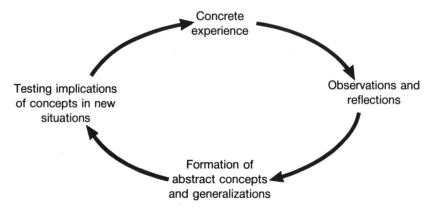

Figure 7.1 *Kolb learning cycle*

ences from many perspectives, so as to have the chance to gain new insights from them. Abstract conceptualization is the ability to integrate experiences into theories, and active experimentation is the ability to use theories to make decisions and solve problems.

Different people have different emphases in these stages; in particular, some people will tend to be sparked off by events in one part of the learning cycle. But for gaining any kind of knowledge, the person needs to go through all stages of the cycle.

THE POWER OF KNOWING, AND OF NOT KNOWING

'Knowledge is power', runs the old cliché. Is it true? Why do people want knowledge? Why do people want to show off the knowledge that they have of what is going on in the company, of deals being struck, of liaisons being carried on?

There is a very obvious sense in which knowledge is power. Like money, it is a currency that can be traded. **Gossip** tends to be traded like this; I will tell you a story I have heard about what is going on, and will expect you to tell me one too. The resulting information can be used coercively or punitively. For example, if I know more about the context of a decision than you do, I can always ask questions in a meeting which will make your proposals look silly. 'Have you considered the implications for your proposal of the . . . (and then comes something obscure)?' This can unpick all the hard work you have been doing in presenting your case.

There is also the paradoxical situation where no knowledge, ignorance, is a source of power. For example, a new manager can come into a company with very little direct knowledge of what has happened, and be more powerful as a result. If the manager knew everything that had been tried in the past, and why none of it had worked, then he or she would probably have been as disabled as their predecessors. Also, he or she is given more leeway by their staff, who may give the new manager a 'honeymoon' period, seeing how their approaches and frameworks feel or work. In fact, **consultants** are sometimes hired by a company for their ignorance. Their lack of knowledge about what will not work is what makes them useful to the company.

Because they are not supposed to know all the context, they can come out with new ideas. We know an organization which appointed a new chief executive two years ago. He was brought in from outside (see Chapter 15, Looking outward), and from the start made a virtue of the fact that he did not know all the history of the company. He got away with a lot of actions which he could not have taken if he had been around for longer, and he would occasionally let slip a boast: 'They won't try to stop me, because they think I don't know my way round yet!'

Knowledge may be power, but paradoxically there is another kind of power – the power of the innocent. This may be seen in the person who has no managerial or organizational knowing, while having professional knowing. This is the power of the boffin. The most powerless position is having to pretend to a degree of knowing that you do not yet have. We saw a meeting in which the boss presented several pages of neatly charted figures, purportedly showing why the direction he wanted to go was good. One of his staff pointed out that the figures did not add up. It became clear that the figures had not been checked or fully understood. Since the meeting this manager has been taken as a standing joke, and has been sidelined from his organizational responsibilities. As one of his colleagues said, 'When you see Jim, there is always a whiff of bullshit.'

- There are several different kinds of knowing in an organization: professional, managerial and organizational.
- Professional knowing is usually what gets people started on a managerial career.
- Managerial knowing involves understanding other people, and knowing how to work with and through them.
- Organizational knowing is knowing the systems, structures, people and politics of the organization.
- Knowledge is not always conscious; we may take a particular view of the world for granted.
- People may build up their stock of informal knowledge in much the same way as scientists build their expertise and knowledge.
- Knowledge by acquaintance may be different from knowledge by description.

- 'Knowing that' may be different from 'knowing how'.
- It is sometimes possible to make good use of *not* knowing something; judicious use of ignorance or innocence can be powerful.

THESAURUS ENTRIES

action	leadership
change	learning
cognitive	management
communication	motivation
conflict	organization
consultant	perception
culture	personality
decision making	power
gossip	professions
group	role
implicit personality theory	skill
informal networks	team work
interpersonal attraction	training
knowing	

8

MACHINES AND MECHANIZING

Man is a tool-using animal. . . .; Without tools he is nothing, with tools he is all.

(Thomas Carlyle, *Sartor Resartus*)

K woke up with a start; his alarm had not gone off. K looked at it accusingly and noticed that both hands were rigidly stuck on 12 o'clock. He jumped out of bed looking at his watch, but that too had stopped at 12 o'clock. He dressed in haste, remembering that he had an important work appointment that morning. He picked up the phone, thinking of suitable excuses, but it was dead. Over the next few minutes, K realized with rising frustration that his electric razor, the kettle, the radio, the TV, the fridge – and all the machines in the house – were not working. He slammed the front door and left his flat. As the door smashed shut, it set off the burglar alarm, whose shrill monotone pierced his skull. He woke up for real this time, the alarm buzzing noisily.

Life without machines has become inconceivable. Our age has been described as 'The Age of the Machine'. Machines dominate our physical landscape, they **control** our daily routines and affect every moment of our lives. Machines have enabled us to fulfil some of the oldest dreams of our species and have given us powers which our ancestors reserved for gods. With the help of aeroplanes we can fly, telephones help us to communicate across vast distances, and computers provide huge amounts of information at our fingertips. Jupiter's thunderbolts look rather tame in competition with the weaponry available to today's warriors and Vulcan's magic bellows are pathetic compared with the robots that fill modern factories.

Alongside these visible, physical machines there is a wider

wish to mechanize and routinize. Machines bring a repetitive orderliness to physical and mechanical tasks, and procedures and systems in organizations seek to do the same for other tasks. The internal mail system in an organization tries to treat pieces of paper and objects in as predictable and orderly a fashion as the way a telephone treats speech. With its regular collection times, its rules about what will and what will not be carried, its defined collection and delivery points, it attempts a similar level of efficiency to a machine by accepting similar limitations. In the same way, there are systems for discussing the budget, new products, quality, or staff promotions, all of which seek to give what might easily be chaotic processes the routine character of **work** that could be done by machine. At a personal level, organizing may be done with the aid of time management systems (a way of mechanizing time allocation). The appeal (if any) of the filofax and the electronic diary is that they offer some mechanization for difficult tasks that can be expected to require judgement and care.

HOW MACHINES MADE THE TWENTIETH CENTURY

There are three primary purposes that we hope machines and tools will fulfil for us: to protect us against our natural environment, to help us control it and profit from its resources, and to make our lives easier. Think of any domestic appliance; a dishwasher eliminates the tedium of washing up, a refrigerator extends the life of food, a vacuum cleaner speeds up the cleaning of a house, as well as removing dust which manual methods can only re-distribute. Advertisers emphasize the labour-saving qualities of domestic machines, keen to portray the woman as freed by their latest offering and able to pursue other, more pleasurable interests.

Not for nothing has our species been called 'a tool-making animal', an animal who seeks to fulfil needs not only directly by taking what nature offers, but also by using nature's own resources to control her. Control over fire gave people some measure of control over the temperature of their ambient environment and opened the way towards control over metals, clay and glass. The water mill, invented in the first century BC, made the grinding of corn immeasurably easier, offering welcome relief for women (and especially slaves) who had spent the best part of the day grinding with pestle and mortar to provide for their families and masters. 'Stop grinding, you women who toil at the mill', wrote Antipater of Thessalonika in a poem dating from that time. 'Sleep late, even if the crowing cocks announce the dawn. For Demeter has ordered the water Nymphs to perform the work of your hands, and they . . . turn the axle which, with its revolving spokes turns the heavy Nisyrian millstones. We taste again the joys of primitive life, learning to feast on the products of the earth without labour.'

Since the early days of humanity, however, machines have served another, less edifying purpose. This is illustrated in an early sequence of the classic film *2001: A Space Odyssey*, when the chiefs of two primitive tribes are about to attack each other. Suddenly one of them focuses on a bleached thigh-bone lying nearby, his face lights up, he grabs it and proceeds to beat his opponent senseless with it. A primitive instrument of war to be sure, but it proves to be an effective one under the circumstances.

As the ancestor of intercontinental ballistic missiles and nuclear submarines, the thigh-bone sums up two important features of **technology**. First, it shows how a part of nature, something lying out there, is transformed into a tool through the power of an idea; it is the idea, eventually crystallized into know-how, which turns inert matter into technology. Second, the thigh-bone underlines the fact that fighting, the domination of one's fellow human beings, is a mother of invention, on a par with economic necessity and the desire to dominate nature. War has spawned many new tools, new machines and new technologies. From the primitives' poisoned arrows to Archimedes' catapults and mirrors, and from Leonardo's prototype machine gun to 20th-century developments in explosives, poison gas, nuclear and other technologies, warfare and destruction have acted as a stimulant of human technological genius.

Machines do not just help us go about our business, in peace or war. They also define our business. They shape not only our physical but also our social and psychological world. The lift, invented in the 1880s, did not just help people get from floor to floor; it genuinely revolutionized architecture by paving the way towards 'vertical living' culminating in the skyscrapers of Manhattan.

If the lift was a major breakthrough in dominating vertical

space, a machine dating from the 13th century, whose central feature is a perfectly steady rotation of one or two mechanical hands around a central pivot, has revolutionized our perception of time. The clock, whose failure started off K's nightmare, arose initially from the needs for time-keeping in medieval monasteries. The clock was not merely a means of keeping time, but a means of synchronizing people's actions. The marking of hours and, from the 17th century, of minutes and seconds, turned people into time-keepers, time-savers and eventually time-servers.[13]

In the factory

It is not accidental that the mechanical clock, and the time-keeping and time-saving consciousness which accompanied it, emerged just as the growing European cities were calling for orderly routines. Neither is it an accident that it found its place of honour as the only 'decorative' item to grace the interiors of Victorian factories. In the factory, time is money; it is against the ticking seconds on the clock that work, machines, outputs and money are counted.

Not everyone liked this. In the 1810s, the Luddites, bands of workers who saw their livelihoods ruined as traditional cottage industries were swept aside by manufacture, had roamed the manufacturing areas of England breaking machines and destroying factories.

Philosophers too expressed profound reservations about machines. John Stuart Mill wrote that 'it is questionable if all the mechanical inventions have lightened the day's toil for any human being.' Instead of more leisure time for all, manufacture brought forced unemployment. Moreover, workers found that their role was to serve the machine, feed it with raw material, remove its product, always at the pace set by the machine, on the terms of the machine. 'The machine unmakes the man. Now that the machine is so perfect, the engineer is nobody,' wrote R.W. Emerson, the American poet and essayist.

With the rise of machines, production was detached from the skills and ingenuity of individual workers. The intelligence and craft which had hitherto resided in the operator were now incorporated in the mechanical process. The worker found that his or her specifically human qualities and creative capacities were no longer required.

Owing to the extensive use of machinery and to division of labour, the work of the proletarians has lost all individual character, and consequently, all charm for the workman. He becomes an appendage of the machine, and it is only the most simple, most monotonous, and most easily acquired knack, that is required of him.

(Karl Marx, *The Communist Manifesto*)

Mechanizing management

While industrial machinery had already revolutionized production, a new management movement emerged in the early decades of this century, known as '**Scientific Management**'. Its chief exponent was F.W. 'Speedy' Taylor and its greatest achievement was the 'supramachine', Henry Ford's assembly line.

Taylor argued that managers had been unsystematic in their approach to production. Maximizing efficiency and rationalizing production were the proper tasks of management, and ought to be done in a scientific way. Taylor proposed his principles of scientific management, which included:

1   Remove all brain work from the shop floor; managers must plan and organize production and limit the worker to the task of implementation. 'We are not paying you to think.'
2   Standardize products, parts and production methods. Scientific methods should be used to determine the most efficient options.
3   Fragment the production process to elementary tasks, each of which can be optimally standardized.
4   Select the most appropriate individuals for each specified task, train them to work precisely according to rules and formulae and monitor them to ensure that they adhere to these.
5   Offer financial incentives to the workers linked to their output. Taylor believed that workers, as well as their employers, would benefit from the results of increased efficiency.

Taylor's theory was not about machines but the mechanizing of **organization**. His interest lay in the detailed study and design of often simple instruments, like shovels, and the work activities themselves in the belief that small changes in the planning and organization of production and instruments of work can lead to great changes in output.

An apt illustration is provided by one of Henry Ford's assembly lines. One man took 20 minutes to produce an electrical alternator; when the process was spread over 29 operations, assembly time was decreased to 13 minutes. Raising the height of the assembly line by eight inches reduced this to 7 minutes, while further **rationalization** cut it to 5 minutes. But more planning by management meant less **control** by the worker, who is now further reduced from being a servant of the machine to being a part of it. Like parts of machines, workers are interchangeable, their jobs require little or no **training**, and the speed and quality of their work are easily controlled since no skill or thinking is involved. In the film *Modern Times*, Charlie Chaplin memorably captures and criticizes the spirit of Taylorist ideas and Fordist applications. The worker is seen being fed by a giant feeding machine while working on an assembly line, where his day is spent tightening pairs of bolts with two spanners. One hardly knows whether to laugh or cry as the feeding machine goes berserk scattering bits of corn and tipping bowl after bowl of soup on the worker's face.

The history of 20th-century industry is inextricably connected with Taylorism. Highly sophisticated technological products are produced by workers whose skills took hardly more than a couple of days to acquire, who know virtually nothing about the products they are producing and, at times, do not even know (or care) whether the parts they are making will end up on washing machines or on nuclear submarines.

Assembly lines became the established mode of industrial production, dominating not only manufacturing but also service industries and office work. One ingenious application was in catering, where fast food technology ensured the production of a consistent, standardized product and service with the help of virtually unskilled staff. The process is designed to ensure that the food will be prepared to specific standards by people who may be unable to boil an egg at home. The self-service principle transforms every customer into his or her own waiter.

The ingenuity of this technology, however, leaves the workers with few intrinsic benefits. Whereas simple cooking technologies allow cooks scope for initiative and experimentation, fast food staff are handlers of materials. Their experience resembles that of production line workers, with the additional pressures that direct contact with the customers brings. 'It is not an easy job, but it's very monotonous,' said one who had worked for two years. 'If there was more variety and skill, people here would be less short-tempered. The staff would stay longer too; in this place I've met two or three hundred people who came to work and only five or six of us are still here.' As work becomes more routinized (unlike the work of professionals or skilled craftspeople), it becomes purely a means of earning a living, something to put up with for as long as one can.

THE JOY OF MECHANIZING

But there is another side to machines. Some people like them; they even become addicted to them. For example, new users of computers often make a most uneconomic use of time to explore all the different things their computer can do. Many of these will be things they had never wanted done before. The capacity of a machine to do some clever task proves irresistible. Some people care for their machines, and even seem to love them. They may romanticize their cars, and bestow more time and attention on them than on their partners.

Consider the word processor. For a typist whose work is to put in text which means nothing to him or her, a word processor can have all the **alienating** characteristics we discussed in the previous section. For an academic writing a book, or for a student writing an essay, the relationship may be one of dependency. Many of us now do not know how to produce text without a word processor. For others it can be a fetish. They are so pleased with this machine with its whirring fans and coloured dots on a screen that they find whatever excuses they can to word process memos to others around the organization. They continually explore extra features tucked away in the corner of their software to manipulate text in different ways, and then insist on telling half-listening colleagues about this.

In one of our courses, the amount of computing that students do has been cut back sharply because it was producing too many computer junkies. People would spend hours playing (or working – who could tell?) with computers. Their other work and their sleep would suffer, and still they played.

One of the pioneers of research in 'artificial intelligence'[14] wrote a tongue-in-cheek program to simulate a counsellor. The user would type in a few words about their problem, and the computer would feed back a few of those words at random as part of a follow-up question. He was horrified when he found that his secretary, who was fully aware of the limitations of the program (and that it had been intended as a joke), was using it to get advice about a serious problem, and taking the consultation seriously. People are somehow very reassured by the apparent **objectivity** and cleverness of computers.

There is also an excitement in machines – a 'boys' toys' effect. To be seen as competent with machines is a matter of pride to some. Many motorists like to be thought of as a 'good drivers'; indeed very few take pride in being incompetent at the wheel. There is some **status** in being able to do what you want with computers. However in this case there is another side too, which is that some people like to thumb their noses at computers, and are proud of their incompetence with them. Some people love gadgets, as can be seen from the healthy market for executive toys – electronic diaries and the like.

In one research project, managers were asked to use computers to do a **decision** task they could have perfectly well done with a pencil and paper. The researchers found that it was more fun for the managers to work with a computer. It also gave the research higher status in the managers' eyes.

INFORMATION MACHINES

The technological revolution of our time is that of **information**. This is not the first revolution in information handling. The invention of writing in the fourth millennium BC was seminal, permitting the keeping of accurate records and the development of accounting. In the 15th century, the invention of typography, combined with the production of cheap paper, revolutionized the dissemination of information. The mechanical clock itself is an information device. The invention of the telegraph in the 19th century provided a cheap and instantaneous method of communicating information across vast distances; previously, with the exception of smoke signals, semaphores and drums, information had travelled at the speed of the fastest horse.

Information technology consists of instruments (such as pens, paper and erasing fluid), machines (such as typewriters, adding machines, telephones, computers) and systems for gathering, storing, processing and communicating information. Taylorism in the office sought to emancipate the processing of information from the personal quirks of clerks. Maximizing output and efficiency was pursued through the standard **Taylorist** recipes – fragmentation, standardization and **control**. This approach was suited to large bureaucratic organizations handling vast amounts of routine information. The issuing of passports or of electricity bills, the handling of insurance claims or of mortgage applications yielded easily to long paper-processing lines. Each individual received a set of documents in an in-tray, carried out one or two simple operations or simply signed them, and then placed them in the out-tray.

The shortcomings of this approach are familiar to all whose documents get 'lost in the system', whose special requests cannot be accommodated within the standard forms or who have to wait for ages until their cases are seen. Personal service to the customer is unknown, service of any sort rudimentary. The clerk becomes a 'pen-pusher' or a 'paper-shuffler', enjoying no discretion, variety or security, having little contact with fellow workers and almost none with the customer.

On the other hand there are undoubted benefits to some people. The arrival of electronic office equipment has changed dramatically both the nature of information handling in organizations and also the nature of information itself. Instantaneous access to and updating of records, multiple access to them, processing and communicating capacities previously undreamed of, open new possibilities both for the service offered to the customer and for the planning, forecasting and organizing of production. The desktop computer, at best, enables the clerical staff to process individual cases through from beginning to end, offering a more personal and prompt service to the customer. Errors can be rectified more effectively, and controls can be introduced discreetly.

Mechanized information at work: an example

One of us conducted a research project in which we interviewed 47 managers and clerical staff in a privatized utility. In the space of ten years, most of the office workers had made the transition from working with manual files, cabinets, typewriters and index cards to working with desktop computers or terminals. A mainframe system of customer accounts, enquiries and service records had been installed. The staff dealt directly with customer enquiries over the telephone and planned the work schedules of service engineers.

This is how one of the workers recalled the experience:

We were computerized seven years ago. With computerization morale hit rock bottom, mainly because of the way they were brought in. People were worried about the changes and the machines weren't as easy as we had been led to believe. . . . A group of us were picked for our typing ability and were shown the computer. We had to input all the existing records into the machine. At least, in those days we worked in two-hour stints in front of the machine. It was thought that it is not good for you to stare at the screen any longer. Even later, there used to be a compulsory break every hour. Of course, it is no longer on offer.

While staff had come to terms with the computerized information system, numerous grievances were mentioned. A supervisor had looked forward to computerization:

It meant less paperwork, less files, originally it seemed like a fabulous idea. As time went on, however, we realized that it didn't stop the paperwork, but actually increased it. We get reams and reams of tabulations, most of which are never read. . . . The customer gets a better service; we can provide an immediate response to customer enquiries. If there is a complaint or a disputed account, I have the information ready at my fingertips. But most of the girls in the office would sooner go back to the old manual system; you could moan about that, but it was not bad. The computer makes the job more monotonous; it has decreased **job satisfaction** for the girls. They can't move around any more; they don't have to go looking for files, most of the time they are stuck at their desks. There is less variety, less time spent chatting by the filing cabinet.

Seventy per cent of those interviewed in that site said that they would happily revert to the old manual system. 'Service to the customer has improved but my job satisfaction has declined; mind you, the computer always gives you an excuse why you can't do something,' said another member of staff. 'If in doubt, blame the computer', was a fairly common attitude. In spite of the improved service to the customer, the computer had not reduced the overall number of errors. Wrong bills were still being sent to customers or the wrong appliances delivered, engineers were still being sent to the wrong address, and at times two crews would be accidentally sent to do the same job. The clerk responsible for rectifying mistakes said:

> Work now is quicker and more efficient; there is less duplication, for example I can send bills out to the customer directly through the computer. The computer also covers some mistakes, like wrong sums, no bill goes out if the sums don't add up. But generally there are more mistakes since computerization; there are omissions leading to disputed accounts which means more work for me.

Managers too drew attention to some of the difficulties resulting from computerization. One of them said:

> Since computerization some operations have become more awkward. Travel by service engineers has increased; with the old card system, you could see at a glance how each engineer's day was turning out. This is now computerized, but we cannot get an overview of the jobs planned for each engineer.

A common problem was that the computer treated all engineers as interchangeable, whereas in fact each engineer had his preferences in terms of the type of work he did and the location of the job. Of course this *could* have been built into the system, but it had not been; in reality there are always such extra factors that are important, that could in principle be built in, but so far have not been. It may sound unfair to the computer to complain about these, but it does seem to be an inherent weakness of a machine approach that it is insensitive to some of the complexities that can be handled by people. In this case, some managers kept an informal system of manual records on cards or loose pieces of paper, especially when jobs needed to be done urgently or a specific engineer was to be sent to do a special job. This informal system often over-rode the computer causing irritation to clerks, who had assigned jobs through the system.

Several staff reported that they frequently resorted to 'cheating the computer' in order to assign a particular engineer to a job, or in order to give priority to an especially troublesome customer; to do so, they would feed the computer one or two pieces of strategically wrong information, 'forcing it' to do as the clerk wished. The result was that some of the data in the system were not entirely reliable. One manager remarked:

> Much of the time, my staff try to find ways of working around the computer, outsmarting it. For example, when they are dealing with a dodgy case of a customer who complains about something, instead of

entering their initials after the action they have taken, they enter the initials of the person who carried out the original transaction. In this way, when a mistake occurs, it is impossible to establish who is responsible.

Such findings do not support the view that new information technology necessarily liberates the worker from boring and routine tasks, equips him or her with new skills and gives him or her new powers and controls. On the contrary, they suggest that the computer can restrict the worker's mobility in the office, limit informal **communication** and casual chatting, and if anything further dehumanize office work. While it gives more information to clerks, enabling them to accomplish tasks, from beginning to end, it does not increase their overall **control** over the work process. To do this, clerks engage in all kinds of tricks and dodges, some of which are to help the customer, some to protect themselves and some to obtain the satisfaction that they can outsmart the machine.

The conclusion from this illustration is a mixed one. Technology itself is neither enslaving nor liberating. It is the *management* of technology that is important. Information technology, like earlier manufacturing technologies, was used here to replace human intelligence and **skill** and to increase control over the individual. The worker, stuck in front of a terminal, sees the world shrink to a narrow range of symbols on a screen and a sequence of voices at the end of a telephone line. Feelings of **meaninglessness**, boredom and **powerlessness** prevail. It is too early to generalize from this example. It, nevertheless, highlights some serious dangers inherent in current information technologies. In essence they are not so different from the dangers of technologies past, but their magnitude is even more alarming.

The desktop computer generally promotes a more restricted and confusing view of the world. One study[15] suggests that it is generally hard for people to make sense of what they are doing in front of terminals; there are five deficiencies, which together lead to a chaotic understanding of the world:

1 **Action** deficiencies; the operator cannot see, hear or smell data from the outside world, but only observes symbols on a screen;
2 Comparison deficiencies; the operator cannot walk around and look at things from a different angle, but has to rely on one, uncontradicted data source;

3   Affiliation deficiencies; people often work out what is going on by talking to other people, and working at screens discourages this;
4   Deliberation deficiencies; it is hard to see the wood for the trees, to tell the important from the unimportant, on a screen;
5   Consolidation deficiencies; material on a screen does not look like work in progress, and it is hard for people to go away and think about it, as they would with less imposing looking information.

These five points apply generally to the world as mediated by a television screen. The limited world of the television viewer has been brought into the workplace.

BEYOND MECHANIZING

Equally far-reaching are the effects of new information technologies on production. Product differentiation and targeting of consumers, decentralization, the contracting out of products and services, globalization of financial services – all these were logistically impossible before, but have now become possible thanks to the computer. Flexibility replaces standardization and routinization as the order of the day, flexibility of products and production methods, flexibility of working practices and labour markets, flexibility in geographic and financial terms.

Japan has been hailed as the prototype of the new industrial age, in which success depends not on churning out a uniform product cheaply, but on very fast adjustments to market and other external **changes**. New computerized technologies require a new range of industrial skills and attitudes. The worker must have an overall understanding of **systems**, must be able to switch from one area of production to another, from production to maintenance, from maintenance to service, and from service to information processing.

It is becoming popular to argue that the age of mass production is now giving way to Post-**Fordism**, the era of the intelligent machine. While it may be too early to judge how current developments in information technology will shape tomorrow's organizations, certain trends are already apparent. A move away from the **hierarchical** pyramids of the past towards flatter, leaner

organizational structures is widely regarded as essential for survival. While classical **management** theory recommended that each superior should be in charge of between five and ten subordinates, that being the number of people he or she could 'keep an eye on', today's managers might manage a hundred or more subordinates, in different locations, with the help of computerized information processing. Henry Ford's own organization has seen its levels of management decline from more than fifteen to seven, a number which has proved adequate for the Catholic Church through its history, and which would still be seen as excessive by most Japanese companies. Middle management is squeezed out, as senior executives have instant access to information that would have been processed by numerous intermediaries in the past.

The optimists view this as an opportunity to bring the human factor back to the workplace, to restore meaning and dignity to work and to do away with the drudgery and monotony of much manual **labour**. The **alienated** mass production worker will be replaced by the expert information handler. Just as a very few farmers can provide enough to feed a nation, it is argued, in future a few manufacturing workers will supply most of the material commodities required. The rest will be engaged in managerial, service and information-processing work.

The pessimists take a different view. They regard the information technology revolution as yet another step in humanity's subordination to its own creations. It takes the process of **deskilling** to ever larger sections of the workforce. The supramachine of the present, the computer, threatens the last vestiges of privacy, freedom and independence. Electronic spies monitor our every move, huge databases maintain records of our every credit card purchase, computers decide where and how to commit vast sums of capital which sooner or later are translated into jobs lost and gained, livelihoods created or destroyed. This is not flexibility but perpetual insecurity and suffocating impotence.

- Technology is not just tools and machines, but recipes, techniques and know-how.
- While many tools and machines make our lives easier, technology has for a long time been linked to the requirements of production and warfare.

- The application of new technological methods in production has, under capitalism, led to some deskilling and degradation of work.
- Taylorist principles and Fordist mass production subordinated the worker to the mechanical requirements of production.
- This has resulted in alienation and feelings of powerlessness and meaninglessness.
- Technology, and especially information technology, can create strong dependency; people become unable to function without mechanical supports.
- Computerization may offer some relief from monotony at the workplace.
- But computerization often reduces people's control over their work and severely restricts awareness and understanding of what they are doing.
- Developments in information technology facilitate changes in organizational structures, notably towards greater flexibility and shorter managerial hierarchies.
- It remains an open question whether technology offers solutions to today's social and organizational problems or whether it stands at the very root of these problems.
- But there is abundant evidence that machines can end up becoming the master of humans rather than their servants.

THESAURUS ENTRIES

action	management
alienation	meaninglessness
artificial intelligence	objectivity
change	organization
communication	organizational structure
control	powerlessness
deskilling	rationalization
decision making	Scientific Management
Fordism	skills
hierarchy	status
information	system
information technology	technology
job satisfaction	training
labour	work

9

LEADING AND FOLLOWING

So there is a boss, sitting in a comfortable chair, in a fine office, telling others what they should do. He (rarely she) is world-weary, gets frustrated and stressed, and shouts a lot – at people – because they often do silly things. This is a favoured, but predictable, image of organizational leadership amongst writers of television soap operas. It makes good drama. It is saturated with coercive power – the wielding of decisive **influence** over people's lives. Many of the early industrial barons were well practised at such leadership, as are some of their late 20th-century descendants. Lee Iacocca, reflecting on his executive career in the Ford Motor Company, tells us . . .

> Each time Henry (Ford) walked into a meeting, the atmosphere changed abruptly. He held the power of life and death over all of us. He could suddenly say 'off with his head' – and he often did. Without fair hearing, one more promising career at Ford would bite the dust.[16]

Pushing people hard, with threats, can certainly get them moving; but in what direction? It has not proved a very successful strategy for engendering commitment and creativity, or reducing **conflict**, being based on a very crude **psychological contract** between boss and subordinate. The boss is doing just that – bossing. If we regard **leadership** as a process of helping others to do things in a direction which serves the aims of the organization, then coercive power is simply out of place.

WHO *IS* IN CHARGE, THEN?

As the image of the omnipotent boss fades, we have to search harder in the organization for the leader. The following is typical of recent conversations we have had with some of our management students when we visit them on industrial placement:

Tutor: Who's looking after you here?

Student: Well, no one really. I suppose Bill is, officially.

Tutor: Yes, but who guides your work?

Student: Oh. Quite a few people. We all help each other.

Tutor: But the project you're on. Who's in charge of it?

Student: It depends what you mean by 'in charge'. As we work in a mixed team, there are several different managers who are looking after different bits – one on design, one on production, and one on marketing.

Tutor: OK, then, how do you get your instructions on what to do?

Student: It comes from several sources – I usually have to go and ask, and the n make my own work.

*Tutor:*What happens if you can't do the work?

Student: I just say so. We then work out something between us.

What this student was trying to convey to her tutor was something about the quality of working in an organization which had little of the traditional **hierarchy** of **control**. She worked in a project team. Leadership was not the prerogative of a single boss; it was distributed across managers and team members. She went on to describe how, in meetings, senior managers seemed to 'just chat' with them, after a lot of listening to their issues and problems. She could not remember many times when she was actually told what to do: 'It feels as if I'm being given space to draw my own conclusions and work schedule – which is nice. Sometimes I can even help others.'

Not everyone would feel as comfortable as this student with the kind of direction she was receiving, but she illustrates two important features of leading.

Firstly, leading is a two-way process, of mutual influence. What happens (and we shall come back to this) is often a subtle shaping of another's world, *but only in so far as both parties wish this to occur.* An influential theorist on organizational behaviour, made the important point that 'executives are essentially powerless until the time comes when followers grant their leaders the **authority** to lead'.[17] In other words, if everyone refused to be led, then the leader is pretty much disabled. A supervisor in a large chemical corporation told us of her shock when she first discovered this simple principle in her early career: 'I said "do this" and "do that" to someone and he simply said "No". I was stumped. I could have said "Well, I'll go to Personnel" or something like that, but what kind of atmosphere would that have created?' The effectiveness of a leadership act is evident in what others, on the receiving end, do and feel. In order to gain maximum commitment, the influencer somehow has to hit what is important and relevant to those involved, while also steering them in a direction that he, she (or 'the organization') desires. No easy task.

Secondly, leadership, in some form or another, is an essential ingredient·of social organization – but you do not have to be a designated leader to lead. Working relationships involve a myriad leading–following interactions, often aimed at meeting different needs – **emotional**, task, organizational. Within **groups** or teams different people can play different leadership roles at different times; leadership is 'distributed'. In fact it is hard to imagine a social situation where there are no attempts at organization through leadership . . . but let us try:

> You are asked to attend a managerial training meeting. Around the table are six people you have not seen before, but you know that they work for your organization.
>
> A trainer (you have not met) is sitting there, the obvious leader, you think. But he does nothing, says nothing. There is silence; an extremely long silence. You feel uncomfortable. Others look uncomfortable too. Where is the agenda? What are you supposed to do?

This scenario is, in fact, not fictitious – it happens in **'t-groups'**. These are training events specially stage-managed to be free of obvious **structure**; free from formal leadership. They create a social vacuum – which, like its physical counterpart, is very soon filled. Leadership just happens. People begin to talk, laugh nervously, get angry – anything to produce some structure and meaning out of the highly ambiguous situation. In doing so they reveal something of their own style and anxieties. Some will specifically try to influence the direction of affairs; others will gratefully fall into line. A few may protest, offering their own ideas about what everyone should do.

The effect of a leadership vacuum on people's desire for leadership is pervasive. Populations in countries which experience long periods without stable leadership will often look appreciatively – for a time – on anyone who is willing to pick up the mess (a fact not missed by opportunistic dictators). One of us took up a directorial position in his own academic department following a long period of organizational uncertainty. He was astonished to find how willingly people, well-known for their recalcitrance, would respond to his requests for co-operation. His tale is worth recounting – in his own words:

> The department had gone through a long period without a head, and was now facing the prospect of no director of studies – a key role for the functioning of the academic programme. Normally, the position is filled from the ranks of academics, on a rotating basis. However there was no-one who relished the prospect of the high administrative load, preferring instead to do their research and teaching. The department was at crisis point: everyone acknowledged the need for a director, but no-one wanted to be one. Staff were mysteriously unavailable when needed, and tension was high. Finally, the matter was resolved bureaucratically. Although I have only modest administrative skill and zero inclination in that area, I was nailed – following vague threats of the sort 'we will have to look carefully at your contract of employment if you refuse'. The word got round fast that there was now a director of studies and colleagues appeared, as if by magic, from their hiding places. I was heartily congratulated for my good fortune. Ha! Significantly though, for at least a year, not one of my actions, requests, or initiatives was queried. Co-operation was amazing from a department usually full of divisions and conflicts. Colleagues were much relieved that someone was now in charge – and that it was not them personally.

THE GOOD AND THE GREAT

Will you make an effective leader? Have you got what it takes? There are many lists of desirable **personality** qualities reeled out by personnel specialists and psychologists which can make even a saint look suspect. Some can be found in job advertisements – 'reliable', 'initiative', 'self-starter', 'effective in groups', 'firm under pressure', 'good communicator', and so forth. Despite many studies which show there are no such things as universal qualities of leadership, many of us cling to the firm belief that we can spot a leader when we see one. But, it seems, different people spot different things, and it is not uncommon for 'experts' to disagree.[18]

Leadership is a *process*, not a personal trait. That process takes place within a particular social context of which the people to be led are an obvious, but often forgotten, part. It does not make a lot of sense to analyse leadership without reference to what is going on between leader and led. For example, so-called wondrous leader qualities, like charisma, are only detectable in their effects on *others* – such as in their blind trust and awe of the leader. After the Second World War Winston Churchill's charisma faded – not because he had suddenly become a different person, but because he was perceived differently by a peace-time constituency who had peace-time needs.

But this is still only part of the story. Being influenced by a leader does not necessarily make that leader *effective*, or his or her actions **ethical**. Somewhere along the line a judgement of quality has to made. Effective by what criteria and in whose terms? A manager may be regarded by his or her staff as delightful to work with and attentive to their needs. However, the manager's manager may see things differently: 'A nice person, but perhaps too nice; a low-productivity section.' Different people can attribute different qualities to a leader, according to what *they* think is important.

TODAY'S HERO; TOMORROW'S FOOL

Audiences can, on one day, praise the leader and on the next castigate the person, branding him or her as fool or villain. This shows that leadership is a partly a reflection of the social times. Politicians who say the wrong thing at the wrong time (or the right thing at the wrong time) can be fast eased out of prominent positions. National heroes, whose words, wisdom and faces become immortalized in books and stone, can face sudden obliteration when their message is no longer seen to be appropriate: tumbled effigies of Lenin now litter the junk yards of Eastern Europe. Clive Sinclair, the British inventor and entrepreneur, has, on a number of occasions, been the focus of intense media coverage and praise for his brilliant electronic innovations – from miniaturized television to battery-powered vehicles. Often, though, in just a short period of time, his products hit problems of reliability, delivery or credibility – and sometimes all three. The news about him then fast switches from praise to ridicule.

Again, we return to attributions – what people choose to ascribe to the leader, and how fickle a process it can be. As part of this, one burden for the leader is to carry the projected disaffections and inadequacies of organizational members. This means he or she is a visible focus for blame, as well as a source of balm. Organizational leaders will often find that they inherit a history of problems in working relationships, which they are expected to shoulder. In this manner we can dump our most intractable **problems** on the leader and pretend they are his, or hers, to fix. But they are rarely solved in this manner, because the difficulties lie within us, not with the leader. Many an energetic, but naive, company director has enthusiastically re-structured the organization to improve its effectiveness – while old hands quietly look on. Sure enough, after a short period of time, the old patterns re-emerge. Sometimes this is because people gain a vicarious pleasure and **power** from helping them to re-appear (see Chapter 6, It's not my problem); other times, it is because shifting the organizational pieces around does not touch *underlying* **cultural** beliefs and tensions. So the weary adage: 'The more things change around here, the more they stay the same.'

MANAGING PEOPLE OR MANAGING MEANINGS?

Followers, of course, do not do all of the work in creating leadership; the leader is the other half of the equation. How can we envisage the leader's **role**? Organizations comprise different groups of people with different beliefs and interests. People vie with each other for influence and power. In this environment few leaders can expect automatic compliance with what they personally think is important. Leaders need to know what is important and meaningful to the people they work with, and somehow shape their beliefs, or **'meanings'**, in a direction which makes organizational sense. In other words, it is the world as seen through the follower's eyes that the leader has to appreciate – first and foremost.

The psychological logic here is fairly straightforward. We are likely to be more committed to actions which have been crafted and steered subtly by a leader than to actions that have been thrust down our throats; and the shaping starts with what we, not the leader, think is crucial. This involves an interesting reversal of the old maxim that power can corrupt; powerlessness too can corrupt, in that it leaves people weak, and out of control of their own destinies. The paradox of the kind of leadership we are discussing is that the leader needs to turn his or her so-called followers into leaders; to 'empower' them to use their talents to serve themselves *and* their organization. The notion of **empowerment** is appealing, and it is a fashionable one in current leadership thought. However, it should be borne in mind that in re-setting the power balance the leader's hand is still firmly on the steering wheel – which leaves empowerment open to the accusation that it is but a subtle form of manipulation – where some people remain 'more equal' than others.

Nevertheless, powerlessness can be corrosive, and its effects can be observed in many organizations. Powerless people feel insecure, and one response is to cling to whatever fragment of control they can acquire. It is as if they are saying: 'Well, if I'm valued no more than a cog in a machine, someone to be ordered around, then *I'll* show you how valuable I really am.' The janitor will make himself very hard to find when someone wants his services. The secretary will point to the backlog of work on her desk when asked to do an urgent job.

THE LANGUAGES OF LEADERSHIP

The shaping of what other people think and feel is central to the leadership process. It is accomplished through the skilful use of **symbols**: talk, stories, visual images, ceremonies, writings and rituals. These are the essential tools of the leader's trade. They are used variously to represent the leader's aspirations, visions and beliefs.

Talk

Organization leaders appear to spend an inordinate amount of time talking. In meetings, in corridors, over lunches, at conferences, in cars, on trains, in planes, and on telephones – they talk. **Talk**, and its words, is the most basic symbolic process through which leaders define, and re-define, their ideas, and those of others. For leaders, all this talk *is* their action, and their action *is* the talking. Effective leaders are able to combine listening and talking in a way which gently shapes a direction which offers mileage to both leader and led. We can eavesdrop on a (fictitious) conversation between a managing director and her marketing manager to see the process at work:

MD: So what you are saying Joan is that you would like a marketing strategy for our magazine which extends the age range of readers.

Joan: Exactly! I've been feeling for a long time that we need to take into account the shifting attitudes of youngsters. Today's fifteen-year-olds think like eighteen-year-olds did when we launched this magazine in the 1980s. Their attitudes to sex, personal relationships, work, education, the family and so forth, are nothing like ours were!

MD: Mmm. That's a good point.

Joan: And I really would love to have a go at re-framing our advertisements and feature articles with a younger market in mind.

MD: Joan. I really think you could be on to a winner. But first of all I need to get straight the financial implications. Our parent company is unhappy about our turnover and profit this year, and I'm keen to find a new image. Your idea could be the answer. I wonder if there's a way in which you could do a trial run to test the water first?

Joan: I hadn't thought of that. I suppose we could do a supplement to our November issue – say one special feature with ads.

MD: Fine. Go ahead. Meanwhile, I do need a long-term financial estimate to prepare my case for the Board – as soon as possible. Why don't I arrange a meeting between you, me, and Mark from Financial Planning? He can help us put the financial flesh on your idea. . . .

In this exchange we witness the managing director building on an idea suggested by her marketing manager in a way which (a) supports the marketing manager's initiative and (b) re-channels it in a form which meets the MD's own objectives. Notice that the MD shifts Joan's initial expectations to a rather more cautious position, while also setting up a structure to keep her involved in the development of *her* idea. And it is all done with the careful use of talk.

The way a leader crafts his or her words has much to do with **rhetoric**. By this we do not mean rhetoric in the pejorative sense of deception, pretence and bombast (although we acknowledge that many leaders, political and organizational are well practised at those). Rhetoric, in its nobler form, is the refined art of persuasion – to some extent reflected in all social interaction. The skilled leader exploits the resources of ambiguity in language to suggest and steer meaning; *how* things are said can be as important, if not more important, than *what* is said.

Persuasion, in a brasher form, is evident in the ethos of effective public speaking, a strictly one-way skill which is much valued in managerial circles. The effective leader, goes the argument, moves hearts and minds by offering stirring, polished, performances. And some certainly do. In 1978 Jan Carlzon, then president of Linjeflyg, Sweden's domestic airline (affiliated to SAS), made a stirring speech in a huge aircraft hanger to his assembled staff, an oration which signalled a turning point in his company's fortunes. Standing on a tall ladder he opened his speech, 'This company is not doing well . . .', and closed with 'I have some ideas of my own, and we'll probably be able to use them. But most important, *you* are the ones who must help *me*, not the other way round'.[19] The powers of oratory are mentioned by many high-profile business leaders. Lee Iacocca, chief executive of the Chrysler Corporation, claims that a public speaking course was instrumental in putting him on the right track. His faith in such training has been such that he has sent 'dozens of introverted guys' on courses, and 'for most of them it made a real difference'.[20]

Evocative imagery

Imagine being summoned to a key departmental meeting on the future of your organization. You get there, and one hour later it is all over. You have a headache and eye strain. It was a low key affair. You have been listening to financial forecasts, peering at pages of statistics on the company's declining performance, and hearing a long diatribe from the MD about the poor effort everyone has made (which includes you). You feel depressed and overwhelmed. Now imagine a re-play of this event, but with a new script. This time you leave the meeting fired with enthusiasm and motivated to do new things. Your MD has acknowledged 'everyone's extraordinary effort in keeping the ship off the rocks in these hard, recessionary times'. He talks sincerely, and confidently, of the 'talent in the company which has now got to face new challenges, and take new opportunities'. The competition is fierce, but he is 'convinced that everyone has something important to offer'. The company 'needs to work as a solid team to climb to new heights of excellence and quality'; and he will 'do all he can to build that team – with your help'.

The contrasting scenarios reveal the effects of using very different symbols in managing meaning. In the second setting the MD is using word pictures as a rhetorical device, especially

metaphors (ships, climbing, building) to create a **reality** which looks attractive and possible. In the first case, the images are more rational (lots of numbers) than emotional, and have a grey, punitive, tone about them. This latter approach was starkly portrayed recently by the Chief Executive Officer of an ailing electronics corporation who spoke confidently of having to 'kick arse' to get **change**.

Writings

The written word is almost as prolific as the spoken one in the daily business of organizing. Some managers manage by memo. Each morning there can be a new flow of directives and suggestions on paper and/or electronic mail, for staff to collect, collate and consider. The actual flow can symbolize something about the manager's style (intentional or otherwise). A constant stream suggests a possibly nervous individual, desiring to exert control over affairs: it is as if to say 'don't forget I'm here and I'm in contact with all key affairs'. On the other hand, rarity or unusualness of a written **communication** can signify the importance of the message – 'if the MD has taken the trouble to write it must be something crucial'. Employees of a leading British computer company told us of their special version of such missives – Stanograms. The label was coined whimsically from the name of the Managing Director, and they were yellow pieces of paper containing his cryptic thoughts or key messages. No-one could miss them.

The style and tone of correspondence from a leader can be manipulated to set the psychological distance preferred. Does William Draycot receive messages from his boss addressed 'Dear Bill', 'Dear William', 'Dear Mr Draycot' or even 'Draycot'? Does the boss always feel impelled to write out his or her title in full – as if to reinforce the **status** of the position? Or perhaps the boss is the only person *not* to do so, which ends up having a similar effect. Does the message invite a reply, and will that reply be acknowledged? Is it only the bad news and personal criticism which gets put in writing? Dismissal or redundancy is a case in point. Rather than face directly the shock or discomfort it can cause, a manager might choose to do it all in writing – regardless of the effects on the receiver of the news. For example, we know of a senior manager from an engineering company who received his dismissal notice by personal delivery at his home. What made the event particularly poignant was that the letter was carried by his boss's secretary in the very early hours of the morning; and up until that moment the man had felt perfectly secure in a job he had held continuously for eleven years (see also Chapters 2, Entering and leaving and 5, Morals).

These various manifestations of the written word are normally taken for granted in the daily mêlée of organizational life. To the student of organizations they are, however, small but significant clues to the texture and health of the leadership process.

Physical settings

Monarchs and dictators have long symbolized their authority by grand physical props: a palace, a throne, lavish furniture and décor, luxurious transport, expensive clothes . . . the physical setting speaks for itself. The corporate manager has followed suit. Sometimes the whole building does the job, becoming more luxurious as one moves up the floors. One company chose to construct its headquarters to resemble a vast set of steps, like a stairway. No visitor, or employee, could fail to know who was more important than whom. Divisions of corporate status have long been marked by what and where people eat – from works canteen to plush dining room. The very occupancy of a four-walled office amidst an open-plan layout can immediately mark out who is a leader. Gradations amongst those leaders is shown by the degree of opacity of the glass walls: the higher the manager, the more privacy they get.

All offices say something about their occupants; some ooze authority and **authoritarianism**: the huge desk, the thick carpet, the original paintings, the dark wood panelling, the carefully placed fresh flowers, and the throne-like chair behind the desk where the manager sits. Contrast the room which has light, bright colours, easy chairs and a coffee table in the centre; the desk is tucked away in a corner – all suggestive of someone who is comfortable with a relaxed, consultative style of **management**.

The acquisition of material **symbols** of power and **status** can turn into something of an obsession. The square-metreage of the room, the cubic capacity of the company car, personal parking space, access to privileged dining areas, first class air travel, are just a few of the outward signs of having 'arrived'. They are often jealously guarded by their owners, while envied by those without them. Likewise, they are carefully dispensed by the organization. A middle grade civil servant arrived at his new office one morning to find a workman carefully snipping 25 centimetres off the perimeter of the fitted carpet. 'Sorry about this. This room was an Assistant Secretary's', explained the workman. 'Five grades higher than you. You're not allowed a full-size carpet.'

MESSAGES FOR SHOW, AND MESSAGES YOU BELIEVE

The symbols of leadership have to be carefully managed to convey the meanings they intend. A slip, an over-usage or a misusage can render them invalid. For example, we know of one company director who ends memos to his staff with the statement: 'If you have any problems or queries about this, do not hesitate to contact me.' At first this sentiment was well received; an indication of a person who would listen. After a time, though, it was presented ritualistically on all correspondence, on virtually every issue. It lost its impact. Some began to see it as a cover for the director's lack of consultation with them in the first place. This reaction runs close to the 'I've heard it all before' one. The leader makes a bold speech, full of fine sentiments and imagery – but fails to stir hearts and minds. The imagery fails to connect – because the previous fine speeches were seen to have come to nothing – 'It's all words', mumble people as they leave the conference room.

Those much prized physical symbols of power can also backfire. How, for example, can the director whose office is full of fine objects and whose expensive car sits the courtyard preach to the workforce on the virtues of austerity and economy?

Perhaps the most powerful image a leader can create is a vision which others can identify with and carry forward. Such 'envisioning', the offering of a major creative idea, was what Jan Carlzon, as mentioned earlier, was trying to do for his airline in the late 1970s. It is also the trademark of other high-profile executives, such as Anita Roddick of The Body Shop, Richard Branson of the Virgin Corporation and Lee Iaccoca of the Chrysler Corporation. All, in their own ways, have offered a vision of the shape and style of the company they want, presented in a form which aims to tap into the desires and values of the people who work for them, or simply to catch the mood of the moment. Anita Roddick, for example, has attempted to demonstrate – by personal example, by her products, and by her whole business policy – that ecologically sound principles should govern all aspects of her enterprise. Contrast a recent television interview with a senior director of ICI who, when challenged about his company's publicly declared 'green' credentials, stumbled when asked for his target for waste reduction. After an embarrassing silence he stated a generous-sounding figure – which later turned out to be untrue: no specific target existed. And contrast the Jan Carlzon of the 1990s, now presiding over an ailing airline business and a demoralized workforce. He has talked of the difficulties in maintaining the 'big idea' – and in finding a new one. Clearly, leadership credibility means that grand words have to be matched by grand deeds – and both can decay in plausibility and attractiveness as time goes by.

- Leaders now have to rely less on hierarchical power; there are other ways to manage people.
- Leadership involves managing with symbols and managing 'meanings': the skilful use of language, images, writings, physical settings and rituals.
- Leadership is an interactive process – followers have to grant leaders the right to lead.
- A vacuum in leadership soon gets filled.
- You do not have to be a designated leader in order to lead.
- There is more than one way to judge the effectiveness of a leader's efforts.
- What followers attribute to leaders is crucial – and fickle: today's hero can be tomorrow's fool.

THESAURUS ENTRIES

authoritarianism	conflict
authority	control
change	culture
communication	emotion

empowerment
ethics
group
hierarchy
influence
leadership
management
meaning
metaphors
personality
power

problems
psychological contract
reality
rhetoric
role
status
structure
symbolism
talk
t-group

10

JUDGING OTHERS

- 'Anooj would make a good accountant.'
- 'Mary is extremely bright.'
- 'You can always rely on Colin in a tight corner.'
- 'Older men cannot accept women in managerial positions.'
- 'MBA graduates expect to be given all the interesting jobs.'
- 'The Japanese are very hard workers.'

We are all engaged in multiple judgements about each other. as you read this book, you may have been making judgements about us, the authors. Some of these judgements may have been about our intellectual ability, some about our personality, some about our views of the world. From our perspective, there are implicit judgements that we make about you, the readers, as we write.

In this chapter, we shall look first at the *means* by which judgements are made:

- How do individuals come by their judgements, and particularly the dimensions on which they judge others?
- What is the role of measurement in making judgements about people?
- Can we judge people by results?
- What effect does the way we talk about people, the language we use, have on the judgements that are made?

We then go on to apply some of the answers to these questions to different *areas of judgement*; how do they apply when people are judging groups such as teachers, students, employees, bosses and themselves?

THE MEANS OF JUDGEMENT

Personal judgements

What sort of judgements do we make about people we know well? Think of a group of people you know well, such as fellow students, colleagues, lecturers or friends. How do they compare with each other? 'Alan tends to be a bit stuffy'; 'Anne is an athletic type, and Sue has a good ear for jazz'; 'Charles has a pretty cynical view of the world'. These reveal some of the *dimensions* on which you judge those people. The actual judgements that you make are likely to be different from someone else's judgements; and so are the dimensions on which you make those judgements.

But personal judgements can be explored more systematically than this. Try this out. Take about eight blank cards. Write on each one the name of one member of a group of people. Then draw the cards randomly three at a time, and ask yourself, 'In what way are any two of these similar to each other, and different from the third?' Note down your answers, in the form 'two of them are ——, while the third is ——.' Do this a number of times, trying to come up with different answers for each set of three cards as it comes up. It does not matter if the same set of cards comes up twice – you may be able to give a different answer. Similarly, if you cannot think of anything at all, put those back and draw another three. Go on until it is getting difficult to think of any more, or until the differences and similarities that you can think of seem rather silly to you. You can then proceed to see how widely these dimensions apply to different people. Lay out a grid, like Figure 10.1, with the people along the top, the pairs of words or phrases you have produced down the side, and fill in the matrix with 'y' if the first word applies, 'n' if the second word applies, and leave it blank if neither seems to apply.

What you have just done is called a **Repertory Grid**, because it lays out in grid form the repertoire of personal constructs that you use. It is a basic technique in a theory of **personality** called personal **construct** theory. The theory holds that the best way to think of people is as if they were scientists, continuously trying to improve the quality of the theories by which they understand the world (see Chapter 7, Knowing the ropes). In this view, what scientists (that is all of us) do is to categorize the elements of their world into constructs, and then use those constructs to help them

	Alan	Jim	Jenny	Rajeesh	Paul	Helen	Tom
Indecisive – decisive	n	n		y	y	n	
Unreliable – reliable	y	n		n	y	n	
Quiet – talkative	n	n	y	n		y	n
Secure – insecure	n		n	y	y	y	y
Thoughtful – productive	n		n	y	y		y
Straightforward – pompous	n	y		y	y	n	n
Energetic – tired	y	y			n	n	n
Dishonest – honest	y	n		n	n		

Figure 10.1   *A Repertory Grid*

understand what is going on. When their constructs are not clear or detailed enough to help them to understand, they develop new, usually more complicated ones. For example, some people assume that all bright people will agree with them, and learn by painful experience that there can be people who they think are bright, yet who disagree with them. When they learn this, they split the single construct 'bright and agrees with me' into two separate constructs 'bright' and 'agrees with me'.

What you should have discovered through the exercise with the cards is your own **implicit personality theory**. Theory does not have to be something that is written down formally. If we have a general set of beliefs or ideas about something, that can be regarded as a 'theory'. So the theory that you have just discovered is a theory of personality that you hold implicitly. It is the theory on which you base the judgements that you are making of people around you. It is *your* theory of personality. Because your system of dimensions, or constructs, will (like your fingerprints) be different from anyone else's, this construct system is *personal*.

MEASUREMENT AND SCALES

The Repertory Grid is a way of identifying the dimensions on which we spontaneously judge others. As we have said, these dimensions are personal, and often idiosyncratic. But in organizations our judgments of others often have to be more formal, more systematized and **ethical**, more **'objective'**. Organizations are places where **perceptions** and the judgements that are based on them can have a crucial impact on people's lives. Appointments, promotions, dismissals and other vital **decisions** are based on judgements. Many organizations like to present themselves as places where hard work and ability will be rewarded, and where no-one needs to depend on nepotism or the 'old school tie' to get on. The judgements that people pass on others are often open to inspection. Recruitment officers, admissions tutors, promotion boards and disciplinary panels are required to justify their decisions with something stronger than 'it felt right at the time'. The prevalence of **racism** and **sexism**, and attempts to outlaw them, have led to a need for explicit standards of judgement. Judgements must sometimes be justified; they must not be entirely 'personal'.

Yet, the whole business of making judgements about other people is so difficult that we sometimes grasp at straws. We know how easy it is to favour those we like or admire, and discriminate against people who offend us in quite small ways. We also know that we can make judgements about people that turn out later to have been completely wrong, and we regret these. So we are often glad to resort to 'objective' tests, rather than rely on the much more subtle judgemental abilities of a human being.

Measurement on a clear set of 'scales' has become a strong tradition in most assessment systems. The principle is that the strength or degree of one's specific abilities, **personality** qualities, **skills** or **competencies**, can be measured in quantitative terms. So how friendly, numerate, neurotic, creative and so forth you are can be assessed with the appropriate **psychological test**, and the statistical 'norms' that go along with the test will reveal where you stand relative to others. To a large extent, therefore, judgement is independent of the specific observer.

The process, however, is not without controversy. Take **intelligence** as an example. Intelligence testing is a small industry in its own right, and has been used in many countries as an integral part of the selection system in education and employment. It becomes even more attractive to employers when it differentiates between different types of intelligence, as this can then be used to consider the individual's aptitudes for particular kinds of work. Usually three separate dimensions are tested: numerate, verbal and spatial. Intelligence testing has a colourful history. The early tests showed that women were more intelligent than men. The men who constructed them therefore changed the test items until they came out with the 'right' answer – that men and women do not differ in intelligence. Many intelligence tests have shown consistent (otherwise known as 'reliable') results. However, some researchers suggest that reliability is more a measure of how *insensitive* these tests are to important human qualities, rather than a point in their favour. It is like saying that a crude thermometer will be very reliable because it will consistently give the same reading no matter what the temperature. Maybe there is no such thing as a stable level of intelligence; maybe the word itself is misleading, because it suggests that there is something there to be measured. Perhaps the reliable tests are reliably measuring something quite different – such as whether people can motivate themselves to take pencil-and-paper tests seriously.

One of the reasons for people's confidence in testing is known as 'scientism' – the tendency to have faith in statistics, numbers, graphs and the like, because of their association with careful scientific work. Numbers are taken to indicate that the work that produced them is 'scientific', and the conclusions from it therefore 'true'. To feel we are doing things properly, we should be 'scientific'. The use of tests shows that we are serious professionals whose views should be taken seriously. The pressure to be scientistic often comes from the users, who like the certainty of quantification, and may not listen to the professional tester's caveats about what the figures do and do not mean. The opposite pressure, to trust 'professional judgement', has become somewhat debased because of the suspicion that **professionals** use this as a smoke screen to avoid having to justify what they are doing.

Judgement by results

One particular form of judgement, which sounds very measurable, is of 'results'. Some organizations give 'payment by results', and others promise that promotion will depend on results. This sounds so eminently fair that it comes as a good example to show why measurement of judgement is such a fraught issue.

There are two factors which make judgement by results more difficult than it at first sounds. Firstly, 'results' are caused by many different things, of which the efforts of an individual employee may or may not be the most significant. If people are selling encyclopaedias, their results are very clear. But are they responsible for these results? Two salespeople might have equal sizes of population to sell to, but if one of them has a wealthy middle-class district and the other an urban district centred on a factory that has just closed, their results could be very different without telling us anything about the relative skills and efforts of the two people. Many decisions in organizations are made in conditions of uncertainty. We are not sure what our competitors will do next, or what will happen to the national economy, or (if we are in a seasonal industry) what the weather will be. Decisions still have to be made, and it may be that the best possible decision turns out to be wrong in terms of its outcome. An attempt to judge a person by results could end up being very unfair, and could discourage people from ever taking risky, enterprising decisions.

The second difficult issue in judging by results is that there is still personal judgement to be exercised in deciding on which results to judge. Let us go back to the people selling encyclopaedias. Do we judge them by their total sales, or by the share of the encyclopaedia market that they obtain, or by the comparison between this month's sales and last month's, or by the profitability of those sales, or by how pleased their customers are? That is just a small sample from the many different kinds of 'results' that might be considered – from people selling just a single product. The complexities multiply when we try to pin-point the results of people who carry a wide range of different responsibilities, such as managers and executives

Judgement by results, like other types of judgement in organizations, entails organizational **politics** – the personal preferences and hidden agendas that determine how the judgement is finally made. Some people may 'need' to be pleased more than others; 'explanations' of poor performance may have to be carefully phrased.

The language of judgement

The **language** in which judgements are discussed is important. Once phrases are accepted as a way of speaking in an organization, ideas can become current which would have been laughed at before. In some organizations, the phrase 'I like John' would be improper. It would suggest that personal feelings might be coming in the way of objective judgement. For example, it would be surprising if this were the justification for John being given a higher class of degree by a board of examiners. In other organizations, such as a small privately owned company, personal language may be regarded as quite acceptable – indeed, as being a more reliable guide to whether it is worth employing John than any test result.

We can see how language shapes our judgements by looking at personal relationships. There is a conventional **discourse** of romantic love, which suggests that 'this thing is bigger than both of us' – a chemical view in which love and attraction are beyond the **control** of those who feel them. So long as people speak in this way, they are likely to fall 'chemically' in love. If they speak a language of choice and personal responsibility, their judgements about their own behaviour will be different. All judgements are made within a particular type of discourse. For example, we know from paintings that different styles of physical attractiveness have been prevalent at different times in the past. At the present time, someone might be referred to as 'slim and attractive'; this phrase would have sounded like a contradiction in terms in the time of Rubens. Equally, it could be a sly and derogatory judgement if it were applied to the new managing director of an engineering company. The phrases that we use, and the way words are grouped, affect the judgements that we make. In a particular **culture**, 'aggressive, mean and hungry' might be regarded as very positive attributes in considering someone for a job; in another it could regarded as completely out of place.

AREAS OF JUDGEMENT: JUDGES AND JUDGED

Many people in organizations have to make judgements about others as part of their work. They may not like this; they may not think they are qualified to make such judgements, but they cannot avoid it. This is one of the common characteristics of organizations – the continuous and systematic assessment and judgement that members make of each other.

Some of the people we judge are well-known to us. They may be known to us in several **roles**, as friend, as boss, and as fellow member of the football team, for example. However, a lot of the time we are judging people who are *not* well-known to us. These are people (students, teachers, employees, colleagues) whom we only know from one particular role. What we judge is the **persona** they present to us. Some writers argue that we each have a repertoire of different sub-personalities, or personas. Each persona is shown to a different category of people in different situations.[21] For example, some students behave quite differently with their parents, their fellow students and fellow employees in their industrial placements or part-time jobs. They use different language, express different opinions, wear different clothes, and even drink different drinks. They may not be aware of the differences until they are with people whom they know from two or more situations. Then they may feel uneasy about which of their personas to act out. It can be instructive – or shocking – when we occasionally glimpse a different persona from the one with which we are familiar.

The rest of this section looks at five examples of roles in which people are judged, and considers the positions from which others judge them. It is not exhaustive about the merits and short-comings of examinations, feedback, personnel selection techniques, and the like, but illustrates some aspects of judgement in organizations.

Students

What sort of judgements do lecturers make about students? Some of these judgements may be personal, based on a student's performance in class; but most judgements tend to be based on formal assessment techniques, such as coursework and examinations. There has been a long debate in the educational world about examinations as a means of measurement; what do they measure? Perhaps above all they measure peoples' ability to do examinations – arguably more so than intelligence, application, knowledge or any of the other qualities that we might like to know about. But as we have said, something is needed to help people through the maze of judgements they have to make, whether this be a judgement about the suitability of a candidate for a job, the annual appraisal an employee should be given, the academic merit of a student, or the quality of a person as a potential ally.

As the ratio of staff to students declines in most educational systems, impersonal judgements based on examinations are likely to become more prevalent. Staff will not know enough about individual students to make a more personal judgement, and records of achievement will play a bigger role than memory of a person when it comes to writing references. Such increasing impersonality in the making of judgements may be fairer to the student, although it is likely to be less subtle and revealing than a more personal judgement.

Do students get to know about the judgements that have been made about them, and if so, how? This is generally a sensitive question in organizations. Knowing how well you have done in an essay or in an examination is an important part of the educational experience, helping you to make decisions about how to spend your time, or in what subjects to concentrate your efforts. Feedback is an important part of **learning**. Yet, in many cases people only get to hear about relatively unimportant judgements. Students are often given only the broadest indication of the judgements that have been made about them in examiners' meetings. Better feedback to students would increase their learning, but would also open up the possibility of contesting the judgement – which some organizations prefer not to face. Judgements are never outside organizational **politics** and **conflict**.

Teachers and lecturers

What sort of judgements do people make about their teachers and lecturers? **Repertory Grids** that students have completed on their lecturers have shown judgements about dress sense and hair style, about how entertaining the person is, and about their knowledge of their subject. To find out more about your personal judgements of teachers, you could try the repertory grid exercise from the beginning of this chapter, but using as the set of names a number of present or past teachers.

Increasingly, judgements by students are sought by universities to measure and evaluate the quality of their courses. Most educational organizations now issue 'course feedback forms', in which students are asked to make evaluations of their teachers. Yet, such judgements are usually constrained by the *language* of the assessment form. Like psychological tests, judgements are made in the **constructs** of the designer of the form, not the personal constructs of the student. We have found that only a few people fill in the 'open' section at the end which invites further comments, and permits them to give their judgement in their own constructs.

Again the assessment process has political overtones. For example, the experienced teacher may go in for **'impression management'**, and play for a good evaluation; a few jokes or a lenient assessment can be worth more than hours of hard work spent on improving the quality of the course. However, some students are alive to this possibility, and will judge the teacher by results. These results may be measured by examinations, or by the extent to which students achieve their learning goals.

Employees

The recruitment process highlights the dilemma in using personal and/or impersonal judgements (see Chapter 2, Entering and leaving). Hiring John just because you have known him in the past and like him may not be a particularly reliable decision, unless joining your organization is like joining a club. Hiring him because he scored high on an examination or a test may not be very reliable either, unless he is being hired to do a back-room technical job accurately measured by that test. Hiring him because he 'looked good', and 'came over well' in an interview may not be very reliable either, unless it is a job in which social skills are paramount.

Often, the quality of recruitment judgements can be improved, but at a cost. Some jobs are so important that organizations will use a combination of costly techniques in order to appoint the best possible person. Other appointments, however, are treated in a more desultory way. In one organization that we know of, a boss told one of her staff to throw away all the job applications that were not signed in blue ink. It was not that she particularly liked blue ink, but she thought that this was as good a way as any other to bring the enormous number of applications down to manageable proportions.

Appraisal is another area where important judgements are made regarding employees. In the typical appraisal (but there are many variations) employees make a statement of what they have done over, say, a year, and then discuss it with their boss. The boss gives a view of what has been achieved and what might be improved, which the person being appraised responds to. This is a means of making sure that one of the most important relationships in organizations – the boss–employee – is the subject of a regular dialogue. An appraisal process can be abused, or highly politicized. It is not unknown for an appraisee to have his or her say, while the boss listens little and puts in exactly the judgement that he or she was always going to make. Such mock consultation clearly serves interests other than those of the boss–employee relationship.

Giving negative feedback may not be easy. Neil, a project manager, would talk dismissively to his fellow managers about one of his research teams. The team finished their project, and two members told us how proud they were that Neil thought so highly of it – because he had been derisive about other project teams. We, by contrast, had never heard him criticize other teams, but we had heard him be thoroughly and destructively critical of the team in question. He had lied to them to avoid embarrassment.

Variations on this story could be repeated countless times in almost any organization. Judgements are **communicated** for a variety of purposes, of which the potential learning from the feedback can be low in the communicator's priorities. Avoiding time-consuming debates, avoiding angry scenes, and avoiding giving other people the chance to challenge your judgement in detail can be more significant.

Bosses

People also make judgements about their bosses. A good deal of informal discussion takes place in organizations about the quality of particular managers, and some people will deliberately seek to work for a boss who they think will help them develop their skills and career. Other judgements can be formal. Appraisals can be done upwards ('reverse appraisal') because, goes the argument, management is a service to the managed and the consumers of that service should be the ones to appraise it. One fast food chain, for example, makes use of 'rap' sessions in which groups of staff discuss the performance of their managers with a senior executive from headquarters. This is still rare, but the likelihood is that employees will increasingly be asked to make formal judgements about their bosses.

Most of the judgements made about bosses are informal. These judgements can be strongly influenced by a careful use of language and the skilful presentation of a particular persona on the boss's part. If subordinates are encouraged to feel that they are trusted colleagues, and that they are being told significant pieces of high-level gossip by the boss, they may forgive a lot. If this impression management by the boss is overdone, however, it may be seen as hypocrisy.

One criterion on which superiors are judged is the quality of the links they have with other people. Some are particularly good at finding out what resources are available, and can link with those who are able to release them. They may be able to put together a consortium of interested parties who can achieve something that they could not achieve alone. They may not know how to solve a problem or give direct help, but they may know other people who can help. The links that people have informally, within and between organizations, are part of what oils the wheels of an organization. A boss may be judged by his or her ability to maintain powerful links, if only to defend his or her subordinates.

Self

Our judgements of others, especially the informal and personal ones, often reveal as much about ourselves as about those whom we judge. So a very important judgemental relationship we have is with ourselves, and many of the processes we have described about judging others also apply to self-judgements. For example, in doing a repertory grid, it is worth including 'self' on the cards, and seeing what emerges about judgement of self. Try also 'self as I would like to be'.

Some organizations use self-assessment as part of an official appraisal. But this only highlights further (yet again) the political nature of judgements in organizations. If your self-assessment is too glowing, a superior may conclude that you are complacent and glib. If, on the other hand, you are very hard on yourself, your superior may conclude that you are lacking in self-confidence, and your **career** may suffer. The judgement that has most impact is the one *they* are making, not the one you made on yourself.

CONCLUSION: LEARNING FROM JUDGEMENTS

Judgements are a vital part of organizing. They may promote learning and harmony or they may fuel resentment and discord. For judgements of people to have a positive influence within an organization, people must have confidence in the ability and fairness of those who make them, and an opportunity to correct a judgement if they know it to be wrong. Equally important is to recognize that people will not learn from judgements that are not fed back to them.

In the bustle of everyday life, this feedback may seem a luxury. It will have no immediate effect on the profit figures. Lack of learning, or learning the wrong things, shows up slowly. If judgements in organizations are fed back to those affected by them, and are open to inspection, comment and correction, both parties may well learn. Subsequent judgements are likely to be of better quality. On the other hand, if judgements are made in a secretive or underhand way, those being judged will be suspicious about why they are not being told about the judgements. They are almost bound to respond by becoming defensive, which further decreases their chances of learning to do better.

- There is no way of avoiding making judgements about other people.
- People do not only make different judgements; they have different dimensions on which they exercise judgement.
- Each of us has our own implicit theory about different people.
- Much work has been done on developing tests and objective measures for judgement.
- Even something as fair sounding as 'judgement by results' involves individual judgement about which results to judge by.
- People may learn from the judgements made about them, but only if they get to know those judgements, the basis on which they are made, and if they have confidence in the person doing the judging.
- People may learn to be better judges if they are open to feedback about the quality of their judgements.

- However fair the intention, judgements of people always have political overtones.
- There are different types of judgement made in different relationships.
- For many people, the most important judgement is the one they make of themselves; others' judgement of them may be part of how they make a self-judgement.

THESAURUS ENTRIES

career
communication
competencies
conflict
construct
control
culture
decision making
discourse
discrimination
ethics
implicit personality theory
impression management
intelligence

language
learning
objectivity
perception
persona
personality
politics
professions
psychological testing
racism
Repertory Grid
roles
sexism
skills

11

FEELINGS

Feelings can be a nuisance. We get fed up at work, angry, stressed, hurt, bored. We can feel malicious, vengeful, embarrassed, fearful or hurt, especially if we are judged negatively. We can feel torn between the demands of our career and family. These sorts of feelings can gnaw away inside us – before, during and after work. They can be exhausting. Other feelings hit us rather differently, more positively. There is the happiness, joy, love, excitement, pride or elation – the up-side of working life when things are going well, such as when we are praised or complimented (see also Chapter 17, Working and living).

Sometimes people seem to want to talk candidly about their feelings – perhaps quietly in corridors, coffee rooms, pubs and dinner parties. In other settings, however, talking about feelings takes the form of an oft-repeated, but hollow, ritual:

> Alice's boss strides purposefully up to her desk: 'Morning, Alice, how are you today?'
>
> Alice replies quickly, with a broad, confident smile: 'Oh, I'm fine thanks, John. It's a great day, isn't it?'

What John does not know (and does not want to know) is that Alice does not feel at all fine. He would be more than confused if Alice said what is really on her mind, which would be this:

> 'Well, John, I had a terrible time last night with my boy friend. I think we're going to break up. I feel shattered. I feel really pissed off working here too, especially the way you treat me, John; how you seem to take me for granted.'

The exchange of pleasantries is just that. They are designed to mask, not reveal, our inner feelings; to create certain **impressions**. Why should this be the case? What happens to our feelings when we become 'organized'?

'STAY COOL!'

Exhortations to be calm, to think things through, not to get upset, run deep in the education and training of most of us. They are strong social **values**. We may harbour strong feelings – fears, passions – but they are to be kept under **control**, and carefully managed.

Feelings are essentially private affairs, not to be presented publicly without careful stage management. Top managers often have to demonstrate they are clear, decisive thinkers, not simply victims of their feelings. Female leaders who show 'decisive' characteristics win a certain ironic praise – such as the 'iron lady' descriptions of British Prime Minister Margaret Thatcher in the 1980s. While women may be permitted to be rather more emotionally expressive than men, they are to contain their 'unreliable' feelings in public in the interests of logic, **rationality** and decorum. If they do not they risk confirming the negative **stereotype** that people, especially men, hold of them (see Chapter 12, Sex). This becomes especially crucial in public events, like conferences, or important speeches. Politicians and organizational leaders often plan carefully their presented image, sometimes down to minute details – gestures, tone of voice, dress, words. It can make all the difference to the way they are **perceived**, such as emotionally sensitive or firm, and to the kind of emotions mobilized within the audience.

The social veneer we place on our feelings is most evident when we are permitted a backstage glimpse of the private worlds of public heroes and heroines. They are rarely the cool, clear-thinking souls they seem. They have rows with their partners, they have mental breakdowns, they have depressions, they have fears and jealousies, they have anxieties about their jobs. They are, after all, real people. The most publicly respectable of 'rational' scientists can be ruthlessly competitive, vain and anxious, to the extent that they may resort to faking results to win attention and praise. The media's preoccupation with stripping away public masks of famous people is seductive, and can make compulsive reading or viewing. Why? Maybe it says something about our own emotional lives. Even the great and glorious can be confused and mixed up, like we sometimes feel ourselves. We can safely peer at their distress, and in doing so feel a bit happier about our own messy feelings.

Inside organizations, though, the controlled act must go on. The essence of organization, as laid down in the traditional texts and much current practice, is the creation of structures and lines of command to ensure that A leads to B leads to C leads to D. Material and effort go in one end, and a product comes out the other end. In the strictest **bureaucracies** there is little room for doubt, anxiety or passion. Reliability and predictability are all-important, the mark of good machines and good workers alike. Feelings get in the way of reliability and predictability, so keep them to yourself (see Chapter 8, Machines and mechanizing). Alice knows that her work role would be untenable if she told her boss what she really thought about him. Similarly, John cannot afford to care too much about Alice's (or anyone else's) doubts and worries. If he did he would be unable to function effectively – or so he believes.

There are organizational procedures and terms which help people to operate unemotionally: crisp job descriptions which lay out the demands of the job; rules, objectives and targets to keep us on track; and then the statistics – on profits, growth, sales, share values, waste – to tell us how well we have done. After a while the whole activity can take on a momentum of its own, to the extent that feelings become blurred, or largely forgotten, in getting through the day. We may fumble when trying to express them. At the extreme we become emotionally illiterate: 'I don't really know what I feel about my job; I just do it', is a phrase one hears from people who have worked at the same activities for years on end. At first glance some jobs, such as sacking people, could not look more emotional. But a Senior Personnel Officer from a large car manufacturer put it to us thus:

> I have had to handle literally hundreds of layoffs personally, to tell people face-to-face that their livelihood is going to end. At first it used to tear me apart. Now it's just part of my job. I've seen all the reactions; I know exactly what I've got to say. I know their rights and our rights. Of course I try to be sympathetic and helpful, but in the end it's something that just has to be done.

PUTTING FEELINGS TO WORK

In the late 1950s managers began to acknowledge that trying to engineer people's work to be thought-proof (productivity should not be impaired) was not altogether a clever thing to do. Simplifying, routinizing, mechanizing and supervising work certainly rationalized production; but it also left people with boring, monotonous, meaningless tasks. For some employees it did not seem to matter, as long as they had money to spend from their efforts. Others, though, became dissatisfied and depressed, and showed it by staying away from work, demanding ever higher financial compensation, and fighting the management. That state of affairs spawned much social science research aimed at seeking ways of enhancing **job satisfaction** – from playing music while you work, to splitting assembly lines into 'autonomous working groups'. Jobs became 'enlarged' and 'enriched'. Volvo, for example, broke with the traditions of mass car production, permitting their assemblers to work in teams around separate workstations. Together team members could decide how much they would produce and in what way. **Participation** was seen to be the key to increasing worker satisfaction. And it did for some of them – for a time. For others it did not.

While jobs can be enriched in the manner described, this rarely touches the essential **meaninglessness** of the task; it just rearranges the pieces. Other than in special cultural conditions, such as in Japan, it is unusual to find mass production workers strongly identifying with the product. Overall design, control and supervision still, typically, rest with management. What employee participation provides, however, is an opportunity for workers to come out of their social isolation (standing at a workstation on a long production line) and to enjoy the emotional release of chat with colleagues.

There are **ethical** and psychological issues to face when we manipulate working conditions in order to raise employee satisfaction. Ethically, it is open to accusations of deception if the prime managerial interest – increasing profit and production – is not declared. Psychologically, there are questions about what job satisfaction *is*. Satisfaction is a complex phenomenon, which cannot simply be produced, or induced, at the turn of a managerial key. For a start, most of us experience a range of different emotions as we work; satisfaction may or may not be an appropriate description for what we feel. More crucially, though, our satisfactions are likely to be ephemeral, and fluctuate in quality and degree as the day passes. So your high satisfaction at 11.15 a.m. (you have met a deadline) may drop to mild dissatisfaction at 12.20 p.m. (you cannot contact a key customer), to deep dissatisfaction at 4.00 p.m. (your report has been rejected by your boss). Satisfaction is deeply embedded in the subtleties of our relationship to our work and organization, distinctly coloured by our personal needs, background and non-work-life. Attempts to manage it by simple structural means are likely to be problematic.

SELLING EMOTIONS

> First we *practise a friendly smile* at all times with our guests and among ourselves. Second, we use friendly courteous phrases. 'May I help you?' . . . 'Thank you' . . . 'Have a nice day' . . . 'Enjoy the rest of your stay', and many others are all part of our working vocabulary.

That is what Walt Disney World insists on from all its employees. Similarly, McDonalds' 'Hamburger University' tells its managers to ensure that 'all-American traits' are displayed by its counter staff – 'sincerity', 'enthusiasm', 'confidence' and 'a sense of humour'.

Here we witness an extreme form of commercialization of emotional display. You have to express the *right* emotions in order to survive in the job. The rules about what to express, and how to express them, have been decided in advance by executives in a boardroom, and you have to learn them by heart. Effective restaurant waiters and salespeople have long had an intuitive appreciation about the importance of displaying the right 'interest', 'concern', 'understanding', and 'warmth' if they are going to clinch a sale or get a good tip. What has changed, however, is the extent of corporate control over what an employee should or should not feel.

The point comes over strongly in a study by an American sociologist. She studied what happened to flight attendants in an American international airline. The flight attendants are pushed very hard by their company to practise an 'inside-out' smile. They need to believe the act, and take it inside themselves. In this way they should *really* feel OK about the crowded, hectic life in the cabin of the aircraft, and they *really* should not mind whatever a passenger throws at them – literally and metaphorically. Flight attendants are taught to perfect their emotional performance, which is kept up to par by regular refresher courses. In this way, as super-heroes and heroines of the aircraft, they receive adversity and abuse and re-process them with a smile and a kind word. For the airline, it makes commercial sense. If customers feel good about the nice-looking people who serve them, they will (it is believed) be more likely use the airline again. The flight attendant's emotional performance is thereby linked with the company's profits.[22]

The required emotional performance can be achieved more subtly than via smiling lessons. It can be part of a deeper cultural change in the whole organization where top management offer a vision of the emotional atmosphere they wish to create (see Chapter 9, Leading and following). In the 1980s a major British airline attempted just such a programme, with some success. However, this did not prevent private feelings bubbling to the surface when the reality of sustaining the emotional performance took hold. A senior flight attendant, with nineteen years' flying experience in the airline, explains:

> You try saying 'Hello' to 300 people and sound as though you mean it towards the end. Most of us make a game of it. Someone – probably a manager – said, 'This business is all about interpersonal transactions.' He was wrong. It's all about bullshit. If life is a cabaret, this is a bloody circus.[23]

Her colleague, equally cynical, describes her economy-class passengers as 'an amorphous mass of inconsequence'. Over time, and under pressure, the constant strain to keep up the emotional front leads to an ever widening gap between inner feelings and outward display. Sometimes, the mask slips:

> A young businessman said to a flight attendant, 'Why aren't you smiling?' She put her tray back on the food cart and said, 'I'll tell you what. You smile first, then I'll smile.' The businessman smiled at her. 'Good,' she replied. 'Now freeze and hold that for fifteen hours.'[24]

Getting by in such work means keeping up the act, but not taking it too seriously.

EVERYDAY EMOTIONAL CONTROL

Organizations which are out of the direct eye of the consuming public are less concerned with these very obvious forms of emotional control. Control still exists (as Alice and John show, at the start of this chapter), but the processes are more subtle and implicit. We **learn** the social **rules** of appropriate emotional display by trial and error, revealing too much or too little, in the various settings and circumstances of organizational life. We learn where humour, seriousness, anger, despair, joy and so forth can and cannot be expressed, and the verbal and non-verbal displays that are acceptable. The settings are particularly important. What is right for the coffee room does not necessarily work in the committee meeting. What can be said in your own office cannot always be said in your boss's. An unburdening of worries in a car ride with a colleague cannot necessarily be repeated elsewhere. After a time we take these things for granted, and it can come as something of a shock when we find ourselves confused as to the correct emotional response for the situation, and feelings of embarrassment begin to show. One of us was faced with just such an event:

> What do you do when a policeman takes his trousers off in front of you? I was with this police superintendent in his small, well-ordered, office – a first meeting – conducting a research interview with him. He was in full uniform. He was a very formal man, and quite proper in his style. After about an hour and a half he invited me to go lunch with him at a local restaurant. I was pleased to accept. He said he would have to change out of his uniform, and made as if to go to another room. Instead, he stopped at a large wardrobe in the office, took out his civilian clothes, and slowly started to change in front of me, removing his trousers first of all. I was suddenly struck by the absurdity of it all. This sober, authoritarian man silently performing a fairly private act in front of a relative stranger – and in a work office. I felt embarrassed, but I did not want to show it. I stumbled for something to chat about, but I just couldn't continue the interview while he was standing there in his underpants. It felt like a sketch from Monty Python! I tried to hide my embarrassment (he wasn't the slightest bit ruffled) by getting up, talking about the weather, and then, strolling as casually as I could into an adjacent room – until he had finished changing.

Fear of embarrassment is an **emotion** which, in many cultures, controls social behaviour. It is learned fairly early in life; only very young children do not get embarrassed. Looking socially competent becomes all-important in itself; gaffes or cracks in one's social poise have to be disguised with face-saving routines. Thus we see people in boardrooms, committees, coffee groups or classrooms, trying to look and perform the part. To avoid the embarrassment of ridicule or censure they may sometimes overperform, deflect attention with humour, justify themselves, or simply say or do as little as possible.

OFF-STAGE RELIEF

Playing our emotional parts in organizations involves knowing what not to express, as much as knowing what to express. But what happens to Alice's dislike of John, her boss? What do flight attendants do with their distaste about their false smile? What does the calm-looking waiter do with his frustration at pernickety and critical customers? How do production operators handle their long hours of boredom, or anti-management feeling at work? And how does a person handle feelings of sexual attraction to someone else at work?

As a rule, the direct, up-front, expression of any of these feelings could seriously compromise a working relationship. Typically, therefore, the feelings are suppressed, held to oneself – at least in the work setting. Some will be too sensitive to share with anyone else. Others will surface and be re-worked outside the organization – with a partner, friend, doctor or therapist. But the very need to express hidden emotions can also spur the growth of informal organizational processes which help give indirect voice to inner feelings. For example, stories and **jokes**: the telling and re-telling of tales about the 'utter incompetence of management', 'that dreadful speech by the MD', 'the sales department where no-one answers the phone' or 'Bill, the engineering foreman, who can't fix his own car'. Stories can carry, in coded form, people's worries, disaffections, desires or ignoble thoughts, which otherwise could not be expressed. They can, symbolically, compensate for the **power** imbalances in the organization. So the secretary who feels put upon by her powerful boss vents her feelings by telling tales which demonstrate how awful and insensitive he is (see Chapter 13, Serious joking).

Off-stage relief can also be seen in **games** (see also Chapter 3, Rules are rules). Not the conventional ones like sporting activities (although these no doubt play their part), but creating games out of the everyday tedium. Production workers may compete with one another to produce the most unusual rogue product – like a cake which is extraordinarily deformed, or a mis-shapen package. The organization's communication technology is ripe for fun: computers on which one can load absorbing games, telephone systems where colleagues' calls can be mischievously diverted (to the elevator in one company we know), and faxes through which friends can be sent silly messages. While providing emotional relief, some of these games become a strong part of working **culture**. For example one organizational researcher [25] describes the cosy atmosphere of a patient-records office in a hospital where, for years, clerks had contributed to an office 'doughnut fund' each time a paper pellet they threw missed a target bin. This practice had to stop when the department was streamlined by management – and morale plummeted.

Sometimes games have a sharper edge, being aimed punitively at the person to whom one's real feelings cannot be directly expressed. For example, creating a recurring breakdown which a supervisor has to keep correcting, or deliberately arriving late for a meeting – which prevents a boss starting on time. Some games can be at the expense of the weaker members of a workgroup, especially the novice. On joining a steel company one of our students received a phone call from an important client, asking for 'special steel with a pink and green speckled surface'. The student expressed puzzlement at the request, whereupon the customer snapped angrily at him for his equivocal response. Frantically, the student called all the managers he could find to get an answer to the query. What he did not know was that the colour was absurd, and the 'client' had been put-up to the hoax. The student's embarrassment was his colleagues' delight.

Some organizations have clearly demarcated settings where the public courtesies of emotional control can be relaxed. The school staff room, the restaurant kitchen, the nurses' rest area, the works canteen, the galley on an aircraft – are all no-go areas for the public. There the pupil, customer, patient, manager or passenger can be chided, cursed or reviled – with impunity. The professional mask is dropped for a while, and private feelings can spill out. There is usually a willing audience. The switch from public mask to private, and back again, can occur many times in a working day. The waiter epitomizes this as he or she crisscrosses the boundary between restaurant and kitchen – cool, calm and collected at one moment; shouting for orders the next. Similarly, a police officer can show restrained politeness to an abusive motorist whom he has just caught for speeding, but then 'return' the abuse in the privacy of his patrol car – to the eager ear of a colleague.

Now and again we witness some remarkable, accidental, off-stage revelations, cracks in the mask – such as the private and confidential tape recordings of President Nixon of the USA in the 1970s. We hear his anguished words as he struggled desperately to cover his tracks on his own illegal activities. More whimsically, a television broadcast a few years ago showed another ex-President of the USA, Ronald Reagan, very jittery and roundly cursing his audience. Someone had inadvertently thrown a switch, transforming a private rehearsal into a national live broadcast. The emotional import of these events was accentuated by the 'real' public performances of the presidents – which were calm and reassuring.

CHANGING THE EMOTIONAL RULES?

Can work organizations operate with more emotional freedom? Should they? A few practitioners have asserted that what employees feel, and how they can express those feelings, must be very much more than an add-on feature to the economic or management purpose of the organization. However, the most influential force for change has come from **feminism**. Feminist writings are now part of most business school curricula (reaching student audiences comprising around 50 per cent women), and they regularly feature in the national press. Questions concerning the interests of women at work have been debated at national level, especially the poor representation of women (and ethnic minorities) in senior posts in corporations and government.

From an emotion point of view, feminist thought draws our attention to the contrasting **socialization** of the sexes, and different ways of valuing and showing feelings. The meaning and expression of emotions such as care, pain, love, sensitivity, aggression and anxiety are massively influenced by **gendering** – what is regarded as appropriate for a man or a woman. The differences can be found in statements such as: 'the sweet smiles of women'; 'women should be demure; men should be forth-right'. Women can reveal their pain and distress; men should hide it. Women can cry (only to be judged by men as 'emotional', which they resent); men should not show tears. Arguably, such gendering of emotion impoverishes both men and women, and encourages occupational stereotyping: 'women's jobs' and 'men's jobs' divided according to supposed emotional and skill requirements. Indeed the latest surveys of job attitudes reveal a persisting belief that women are more suited to occupations such as nursing, personnel work, domestic work and secretarial activities, while men should be the mechanics, commanders and engineers. There is no biological or emotional necessity for such gender divisions, although it may be convenient for men to believe that they are more temperamentally suited to jobs which happen to have the most power, pay and prestige in our society.

Typically, corporate success for women has meant learning male-type behaviours and male emotional expression: competing with men on men's terms. A female middle manager in a dominantly male, and macho, car retailing organization, described her position to us as follows:

> They call me 'dearie' or 'young lady', even those who are much younger than me. If I'm ill or a bit off colour my manager keeps asking me whether I'm pregnant. They have reluctantly agreed to pay for me to study for a part-time MBA, but only if I sign a pay-back clause in case I leave the firm within two years. The interesting thing is that no male manager has ever been asked to do this. I need to swallow all this stuff, and meet them on their terms. I have to show that I'm one of them even though I feel I'm not. So, for example, I've taken to putting on overalls, going down to the car service bay, driving onto a ramp, and saying to the boys there, 'OK, I want to learn to service it; show me.' They're amazed – and it works a treat.

There is evidence that, to be taken seriously, women have to be noticeably better than comparable men. Alternatively, women may conform to the female stereotype and, by sheer force of **personality** and shrewd political judgement, steer their way through the corporate networks. Furthermore women, more than men, will have to cope with the conflict of split loyalties between job and family – which can be perceived by an employer as evidence of their potential unreliability (see Chapter 17, Working and living). The woman (or man) who wants to create an open emotional climate, with bonds based on care and concern for the organization as a community, usually has to stand alone – and experiment.

- Emotions, and their control, are intrinsic to human organizing; organizations have rules of emotional display.
- Many jobs involve the creation of the 'right' emotional expression for the right situation.
- Some jobs and roles require more personal effort than others to control one's private feelings. This involves continuous acting, which can be stressful.
- Some organizations systematically manipulate employee feelings for commercial gain.
- We learn the rules of emotion display – according to our culture, our gender and our work organizations.
- Many organizations develop informal rituals through which private feelings can be more easily expressed.
- Social changes, especially from feminism, have challenged traditional assumptions about emotionality and rationality in organizations (but male ways still prevail).

THESAURUS ENTRIES

bureaucracy	learning
control	meaninglessness
culture	participation
emotion	perception
ethics	personality
feminism	power
games	rationality
gender	rules
impression formation	socialization
job satisfaction	stereotyping
jokes	values

12

SEX

'Well, I'll sit here to look at Vanessa's legs', announced the ageing director of a manufacturing firm as he sat opposite the student trainee at the start of a meeting. Vanessa was not impressed. 'Before I worked at Powertech', she said later, 'I did not have much sympathy with women who complained about sexism in the workplace as I really did think it was a thing of the past. I was absolutely unprepared to deal with all the comments and attitudes I encountered on placement. Many of these attitudes are very subtle. Many of the offenders do not understand that they are being sexist, they just feel they are "having a laugh", or being friendly.'

The issue of sexual harassment has lately placed sexuality in the centre of discussions about organizations. For a long time, sexuality in organizations has been a non-topic. Try looking at the index of any Organizational Behaviour text. It is as if people lock up their sexual thoughts and desires the minute they walk into their workplaces. After all, workplaces are not places for pleasure, romance or sensuousness, let alone sex. Most people see sex as a private matter, not as public business (see Chapter 5, Morals and Chapter 17, Working and living).

SEX TALK

Looking at organizations purely as places of work is almost as naive as looking at **sex** purely as sexual intercourse. Men and women are sexual beings. Our sexuality is a central part of our **personality**. We all have sexual desires, anxieties and **fantasies** and we spend some of our working time talking, joking and thinking about sex. The graffiti in toilets and lifts, the pin-ups in lockers and workshops, the sex gossip and casual conversations, provide ample evidence that sex is very much on people's minds during their time at work.

In some organizations, sex talk goes on incessantly. Its variety is enormous, ranging from the subtle to the explicit, from the friendly to the hostile to the downright nasty. Consider the following two examples:

> I had been doing consultancy for the launch of a US software product called Soft-tool. With a name like this you don't stand a chance, I told the manufacturers, you have to change the brand-name. No luck, it was company policy to use the same name in all its geographic divisions. My job was to come up with a logo for this product, imagine now 'Buy Soft-tool to increase your performance'. When they realized their gaffe, they changed the name to . . . Hard-tool!
>
> (Computer executive)

> I think it's mainly me really they tease, about the postboy. Because he's so sweet, you know, I say he is my toy boy, and the others ask me 'Have you seen your toy boy today?' Silly things like that, it just lightens the day up. . . . Or the gentleman across the corridor, I notice him because he is always working, he's such a nice gentleman, such a nice character, and I always say 'I just met him on the first floor, I think he's madly in love with me!' Silly things. We just laugh about them.
>
> (Office worker)

It may come as no surprise that the first story was told by a man and the second by a woman. Men and women do not often see the world the same way. They do not think in identical ways about sex, nor do they talk about it the same way. The explicit sarcasm of the first quote contrasts with the delicate innuendo of the latter. Yet, in their distinct ways, both narratives reveal sexual anxieties – the man's worry about masculinity and the woman's concern about being loved. They both suggest fantasies, the first a fantasy about sexually inadequate men, the second about an innocent postboy and a romantically inclined 'gentleman'. Both stories court embarrassment as they shake some taboos and use potentially risky words. Told in the wrong way to the wrong audience, they could lead to stony silence and embarrassed glances. Told in the right way to the right audience, they generate a unique kind of pleasure, strengthen the sense of intimacy among those present and bring femininity and masculinity into the heart of organizational life.

Wholly male and wholly female work environments spawn distinct brands of sex talk. Yet, sex talk is not confined to groups of the same **gender**. In some mixed offices continuous sex teasing goes on between men and women. Men may tease women about their appearance while women may tease men about their virility. In two district offices of a privatized utility, sexual banter and obscene jokes were traded endlessly across the genders in apparently good humour. Not one of the 47 people interviewed by one of us admitted to being upset about them. For Andrew, fresh from university, the office had been a **culture** shock.

> *Andrew*: When I first came here, I just couldn't believe the language people used. Gossip about who's going out with whom, who fancies whom, it's just like school. The jokes! Not down to the level of whistling, but about how people look.
>
> *Interviewer*: Do the women mind about it?
>
> *Andrew*: I'd say they enjoy it. I've got to be honest, the difference between here and college is huge, people could no way get away with some of the jokes. The attitude here is totally different. It's horrible saying this but most of the women seem to enjoy it. Totally sexist thing to say. But it goes on and on and on. Like the story about two people who are having an intimate situation, this is how it started, and people just constantly crack jokes about them. It's become like a serial. Probably none of it is true.

Nicky, a 21-year-old clerk who had joined the company as a trainee four years previously, said:

> I don't mind sexist jokes, I make them myself. Men tease me about the size of my backside but it's all in good spirit. Mind you, I have taken down the nude calendars. I wouldn't like nude men on the walls either, in fact, I'd rather have the women!

OFFICE ROMANCES

Much of the sexual behaviour at work takes place at the level of talk and fantasy. Nevertheless, physical display and contact are not entirely absent. Touching, hugging or kissing may not be much in evidence in most workshops or offices, but many have apocryphal tales, such as what went on at the Christmas party, or during the residential conference, or behind the closed doors of the office. In the organization above, in the interest of better understanding between clerical and technical staff, once a year each clerical worker accompanies a service engineer on house calls. On a different day, each engineer sits in the office paired with a clerical worker. The joint house calls fed a constant stream of innuendoes. Eventually, one of the women in the office married 'her' engineer, providing a happy ending to another local soap opera.

This type of sexual chatter is generally thought of positively by men and women in the workplace. Sexual fantasies are an escape from the ordinariness of work. Sex talk breaks the monotony, introduces a playful element in a highly controlled environment. Sex talk also reminds people that their bodies are not just labouring instruments hiding inside uniforms and suits, but are also sources and objects of pleasure and **desire**.

This is half the story; the other half is less agreeable. Sex in organizations goes far deeper than being a mere diversion from the monotony of work. Discrimination, AIDS and harassment point to some darker aspects. The rest of this chapter explores some of the ways in which sex cuts across and strengthens the **power** relations in organizations.

SEXUAL HARASSMENT

Increasing awareness of the dark side of sexuality within organizations has coincided with an explosion of concern about sexual harassment in the United States, and to a lesser extent in Britain. Sensitivities, **attitudes** and feelings are changing. On the one hand, there is an increasing recognition that **sexual harassment** is not an exceptional occurrence but a routine phenomenon in many workplaces and that large numbers of women (and to a lesser extent men, especially gay men) suffer in silence. On the other hand, there is a sense that forms of behaviour which used to pass as 'innocent' and 'well-intentioned' involve a covert attempt to humiliate women, to bolster negative stereotypes and to preserve organizational forms in which men generally occupy superior positions to women.

The norms of permissible and abusive sexual behaviour are changing. What used to pass as 'innocent banter' is rapidly being re-classified as offensive behaviour. 'Friendly' compliments are frequently resented, either because they are perceived as implied propositions or because they are seen as devaluing other qualities. Many women now feel that they tolerated such forms of behaviour in the past, pretended not to notice or felt ashamed about it, instead of recognizing the hurt that it caused and fighting back.

Sexual harassment comes in many forms. At its worst it amounts to nothing less than rape, or the demand for what some call 'sexual favours' in return for promotion or other material benefits. This is sexual bullying, the abuse of power to exploit, humiliate or hurt and the pleasure of doing so. Sexual harassment may, equally, assume more subtle forms. Persistent compliments can be irritating as can excessive familiarity, exaggerated intimacy or physical closeness. One of the commonest forms of harassment, however, lies in sexist remarks which either reduce women to sex objects or re-affirm unpleasant **stereotypes**. These put women in a rather invidious position; if they express disgust or disapproval this tends to reinforce the stereotype ('women lack a sense of humour', 'they are emotional' and so forth), while if they bottle up their feelings they offer tacit encouragement for their aggressor.

One of our students reported three incidents that took place in quick succession between her and her manager in a bank.

> I came to work in a smart trouser suit and Paul greeted me with 'Did you forget to take your pyjamas off, Suzie?' (he knows I hate being called Suzie.) A little later I was trying to print some documents and said 'This printer is so temperamental!' and Paul quipped 'It's obviously female.' Eventually, the fault was found to be in the computer and he said 'Have you broken it already?' Me: 'No'. Paul: 'Ah! that's what happens when you let women near machines.'

Susan tolerated this type of put-down for several days. The worst thing, she explained, was not knowing whether these comments were meant as friendly teasing or as serious criticism. She put on a brave face, hid her feelings and tried to 'rise' above this baiting. One day, however, she felt especially annoyed and when Paul told her that he planned to take a three-week holiday, she quipped: 'Why, visiting your Spanish sweetheart again?' before she had time to check herself. 'Don't be cheeky!', said Paul. 'I can remember experiencing mixed feelings about what had happened. Perhaps I overstepped the mark, the fine line between what an employee can and cannot say to a manager. As a result I told myself off for not checking myself, I blamed myself. But I also felt that it didn't seem fair that I had to take his jokes in good humour, no matter how bad they were, while his position meant that I couldn't give as good as I got.'

THE AMBIGUITIES OF HARASSMENT

When does a well-meant joke or compliment become sexual harassment? This is a thorny issue. A joke which in one organization may cause amusement may cause offence in a different one. During a workshop run by one of our colleagues, a participant told of his plans to tour the Far East, 'just three men, without women to complicate the party or disapprove'. Challenged to say what they intended to do, he casually remarked 'Oh, a little bit of rape and pillage!' The comment outraged many of the others and led to a heated debate in which men and women were sharply polarized. What seemed like an innocent joke to some of the men was felt to be a vicious sexist and racist comment to the women. Whether or not the teller of the joke had meant it as an abusive comment to the women present, this is exactly how they experienced it.[26]

In normal circumstances we rely on social **norms** to guide us through what is acceptable and what is unacceptable social behaviour. Tact and sensitivity alert us to the needs and feelings of others. In the area of sex, however, norms vary enormously from place to place and leave a lot of ambiguity. What is more, this is an area where many men have not had to think about or do not realize what issues are involved for women. All the same, the excuse 'I didn't mean to hurt you' sounds highly unconvincing in most cases. Nor does the word 'innocent' stick to the many sexist jokes one hears. The obscenities of the graffiti in male lavatories or many all-male conversations in bars suggest that hate and scorn are as much part of men's feelings towards women as attraction and love.

Men's **emotions** towards women are often ambivalent. Their feelings are often in conflict with each other. They frequently stereotype the women they meet in one of a few basic categories, like mother figure, iron maiden, witch, whore, or defenceless 'pet'. Men idealize 'the virgin' while denying that the 'mother figure' has any sexuality at all. Women with independent sexual desires are often typecast as 'tarts' or 'whores', against whom large amounts of both male lust and aggression are directed. Unless perceived as virgins or mothers, women are often said to be bringing male violence upon themselves through provocative or flirtatious behaviour. 'She asked for it' becomes the stock defence of perpetrators of male violence against women. Instead of the wrongdoer, it is the victim who gets the blame.

SEX AND ORGANIZATIONAL POLITICS

Blaming the victim by turning women into rightful targets for male violence, presents sexual harassment as a purely personal matter. But sexual harassment would not have become a major issue if it amounted to nothing more than the actions of a few male chauvinists, let alone the experience of a few oversensitive females. One of the reasons it has become a central political and management issue is, as **feminist** theorists have pointed out, that sexual politics is enmeshed in organizational **politics** and **conflicts**.

Sex is a feature of many organizational **games**. As Susan noted in the earlier story, men and women rarely enter these games as equals. In competing for jobs in the labour market, women have faced many visible and invisible barriers, **prejudice** or **discrimination**. If direct discrimination is rare these days (women being paid less for doing the same jobs as men), many more or less subtle forms of discrimination make it harder for women to rise to positions of great power or influence (see Chapter 16, Career-ing).

In most organizations, women tend to occupy subordinate positions, either directly 'servicing' male managers and bosses or coming into direct contact with the organization's customers as sales staff, telephonists, air stewardesses, waitresses and the like. **Feminists** have pointed out that women's sexuality is far from peripheral in most of these jobs. On the contrary, it is harnessed either to lure the customer, or to boost their boss's ego/image or to project a glamorous image for a company or an industry. **Femininity** and sex appeal are virtual prerequisites for employment in many such jobs. In many organizations, a 'sexy' secretary is still seen as indicative of the **status** of her boss, while glamour is part of the image cultivated by industries such as cosmetics, airlines, advertising and the mass media.

But women's sexuality is also harnessed by organizations in subtler ways. In jobs involving direct contact with customers, consumers or employees, the 'feminine touch' is deployed to defuse awkward or dangerous situations and to maintain a discreet form of social control. Telephonists, sales staff, receptionists, cashiers, nurses, teachers and police officers are all expected to exercise their delicate interpersonal skills on behalf of their organizations, preventing things from getting out of hand. A feminine presence in most organizations is seen as a civilizing influence and a balancing counterpart to male aggression.

In some organizations, management maintains a low-level sexual 'simmer',[27] placing great emphasis on women's appearance and demeanour, encouraging smart dressing, make-up and so on. One of our students worked for a pizza restaurant which placed high emphasis on the appearance of the waitresses; it also paid minimal wages. Result:

> Some of the waitresses would do anything to earn a tip. Some of the younger ones wore black bras which were clearly visible underneath their pink blouses. Some deliberately shortened their skirts. Some compared this to prostitution, selling yourself in order to make money. I have to agree with them.
>
> Other waitresses adopted their own tip-making strategies. For example, Elaine in her spare moments would go over to the customers and start up a conversation. She would often tell customers about any personal problems that she had. It appeared as though she was begging for a tip.
>
> I swore I would not sink to this level. However, I did and developed my own strategies. One of these was to ask customers with relatively young children whether they would like a bowl and a spoon for the children to use. This was actually quite successful and I believe that it encouraged customers to leave tips.

'USING SEX'

This astute account illustrates sharply the linkage between sexuality and power in organizations. The waitresses were forced because of their inferior positions to adopt sexual and emotional tactics, which could then be used against them (and women in general) to **stereotype** them and disparage them. It also illustrates some of the distress that having to adopt such demeaning forms of behaviour causes women.

Femininity, encompassing physical allure, warmth, tenderness and subtle interpersonal skills, is part and parcel of how some of women's work in organizations gets done. In as much as women's sexuality serves organizational goals it is taken for granted and often encouraged. When the self-same feminine qualities are seen as serving women's own interests, they are frequently turned against women. Women are then placed in a 'double-bind' or no-win situation. The same work environment which encourages femininity and even seductiveness chastises women for using their 'feminine charms' to gain personal advantage and influence. On the other hand, women who suppress their **sexuality** and seek to confront men as equals, are often branded 'iron maidens', lesbians and so forth. Women frequently feel that they are treading a dangerous ground of permissible and non-permissible displays of femininity, between being 'too sexy' and 'not sexy enough'.

There is little evidence that women gain personal advantage against male colleagues by using their sexuality, although they are often accused of doing so. If anything, there is some evidence of the opposite. To the extent that certain jobs emphasize attractiveness, they are seen as requiring little in the way of intellectual abilities, qualifications and motivation. Attractive women in positions of genuine power are automatically suspected of having risen on the basis of their physical attributes, and become the commonest target of male hostility and sexual harassment.

MALE SEXUALITY

While sexual harassment and discrimination have forced us to look at female sexuality in organizations, it would be wrong to imply that male sexuality is excluded from them. To be sure, the stereotypes of men in organizations tend to underplay sexuality, in the same measure as those of women emphasize it. Think of grey-suited businessmen, rational, tough, analytic, and you would be forgiven for imagining that they are pure brain and will, detached from bodies and **desires**. As we saw earlier, however, sexual **fantasies** and wishes are rarely far from men's minds and frequently feed organizational sex talk.

Physical appearance is a central ingredient of male sexuality as it is of female. A computer analyst in a large firm prided himself on his bulging muscles, the product of long sessions spent in the gymnasium. 'I had an office', he recounted not without self-irony, 'next to the girls in the legal department, and they were talking about the sexiest man in the building, and they were coming up with all these men I'd never heard of before. So I went into their office and said "Sorry about this ladies, I thought that I was the real myo-star, the hulk." They cracked up laughing and said "We had a vote and you were voted the most boring old fart in this place." '

Sex teasing in organizations can be good-humoured and benign, but relations between men and women are unsymmetrical and unequal. A woman entering an all-male office saying 'Sorry about this lads, but I thought that I was the sex sensation here', would doubtless elicit a very different response from the witticism of the earlier story. A man who prides himself on his sexual exploits may attract a well-deserved taunt but may be secretly admired as a 'stud' or a 'ladies' man'. A woman doing likewise would probably be derided as fast, promiscuous or worse.

While women have to tread a precarious line between 'not sexy enough' and 'too sexy', displays of masculinity come under laxer controls. Even when it assumes the distasteful shape of sexual harassment it often goes unpunished. There is, nevertheless, a taboo in most workplaces against **homosexuality** and, more generally, against men's displays of physical closeness or affection. Hugging and kissing among Mediterranean men scandalize many Anglo-Saxons, who regard them as a possible blot on their masculinity.

One of us was attending a conference in Italy, in the company of two close colleagues from our university department, and remembers vividly the following incident:

There was Roberto, an old associate, who I met about once a year. He threw his arms around me and gave me an affectionate hug. I was pleased to respond to his warmth. My two British colleagues gave me 'knowing' glances. I was a little embarrassed and they teased me. I

Sage Publications Ltd.,
6 Bonhill Street,
London EC2A 4PU

Telephone: 071-374 0645
FAX: 071-374 8741
Telex:296207 SAGE G

Ⓢ Sage Publications   12/8/93

At the request of Yiannis Gabriel.

Julia Hodkinson
Ed. Asst.

With Compliments

Returning
University
Press —
an address
copy today

laughed it off. Throughout the day, the teasing continued – jokes, quips and innuendo about my 'relationship' with Roberto. I still smiled. After all, I could take a joke, couldn't I?

The teasing, as I recall, resumed the next day. They seemed to be having great fun at my expense, while I felt increasingly uncomfortable. It was now beyond a joke. It seemed curiously childish behaviour, insensitive, silly. Then it was one remark too many. 'I am not enjoying these remarks, could you please stop?' I snapped at Chris. He seemed surprised. Chris communicated my comment to Geoffrey. There was a slightly uncomfortable feeling between us, and then it stopped. A couple of years later, Chris and I discussed the incident. We both agreed about the 'facts'. As for the meaning of the incident, there seemed to be a gulf dividing us.

With few exceptions, Western organizations are neither kind nor permissive towards gays and lesbians, who often become victims of vicious sexual harassment. Gays and lesbians find themselves in especially invidious situations, looking for strategies of **survival** while constantly suppressing their sexuality. Denial, overcompensation, avoidance or straight lying are strategies which take their toll emotionally. Having to laugh at your colleagues' anti-gay jokes (or even initiating them yourself), not disclosing the gender of your living companion, keeping constant vigilance over what others know of your **desires** and **fantasies**, 'splitting' your sexual self from your work self; these are all psychological ways of coping, which exact their price in anxiety, stress and guilt.

But male **sexuality** at the workplace is not limited to displays of **masculinity** and bravado. Throughout the 1980s a style of **management** attracted attention which is widely referred to as 'macho management'. Confrontation, ostentatious use of force and intransigence, contempt for compromise and compassion became the trademarks of this style of management. Its champions included 'hard men' like Michael Edwardes and Ian McGregor in Britain and Lee Iacocca and John Akers in the United States, who introduced new tough regimes in their companies and, in the cases of the first two, broke the **power** of **trade unions**. Talking tough and acting tough became a matter of masculine pride for those who saw it as their mission to restore 'managers' right to manage'. Many macho managers seemed inspired by the confrontational **rhetoric** of political leaders like Ronald Reagan and Margaret Thatcher. Ironically, the latter debunks the notion that macho **leadership** is restricted to men and suggests that a woman can provide a **role** model for ultra-masculine behaviour.

Whether macho management has become the norm or not is debatable, as is its success in restoring order and peace in many organizations. What it does highlight is the fact that aggression, competitiveness, rigidity and hardness are all qualities which are not only accepted but encouraged by organizations which find them as useful as they find the feminine qualities we discussed earlier. The essential difference lies in the fact that while masculine qualities enhance career prospects, feminine ones, though indispensable for many organizations, are frequently an impediment to personal success.

SUMMARY

Sexuality plays a large part in how men and women relate to each other. Whether they meet as colleagues or as rivals, as superiors or as subordinates, as friends or as lovers, gender is ever present. Our ways of looking at things and relating to others is shaped by our identities and our identities are sexual identities. It is not surprising, therefore, to find sexuality in many episodes of organizational life. In this chapter, we have argued that sexuality is not just incidental to organization, but of the very essence.

Organizations harness the sexuality of both men and women, mould it and frame it. The women's and gay movements must claim the credit for demonstrating how sexuality becomes entangled in organizational politics, revealing its ugly side in incidents of sexual harassment and intimidation. Women's femininity is more severely manipulated and controlled than masculinity, with stereotypes from wider culture conveniently invoked as excuses for discriminatory and unequal treatment.

At the same time, we have argued against the view that automatically equates sex in organizations with oppression and exploitation. We have suggested that sexual joking, banter and innuendo are welcomed by the majority as a break from the impersonal routines of organizations and as a reminder that inside every overall, suit or uniform there is a human body, which is not just an instrument of labour, but also the source and object of pleasure and desire.

- Sexuality is expressed directly and indirectly in organizations, ranging from sex talk, innuendo, and office romances to stereotyping, harassment and discrimination.
- Gender issues and sexuality often become enmeshed with organizational politics in which, almost invariably, men have greater power than women.
- Sexual harassment can take many different forms, including exaggerated compliments, offensive language, sexist jokes and sexual blackmailing.
- Sexual harassment tends to re-affirm gender stereotypes and frequently puts the victim in an invidious no-win situation.
- Men's attitudes and behaviour towards women are often conditioned by naive stereotypes of women such as 'virgins', 'pets', 'mother figures', and 'whores'.
- Organizations mould both masculinity and femininity, though in different ways.
- On the whole, the controls placed on female sexuality and homosexuality are tighter and more inhibiting than those placed on what are seen as 'traditional masculine' traits.

THESAURUS ENTRIES

attitudes	norms
conflict	personality
culture	politics
desire	power
discrimination	prejudice
emotion	rhetoric
fantasy	role
femininity	sex
feminism	sexual harassment
games	sexuality
gender	status
homosexuality	stereotypes
leadership	survival
management	trade unions
masculinity	

13

SERIOUS JOKING

Most organizations are serious places. People go about their business with deliberate seriousness. They fill in forms seriously, they answer phones seriously, they write letters seriously, they tap in on their computer terminals or typewriters seriously, they attend meetings seriously, they discuss strategy seriously, they bargain seriously, they operate different types of machinery seriously. An air of no-nonsense fills organizational spaces.

From time to time humour makes a tentative appearance. A joke in the middle of a stuffy meeting or a cartoon on an office wall lightens the atmosphere and raises a smile. But books on management and organizations have not paid much attention to such phenomena, which were not seen as changing the serious business of organizing.

To the outsider, organizations tend to present a uniformly serious front; entering a bank, a hospital or a government department, reading company reports or sales literature, telephoning the local office of the gas or electric company, one finds little that could be described as amusing. But if, with an innocent eye, we glance backstage in these organizations, a rather different picture is revealed, a picture which may combine the ridiculous, the absurd and the funny. For example, there are people being incredibly serious about matters which look utterly trivial, such as a group of executives discussing at length the precise phrasing of a strategy document which they know will have little impact on anybody. Or people carefully filling in forms in triplicate, for no apparent reason other than that they have 'always done it that way'. And there is a middle-aged clerk, in pin stripes, complaining bitterly about the new plastic cups in the coffee machine, while a group of office workers giggle and smile . . .

In addition, unlike the official visitor who sees the serious front of the organization, the insider in offices may share a **joke** about the latest fiasco (10,000 Valentine cards delivered 'as promised' on 15 February), gossiping about the latest come-uppance of the brash young executive ('you should have seen the state of that Porsche after he reversed into the garage wall') or recollect a practical joke played on an awkward colleague ('Do you remember the scream he gave when he opened the box and the severed hand dropped out all covered in blood?').

It does not take long for most of us to discover that the air of seriousness in the majority of organizations is only paper-thin; underneath, a continuous humorous banter goes on, providing an unofficial commentary on organizational life. People joke, laugh, play tricks on each other and generally try to have a good time. Often, the mere mention of an individual or a group, like 'the inspector', 'personnel' or 'the lawyers', is enough to generate a funny story. 'The computer's gone down again; it must be the director pouring another whisky soda on his terminal!' 'No, it's the computer boys trying to wipe out the last three years' accounts!' 'More likely, someone unplugged the mainframe to boil the kettle.'

JOKES AND SURVIVAL

Workers just starting work in an office may find many of the jokes unfunny or incomprehensible. For a time, they may smile to show that they too are in on the joke but soon they will start chipping in. Not being able to share a joke, however unfunny, makes one feel excluded; a person without a sense of humour quickly becomes the butt of many jokes.

Sharing a laugh and a joke, on the other hand, is an important **survival** mechanism, especially for those people who feel stuck in mundane and repetitive jobs. Laughter and humour make light of the many injuries that we sustain in organizations, physical injuries as well as injuries to our pride and dignity. Fred, who has lost part of his finger in a apple-pie-making machine, becomes the target of many good-humoured jokes a mere few days after the accident. The women checking the beans on a continuously moving conveyor belt joke about management's attempt to replace them with pigeons, trained to pick the dud beans, only to find that the RSPCA has ruled that the task is too cruel for the pigeons. Such jokes seem to celebrate survival against the odds.

Jokes and laughter defuse tense situations, break the monotony and let the weak turn the tables on the strong. 'You have to have a sense of humour to survive in this job' is a statement one hears often when talking to people doing jobs that would not test the intelligence of pigeons. 'You don't have to be mad to work here but it helps' proclaim signs in innumerable workplaces, expressing what many people must feel.

Above all, however, humour gives people licence to say things that could not be said otherwise. Organizations require people to keep their mouths shut a lot of the time and keep their opinions to themselves. Criticizing superiors to their face is not a recipe for promotion or success. A joke, however, with people sharing similar views, permits the venting of emotions, such as fear, hostility and contempt, that loom under the surface (see Chapter 11, Feelings).

In a computer company, one of us was told the following joke which clearly expresses the staff's disparagement towards the board of directors. 'Our Chairman meets Presidents Clinton and Mitterrand in an international conference. "My problem," says Clinton "is that I have twelve security advisers. One of them is a foreign spy, but I don't know which." "Funny you should say this," retorts Mitterrand, "my problem is that I have twelve mistresses. One of them is unfaithful, but I don't know which." "Your problems are nothing compared to mine," says our Chairman. "I have twelve directors on the board, one of them is competent, but I don't know which." '

Jokes enable people to test the water and say things that would normally be prohibited or taboo. To exclaim directly 'The manager is a lazy so-and-so' may cause embarrassment even if several people in an office recognize it as true. Saying instead, 'Our boss is an extremely ambitious man; his greatest ambition is how to draw a salary without doing any work' camouflages the hostility and allows the teller to see if others share the same opinion. A joke then offers an amnesty to the teller, enabling a particular view and a range of **emotions** to evade organizational and moral censorship and find an expression. In the last resort, it offers the escape route 'I was only joking.' But if it generates great laughter both the teller of the joke and the listeners have discovered that they have something important in common.

Laughter bonds people as tightly as a shared secret. One cannot tell oneself a joke or a secret, just as one cannot tickle oneself. Jokes and secrets require a social relationship, a shared understanding based on a common **language** which excludes others. Most organizational jokes are also secrets; some people are in and some people are out of these secrets: 'If only the Chairman knew what we say behind his back.' A joke strengthens the sense of *trust* for those who share it. Having shared a joke, especially one that is directed against an excluded party outside the group, generates a tremendous sense of 'usness'. In this way, the joke unleashes two types of emotion, affection for those who share it, and **aggression** for the target (see Chapter 14, Us and them).

Few incidents generate as much hilarity and pleasure as the humbling of a pompous person in a position of authority. Such misfortunes are invariably celebrated by their subordinates and turned into jokes, generating the same type of laughter as pies in the face and banana skins. A manager whose tie gets caught in the office shredder will provide much amusement, especially if he places great store by his appearance. So will an executive who always insists on punctuality and time-keeping, if he/she turns up late for a meeting. The greater our hostility towards the victim of misfortune, the greater our enjoyment. The undeserved suffering of our fellow human beings may trigger in us feelings of sympathy and compassion. Yet, no amount of suffering provides protection against ridicule, so long us we can convince ourselves that the victims brought it upon themselves with their arrogance or their foolishness.

IN-GROUP HUMOUR

While much of disparagement humour is directed outwards, towards members of other social **groups**, some of it is reserved for a group's own members. In particular, individuals who persistently deviate from group **norms** may find themselves on the receiving end of cutting or ironic remarks from their colleagues. Social norms guide our behaviour and shape our expectations of other people's behaviour. Much psychological research has gone into showing how we become **socialized** into the norms of the society and the groups we belong to, so that the norms eventually become part of ourselves. Norms affect most aspects of our life, from relatively minor matters of etiquette to major aspects of our **personality** and life choices, like sexual preference or career choice. Our moral **values** themselves, our sense of what is good and what is evil, depend to a substantial degree on the values of the groups of which we are members. (See Chapter 5, Morals.) Most of the time, social norms guide our behaviour without our being aware of them. Eating with a knife and fork, for example, becomes second nature to us, so that we cannot appreciate how difficult little children may find the mastery of these implements.

Within organizations, as in society at large, our behaviour is regulated not only by written rules and regulations but also by unwritten norms. Not all groups impose their norms with the same severity, but generally deviance from group norms is discouraged. Humour is crucial in both re-affirming group norms and enforcing **conformity**; it is a type of **sanction** relying on embarrassment to pressure the offending individual back into conformity.

An office worker who dresses in an unorthodox manner, a pupil who rushes to answer each of the teacher's questions, a worker who consistently works harder than the rest, a manager who 'crawls' to his/her superiors soon begin to attract disparaging remarks, frequently dressed up as jokes. This acts as a first reminder that such behaviour threatens group cohesion and undermines the group's accepted standards of behaviour. It is surprising, at times, how tiny details of appearance or behaviour become symbolically extremely important for different groups. The college student who drinks half-pints of beer while his/her mates are downing pints will soon be picked on, as if he/she had violated an important group taboo. If sarcastic remarks are the group's first attempt to pull individuals back to the norms, exclusion, verbal abuse or physical violence may follow.

Humour then usually provides the first indicator of the line between acceptable and unacceptable behaviour. It acts as a mechanism of group **control**. People who persistently break group norms face two possibilities. They may be marginalized and ultimately rejected from the group. Alternatively, they may become accepted as 'eccentrics', in other words as exceptions which reinforce the norms.

JOKING RELATIONS

Not all in-group humour functions to chastise deviance and force people to conform to group norms. Much of the humorous banter that can be heard in offices, building sites and other workplaces takes the form of friendly teasing. Individuals are routinely teased for their appearance, their accent, their **ethnic** origin, or their tastes. Such teasing can be quite coarse but is generally good-natured, a sign of trust and intimacy. Targeting an individual, in this case, can be a sign of affection and esteem – the assumption is that the target 'can take it', without offence.

Proving that 'you can take a joke' is often important in order to be accepted as a full group member. New recruits in military or police academies, new boarding school pupils, are often sub-jected to bizarre tests, known as **rites** of initiation or passage, which will later provide the material for jokes. The new police recruit may be asked to go and arrest a supposed criminal hiding on an island in the middle of a lake in the park. A new computer analyst may find that his/her terminal has been tampered with, pretending after a while to delete precious files in front of his/her very eyes. The Chairman's new chauffeur may be asked to go and pick up the Chairman from an address in the red-light district in the middle of the night. The individual who successfully survives these initiation ordeals is then accepted as a full member of the group and as fit to take part in joking relationships (see Chapter 2, Joining and leaving).

Anthropologists have used the term 'joking relationships' to describe relationships which are built around continuous teasing, horseplay, ridicule and jocular repartee that does not result in offence. Such relationships have been studied in factories, offices, department stores, hospitals, shipyards as well as in informal gatherings. Obscenity, cursing, insults and vicious pranks are part and parcel of joking relationships, yet in a curious way the coarser the insult, the greater the affection, warmth and respect it is meant to **communicate**.

THE UGLY SIDE OF HUMOUR

Humour cements group bonds, builds up trust and humanizes **impersonal** relations. Yet, the line between friendly teasing and brutal bullying can be very thin. What passes as an innocent joke may to its target amount to abusive racial or **sexual harassment**. We saw earlier how weak and exploited members of organizations use humour to symbolically turn the tables on those who dominate them. The reverse of this happens when the dominant party of a relationship forces his/her tasteless or abusive humour on his/her subordinates and invites them to laugh at grotesque wisecracks. Under the mock trust of a joking relationship, black employees may be invited to laugh at **racist** jokes and women at **sexist** jokes. Such jokes are expressions of **aggression** and can be the first step of racial or sexual harassment, which may then escalate into more disturbing forms of abuse (see Chapter 5, Morals and Chapter 12, Sex).

Sexist and racist jokes are especially humiliating types of harassment; the target is put in a no-win situation. Laughing at the joke (while secretly despising themselves for doing so) reinforces the joke and makes it socially and morally acceptable. Refusing to laugh, on the other hand, automatically excludes the target from the group and turns them into a legitimate target of sarcasm, apart from anything else, for lacking a sense of humour. Both responses may be adding fuel to the fire and encouraging further insulting jokes.

In such situations it may be best to retort to the joke with a joke; one that twists its meaning and turns the aggressor's ugly innuendo on its head. One of us was once doing research interviews with clerical staff. The atmosphere in the office was relaxed and jocular; many of the disparaging jokes were targeted against the central headquarters (Example: 'What is the difference between HQ and a bag of manure? The bag.') The local managers were in on most jokes, being no mean wits themselves. Much of the banter and teasing in the office was overtly sexual; people's appearance, their secret crushes, the engineers' exploits on house calls, were the source of continuous joking. After Jenny, a young and outspoken office worker had been interviewed, Brian, one of the managers, asked her tongue in cheek in the presence of several bystanders: 'Did you spill the beans, sweetheart?' 'Sure', she replied 'I told him that you are a dirty old man'. 'Me, old?' he retorted without a moment's hesitation. Everyone listening to the conversation burst out laughing.

These three short phrases are charged with danger, innuendo and risk. Each seems to break a little organizational taboo and threaten the established order. The first two generate tension, the third resolves it and in doing so defuses the situation and leaves an atmosphere of goodwill and effervescence.

Jokes and joking then can be liberating and subversive but they can equally be oppressive and humiliating. They can question assumptions and express unpalatable truths or they can reinforce crass **stereotypes** and perpetuate **myths** and untruths. They can provide a cover for the scars of organizational life or can be a prime cause of such scars.

JOKES AND THE IRON CAGE

To regard humour and jokes as a superficial phenomenon of organizational life, as has been the custom, misses the rich undercurrent of **meanings** present. Jokes that people tell at the workplace can reveal as much or perhaps more about the organization, its management, its **culture** and its **conflicts** as answers to carefully administered surveys. If anything, under the moral smoke screen supplied by humour, people can express deeper feelings and views.

Even the scarcity of humour can be extremely revealing about an organization. Joke-free zones have been said to exist, at the level of countries and of organizations (some religious or political sects). People's sense of humour wanes if they are brutalized to quiet resignation or if they take themselves and the organization terribly seriously. The majority of organizations, however, can neither **control** their members to such an extent, nor persuade them of the incredible seriousness of their objectives.

Moreover, we suspect that even the most serious work environments may not altogether lack humour. Instead they may control rigidly those targets of humour regarded as legitimate. One simply does not joke about certain issues, they are taboo. Nevertheless, the wit in the organization will sooner or later find a target which is at least tolerated or even encouraged. If joking about internal matters is severely frowned upon, joking about the organization's rivals may provide an alternative outlet.

Humour thrives as a way of killing boredom, creating solidarity and scoring symbolic points against internal and external oppositions. For these reasons, the different types of jokes examined here seem perfectly suited to the exigencies of organizational life. There is, however, one type of joke which best captures organizational humour and this is the joke against the organization itself. This is the type of joke epitomized in satire, such as that directed at military organizations or at the bureaucratic regimes in what used to be the Communist bloc. The organization, satire proclaims, is an absurd farce. Instead of trying to make sense of it, let us have a good laugh at its expense. Satire celebrates the little and large chinks in the armour of those impressive organizations which dominate our society. It shows that behind the formidable administrative, technical and financial resources of these giants, there are people messing about and making mistakes. Behind their **rationality**, there are absurdities, foul-ups and blunders. However hard organizations may try to eliminate individuality by turning us into extensions of machines and by controlling our behaviour through ever more precise procedures, they can never be fully successful.

Organizational satire can be seen as a protest against the 'iron cage of bureaucracy' and all those who are eager to provide their services to it. **Organizations** themselves, for the greatest part, do little to discourage it. To be sure, a practical joke that results in serious loss of production or the wiping out of the company's records will not go unpunished. However, so long as the work gets done and the orders are obeyed, most organizations are willing to tolerate humour and satire, even if they themselves become the object of ridicule. While offering no prizes to the quickest wit or the most original prankster, they recognize that even defiant humour is a protest, not a rebellion. Its victories are **symbolic**, not material.

SUMMARY

Humour and jokes, far from being inconsequential, are important features of organizational life. They break the organizational routine and enable people to cope with boring or **alienating** jobs. They generate trust and affection for those sharing a laugh and a joke and permit the venting of unacceptable views and **emotions** (like aggression or contempt), by offering a moral amnesty which permits the breaking of taboos.

The targets of organizational jokes are varied, but most workgroups have an individual or another group which serves as the butt of disparaging humour. When directed against superiors or outsiders, jokes strengthen the solidarity of a group and enable the group to score symbolic victories against their psychological adversaries. When directed against members of a group, jokes may be part of joking relations, highlighting the intimacy and trust between the group's members, or they serve to reinforce group norms and force compliance.

Finally, the target of jokes may be the organization itself, whose foul-ups and absurdities are celebrated because they undermine the façade of rationality and seriousness. Such jokes, for a brief moment or two, explode organizational order and give reign to anarchy, disorder and disorganization. In this way, they restore the human factor, in its fallibility and unpredictability, at the heart of organizations.

- Under the veneer of seriousness, jokes, irony and humour play an important part in most organizations.
- Jokes offer a way of saying things and venting emotions which could not be otherwise expressed.
- Humour can provide a way for the powerless to turn the tables on the powerful; having a laugh at their expense. It therefore functions as an important survival mechanism.
- Laughter bonds people, generating feelings of solidarity, intimacy and trust.
- In-group humour establishes the boundaries between acceptable and non-acceptable behaviour and provides a way of testing group norms.
- Jokes and mockery can act as a group sanction against those who violate group norms.
- Racist and sexist jokes tend to rely on crass stereotypes; when addressed at a member of the stereotyped group, they can be seen as a form of harassment.

THESAURUS ENTRIES

aggression	control
alienation	culture
communication	emotion
conformity	group
conflicts	impersonality

jokes
language
meaning
myth
norm
organization
personality
racism
rationality

rites of passage
sanctions
sexism
sexual harassment
socialization
stereotyping
survival
symbolism
values

14

US AND THEM

The director of an engineering firm attended a 'Team Building' course and came back to his office fired up with new ideas. **Team work**, he had heard, is the key to success; everyone within the organization must be made to feel that they are a member of a winning team. From senior executives to part-time clerical staff, everyone has a contribution to make, everyone counts. The director, not an unintelligent man, decided to start by holding a Christmas dinner for his staff to strengthen team spirit. Unfortunately, he was embarrassed when all the workers crowded around one table, while he, his wife and the managers had the second table all to themselves. He commented, with irony, how successful he'd been in fostering team spirit among his workers, only he had been stuck in the opposite team!

Social divisions in organizations, as this director found, can run deep. The idea, or ideal, of bringing everyone together, unified in purpose, is often bedevilled by two social facts. Firstly, that people often feel more comfortable in one social **group** than in another. Secondly, they will resist attempts to bind them with groups to which they feel no particular affinity. From an organizational point of view this is important. People will behave in tune with those with whom they identify most – and this can shift according to place and time. So you might feel one of 'us' when in a committee meeting with colleagues, but a different 'us' when having coffee with your immediate team members. You may see management as 'them' – except when you are invited onto a working party which has a mix of managers and workers.

Although there is a tendency to formalize certain us–them divisions – managers/workers; staff/hourly paid; blue collar/white collar; professionals/unskilled – the lines of them and us in organizations rarely follow the orderly patterns that their **leaders** would wish. Within each organization, different **sub-cultures** may co-exist. Sub-culture is an important concept in that it describes the special understandings, bondings, shared backgrounds and beliefs of particular groups within an organization. They are *sub*-cultures because they exist beneath the wider organizational culture. While the *overall* **culture** of an organization is shared by everyone (they are 'M&S' people, 'IBM' employees, or 'university students'), significant sub-cultures will bind, say, just all women within the organization, all the older staff, all the blacks or all Freemasons. These people may feel that, irrespective of rank or department, they are emotionally bonded through their particular common experience, background or heritage. Alternatively, different departments may develop their own sub-cultures and end up seeing other departments as 'them'.

Some of these organizational sub-cultures may challenge the **values** promoted by management. For example, one of our students returned from her placement with a large accounting firm, the product of a recent merger. The merged company produced a glossy brochure extolling its values – the fundamental beliefs which supposedly underpinned its whole way of working: 'excellence, dedication, team work, decisiveness and integrity.' These values, according to our student, carried little credibility with the staff:

> The merger had produced a company in which people refer to themselves as ex-A or ex-B; different paperwork and different procedures are still in operation. As far as decisiveness is concerned, after nine months of negotiation, no decision has been made by the two rival camps about which computer system should be used. As for integrity, who can forget that the man who masterminded the merger, and who now stands behind the 'values campaign', had told the financial world that there would be no merger, just three months before the event?

Another student who had worked for the same organization reported:

> The tension in the office was only lightened by making fun out of the values booklet. 'Value shifting' became the joke phrase. The booklet was likened to something from the fast food world, and someone suggested that our work should be graded on the McDonald's star rating. The five star award would go to the person with the best values joke.

Values are important to psychological functioning, defining the things in life that we treasure most, which we are unlikely to compromise on, and which are worth fighting for. But, as we see, when values are lifted into the corporate arena their meaning can be easily trivialized or debased. In these instances we can talk of the emergence of 'counter-cultures', which define themselves through their opposition to the dominant value system – or at least to the values of those who dominate.

Sub-cultures and counter-cultures complicate the lines between us and them in organizations. My boss, as one of the managers, may be one of them, yet as a woman she is one of us; as someone who has her own marked parking place she is one of them, as a mother, supporting the setting up of a crèche in the company, she is one of us. At times, the identity switch can be sharp and dramatic; such as when someone turns whistle blower, a shop steward accepts promotion to become a foreman, or a woman testifies in favour of a man in a case of sexual harassment. Such shifts can attract great hostility from erstwhile companions.

Even greater hostility is reserved for those members of a group who are ceremoniously and emotionally cast out, as unworthy of being one of us. This is the phenomenon of **scapegoating**. In the biblical ritual, the sins of the people were symbolically placed upon the head of a goat which was then cast out in the wilderness. Scapegoating is a familiar phenomenon within organizations, especially in the aftermath of major disasters when 'heads must roll' and must be seen to roll. By placing all the blame or the guilt on a single person or group, the rest of the organization can cleanse itself and maintain its unity and integrity. The scapegoat can be a manager (usually one who was not clever enough to cover his or her tracks), a group of employees ('trouble-makers', 'traitors', 'saboteurs') or a convenient third party, such as a consultant, a large shareholder or the government, which becomes the target of hostility. The scapegoat is usually presented in stereotypic negative form, to ensure that no-one can doubt the person's evil or errant ways. Such a process can be observed in high gear during the run-up to a national election. A bemused electorate will watch as candidates aggressively, and sometimes desperately, attempt to scapegoat each other (or a third party) for failings in national social or economic performance. A similar ritual takes place to explain the failure of 'our' sports team, or army at war.

SHARED LANGUAGES

Looking more closely at the nature of the bonds that define in-groups and out-groups, we notice that they involve a **cognitive**, or thinking, dimension. A shared interest (economic or political), a shared body of knowledge, a shared understanding, a shared **language**, bond us to each other. Consider, for example, the jargon used by computer experts. It can act as a barrier to the non-expert and clearly differentiates us, those who understand the lingo, from them, who do not. A senior executive from a leading computer manufacturer, recounted an incident which occurred during the demonstration to a government department of a system called DRS-PWS:

> The presentation went very well, and the department officials said they were impressed with the system, but they couldn't understand who was this woman Doris Pughes, whose name kept cropping up. They had misunderstood the acronym of the system DRS-PWS, for the name of a woman. Obviously they hadn't understood anything, but pretended to have been impressed with the system.

The ability to understand a jargon, a language or a joke which excludes others is a powerful bonding device. You can observe it among audiences of avant-garde concerts, who 'understand' the artists' idioms and are amused by the baffled incomprehension of the uninitiated. In organizations it is 'old hands' who know every three-letter acronym, every bit of jargon and every bit of obscure procedure or regulation. A kind of smug satisfaction, or self-admiration, is a common characteristic of this bond, which others often find irritating.

In this form a shared language is also a source of **power**; the more difficult and esoteric the language the more protected the power. Consider the computer expert's confession:

> DOS [the disk operating system widely used by personal computers] is, I wouldn't say part of a conspiracy, people are not organized or intelligent enough to perpetrate such a large conspiracy. But I think that it conspires in a way that gives people power. Because it is difficult to operate, difficult to understand and difficult to work with, those people who can work with it have power, influence, and they are respected for their knowledge. I personally don't find it particularly difficult because I am an adaptable person, but now having used a Mac computer, where I don't need any of that DOS nonsense, I realize that it's a far superior tool. I think that DOS

proponents believe that Mac computing is Mickey Mouse computing, not serious computing; it's not difficult, so it can't be serious.

SOCIALIZATION

The computer expert illustrates that, within an organization, **learning** the local jargon is an important part of 'learning the ropes', of becoming 'one of us'. In short, it is part of becoming **socialized** (see Chapter 2, Entering and leaving). Socialization goes through many phases. In early life, we each undergo a drastic transformation from our early uncomprehending, impulsive and spontaneous actions into being a member of society. We learn to tame our impulses, to distinguish what is permissible and not permissible behaviour, and to understand the meanings of different gestures and utterances. Within organizations, socialization enables us to make some sense of what is going on, to understand what we may and may not do, what is rewarded and what is looked down on, what is taken for granted, what is 'dangerous' or 'sensitive' territory. Through socialization we learn where we belong. This often involves a change in self-identity where our self gets fused, to a lesser or greater extent, with those with whom we now feel we belong. The tell-tale signs of this are when people start making statements about what 'we' are doing at work; 'our' latest project; the way the government fails to understand 'our' way of working . . . and so forth. The point here is that 'I' is not used; it has become part of a greater whole.

All socialization involves hidden curricula. Just as many schoolchildren absorb (some would say that they become indoctrinated to) the values of time-keeping, politeness, deference to the teacher and so forth, the employees of a work organization **learn** a profusion of things that do not form part of any set of rules or written curriculum. In some organizations, for example, he or she may learn that referring to women as 'girls' is deprecated, that wearing blue jeans is frowned upon, and that mixing with manual staff in the canteen is 'not on'. In becoming part of a new 'us' we must learn a whole range of new words, **assumptions** and values and must adopt a new repertoire of actions. We must also unlearn some of the products of past socializations, assumptions and values.

ORGANIZATIONS AND SOCIETY AT LARGE

Organizations are part of wider society. They continuously engage with the customs and social divisions of that society. Inequalities of **gender, race** and class are not forgotten once people enter the worlds of their organizations (see Chapter 16, Career-ing). In fact, the odds are that most people see many of these inequalities re-created and amplified in their workplace. Black employees find themselves ghettoized in low-income, dead-end jobs. Women find themselves 'serving' male bosses, or working in the 'caring' industries in conditions that almost replicate their subordinate role at home. Working-class people find themselves patronized by middle-class managers, frequently half their age. Pretending that such inequalities do not exist at work, and that everyone is in the same boat, is unlikely to be credible to people who have already experienced very real discrimination or injustice because of their race, **gender**, class or other attributes. Allegiance to these groupings is not easily shaken, as the director of our opening example discovered to his cost.

One strategy for handling **ethnic, gender** and other divisions in organizations is to pretend that they do not exist. Everyone is dealt with as an individual, in matters of hiring and promotion, reward and discipline, being judged on their merits rather than on other criteria. Admirable in principle, this strategy fails to recognize subtler forms of **prejudice** and **discrimination**. Even if they are not directly victims of negative **stereotypes** (like 'blacks are underachievers', 'Greeks are unreliable', 'Poles/Irish are stupid' and so on), members of ethnic minorities often fail to live up to the criteria of 'merit' laid down by dominant social groups. For example, academic qualifications may be used in hiring the 'best' person for a job (see Chapter 2, Entering and leaving). This generally handicaps members of already disadvantaged groups and communities, whose lack of expensive schooling and supportive home environment has limited their academic achievement.

Some organizations adopt more active policies for countering the effects of prejudice and discrimination, like 'affirmative action' or 'positive discrimination'. Such policies usually stipulate that certain quotas from particular groups should be hired/promoted, irrespective of their paper qualifications. These policies have been controversial. Undoubtedly, they enhance the prospects of disadvantaged groups; yet, they perpetuate some of the racist and sexist myths which fuel prejudice of the sort: 'No black/ woman/member of ethnic minority would be employed here if it wasn't for the "affirmative action" programme. They are just not good enough! What is worse, they keep good men out of this company/university.'

Even members of disadvantaged groups who manage to rise to positions of power and high status are often suspected of having got there as part of their company's public relations concern, not on their qualities or merits. This is called *tokenism*. It is good for the company's image to have a black senior manager and/or a woman on the board of directors. Such suspicions poison the climate of an organization, and instead of promoting a corporate 'us' reinforce numerous internal 'us' and 'them' divisions. It is also not uncommon for members of disadvantaged groups who succeed to argue that affirmative action is unnecessary; after all, *they* made it, so it *can* be done. Thus the lone promoted member of an ethnic minority will not always help others from their community to achieve equality, unless their organization adopts special policies to bring it about.

Many middle-class managers, faced with the minefields of class, race and gender, prefer to keep themselves to themselves. Embarrassed to socialize with people they do not understand, they shut themselves in their offices, following a policy of avoidance which is often taken as arrogance by the other side. The lines between us and them harden. Some, however, manage to transcend these lines, effectively bridging the divides. In spite of driving a Porsche, the manager of a team digging holes in the road was definitely 'one of the lads'. Talking their language, sharing their breakfast as well as their **jokes**, he was not averse to lending a hand with the spade, or to sharing a wisecrack at the expense of the pen-pushers at Head Office.

It would be wrong to conclude that managers can do nothing to overcome divisions rooted in wider social inequalities and to foster strong bonds which overshadow them. There is evidence that Japanese organizations in foreign countries have succeeded where local firms failed. The single-status cafeteria or washing facilities, for instance, have gone a long way to bridging many divides. People were sceptical as to whether Sony technical staff would agree to wear the same Sony jacket worn by manual employees. They did, when they saw the senior executives and even the chairman wearing the same jacket. It may be ironic that employees in Bridgend in the United Kingdom find it easier to see themselves at one with Corporate Headquarters, which is in Tokyo, than their counterparts working for a small local firm, whose boss lives just down the road.

Such changes are often most successful on greenfield sites – when the organization, and its new values, can be built up from scratch. Long-established organizations, with very deep them/us divisions, are less malleable. A young, ambitious plant manager in a large, traditional, confectionery manufacturer, explained:

> I look enviously at companies where the main atmosphere is one of trust, where people work in groups or teams, are well informed about all aspects of the company, do not clock in, organize their own hours, and above all welcome, and contribute to, change. Where I work the production line grinds on. Management literally had to force a quality programme – contradiction in terms – because the workers were so suspicious of us. And somewhere between us and them are around a dozen unions and their officials – who seem not to communicate with their members, or with each other. The directors of the company are driven by the latest, short-term, sales figures; if these are down people are laid off. So that doesn't exactly ease tension. But the main problem is that it has been like that for many years, so it's very hard to instigate change.

SYMBOLS, EMOTIONS AND CULTURE

In talking about values in an organization, we have shifted somewhat from the *cognitive* aspect of the bonding process. Values bond us, not just cognitively, but *emotionally*. Becoming socialized implies that the groups to which we belong, and the physical settings and objects about us, will acquire a special emotional significance. They come to symbolize, or stand for, something important, inaccessible to the uninitiated eye. They will evoke special feelings.

Symbols are powerful bonding devices. People have sacrificed their lives to defend a piece of patterned rectangular cloth fastened to a long pole – called a flag. Of course it is much more than this. A national flag can, for some, stir deep **emotions** of pride and belonging. Symbols come in many varieties; think of the cross and the swastika, the BMW and the Citroen 2CV, the designer jacket or the blue jeans. They all stand for something else, something larger than themselves. Words themselves are symbols conveying emotionally charged ideas and values. This is obvious in the case of words such as 'dictatorship', 'justice', 'democracy', 'freedom' and 'success'. Dictionary definitions do not convey their emotional resonance; that requires an understanding of the *culture* within which they are used.

Cultures organize clusters of beliefs and attitudes. They turn simple words into vibrant ideals and innocent images into powerful emblems. Culture infuses everyday events with **meaning** and directs our emotional responses to the world around us. The study of culture, as anthropologists and sociologists tell us, reveals how many of the phenomena that we come to regard as 'biological' may in fact be culturally *learned*. Anthropologists, goes the legend, like to throw spanners in the works of academic conferences. Whenever someone mentions something they have regarded as a timeless truth, the anthropologist will say, 'Ah, you haven't heard about the Marquesan islanders, who . . .', showing that there are exceptions to every rule of social behaviour.

ORGANIZATIONAL CULTURE

Much of this might have been of purely academic interest if it were not for the fact that, since the early 1980s, culture has emerged as a dominant concept in discussing organizations, and central to understanding patterns of usness and themness. This coincided with the emergence of Japan as an industrial superpower. In trying to comprehend the phenomenal success of Japanese organizations, many Western theorists turned to the concept of culture as the key. Japanese organizations and Japanese society, it was argued, foster those values of co-operation, loyalty, innovation, flexibility and sheer hard work which account for their success. Above all, Japanese companies have *strong cultures*, which bond their members into highly cohesive and effective teams (although under fairly paternalistic management). In sharp contrast to many Western companies, they are part of a bigger 'us'. People are inspired to great feats of productivity, seeing themselves as heroes. A slightly naive sociologist asks a British, an American and a Japanese car worker what they do, runs the story. 'I am fitting hub-caps,' says the British worker; 'I'm making profits for Henry Ford,' says the

American; 'I am a member of a team who make the best cars in the world,' says the Japanese worker.

In recent years, management in Western organizations have looked increasingly at **corporate culture** as the key to organizational success. **Leadership** in organizations, it is now argued, is not merely the technical decision making, but the strengthening of organizational **values** and the generation of commitment; in short the **management of meaning** and culture. Resourceful leaders have a profound impact on people's perceptions, through the skilful manipulation of organizational **symbols** (see Chapter 9, Leading and following). In the hands of great leaders, symbols (especially words) can have tremendous power. Senior managers can strengthen organizational culture, manipulate it and control it to generate commitment, unity and meaning, by using symbols. For example, when Lee Iacocca took over the ailing Chrysler corporation he gave himself a salary of $1 for his first year. This was meant to tell the employees that everyone would have to make sacrifices in order to save the company, and that sacrifices started at the top. Similarly, new corporate headquarters, a new corporate logo, company awards to loyal employees, a luxurious restaurant and an imposing lobby, are organizational symbols intended to communicate meanings about the organization and its culture.

The management of meaning is far from simple. When Sir John Harvey-Jones took over ICI, he faced a situation similar to Iacocca. With staff being reduced and their salaries and wages being frozen, he felt that the Chairman's . . . 'Rolls-Royce should be dispensed with, as another symbol of all being in it together' (Harvey-Jones, 1988:292) However, the Chairman of Rolls-Royce phoned and told him that if ICI was to break with tradition, then Rolls-Royce's total business would suffer as other companies cancelled their orders. With a degree of guilt, Sir John changed his mind and ordered the traditional new Rolls. He was relieved some time later, when talking to some shop stewards, to be told that 'they were glad I had decided to buy it, as they did not want to have the feeling that they belonged to a company that was in such a poor way that it couldn't afford a Rolls-Royce for its chairman.'

And this brings us back to the illustration at the opening of this chapter. The director's gesture of a Christmas dinner backfired; instead of fostering organizational unity it underscored the internal divisions. The story suggests that organizational symbolism can be a minefield; at times, a clumsy symbolic gesture means that instead of emerging as a hero, the leader is seen as a fool.

- Emotional bonding, a sense of unity and belonging, feature prominently in most organizations.
- Within organizations people continually cross different mental boundaries between 'us' and 'them'.
- 'Us' may refer to all members of a particular department or trade union, to all female employees, to all members of a privileged sub-group or even to nearly all the members of the organization.
- Bonding is both cognitive and emotional; sharing an interest or a language is strengthened by feelings of solidarity and togetherness.
- Symbols are very important in cementing social bonds; they can be manipulated by leaders to motivate, inspire and strengthen people's commitment to an organization.
- Experiences of 'usness' and 'themness' are sustained by organizational cultures and sub-cultures which encompass shared values and assumptions.
- 'Strong cultures' (cultures with powerful shared values, ideals and symbols) have been hailed as the secret of organizational success.
- Yet, the management of culture is full of dangers and pitfalls, especially if subordinates suspect their leaders of insincerity or dishonesty.

THESAURUS ENTRIES

assumptions	group
cognitive	jokes
corporate culture	language
culture	leadership
discrimination	learning
emotion	management of meaning
ethnic groups	meaning
gender	prejudice

power

race

scapegoating

socialization

stereotyping

sub-culture

symbolism

team work

values

15

LOOKING OUTWARD

We cannot look everywhere. If we are paying close attention to one thing, we may be missing something else. When we are organizing, we attend to some things and not to others. Often this is less to do with negligence than with the limits of human capacity in handling **information** and, consequently, our predilection for what interests or concerns us.

So when we are looking one way, we are not looking another. If all our time is taken up with looking at how to cut costs, we may not notice a new company competing for our market. If we are busy looking to see whether one of our colleagues will be promoted before us, we may not notice a new overseas market for our products. These are results of 'looking inwards instead of outwards'.

It is fashionable to criticize companies for being too inward looking, for not paying enough attention to their **environment**. But what does this mean? We certainly speak of **organizations** as having a boundary separating the inside from the outside. There is the 'inside story'; a new chief executive may be appointed from 'outside'; there is 'inside' information, and someone may be asked to take an 'outsider's' view. We speak of some people as being 'at the centre of things', others 'on the edge'.

The distinction between inside and outside expresses an important psychological reality. To be sure, the organization's world with its edge, centre, inside and outside has no direct physical reality, neatly marked by perimeter fences and factory gates. But it exists in our heads and hearts. It determines our experiences and shapes our actions. This chapter will explore not only how organizations interact with their environments, but also how the lines between inside and outside are drawn.

THE INWARD EYE

An organization we were studying in a research project decided to change the way it worked. To do this, it appointed a steering group of managers to oversee the **change** process. This steering group thought that, in order to change the way the organization worked, they had better get their own way of working right first. So they brought in a small team of experts to help them. The experts in turn brought in a film crew to make a video of what was going on. When we first came across the steering group they were considering what lessons to take from the video to improve themselves. We asked them when they would be able to return to thinking about the rest of the organization. They seemed surprised by the question – this was after two years' work! This may sound extreme, but it is not untypical. Often the act of self-examination can serve as a rewarding end in itself – although there are other satisfactions for the inward-looking. Let us look at some of them.

Firstly, people who 'need to see us' tend to be found 'inside' (see Chapter 4, Dealing and double-dealing). In some ways, being at work is like being on stage. We perform for the benefit of, we hope, an admiring audience. Indeed there is a view that this is true of our lives in general:

> All the world's a stage,
> And all the men and women merely players:
> They have their exits and their entrances;
> And one man in his time plays many parts,
> His acts being seven ages.

> (Shakespeare, *As You Like It*, Act II).

So if we are on stage, who is our audience? This rather depends on our organizational position, **role** and personal needs. But most of the time, the important audience is 'inside' the organization. For example, during a meeting with a potential customer, you may think of yourself as performing to an 'outsider', trying to sell the organization's products. Yet, if the meeting takes place in the presence of a colleague and your boss, it could be that the boss is the most significant audience because he or she holds the key to a much desired promotion. So, first and foremost, the boss needs to be **impressed** (which could be achieved by impressing the customer). Alternatively, the opinion of our colleague, with whom we could be working for many years to come, may be the most important. So we try to look competent in our colleague's eyes, but not *so* competent that we make them feel uncomfortable.

Looking inwards fits the career logic of many organizations (see Chapter 16, Career-ing), in which a key phase of familiarization and **socialization** is getting to know the internal workings of different departments. Managerial trainees in companies such as Marks and Spencer, IBM and major banks are expected to work in all the internal departments before they can be considered for 'wider' things. They will also learn that to do a 'thorough' job they will need to keep their subordinates firmly in their sights – inside the organization.

A further incentive for looking inwards in organizations is that this is where the 'action' is. The daily politics of organizational life may be tiresome at times, but it offers entry to the informal networks of **gossip** and stories, a unique source of organizational intelligence. For example, securing a large deal for an organization may be most creditable, but is it worthwhile if in doing so we fail to pick up the rumour about the new office arrangements which will mean much poorer facilities – unless we protest fast? Or if we miss out on other important pieces of **information** which can only be picked up by keeping one's ear to the ground and one's eye inward.

Corridors and quiet corners of an organization are where much interesting **talk** goes on. Another piece of the action is set in internal boards, committees and working **groups** where the **rules,** regulations, plans and policies are fought over, and **decisions** are made. Being part of those meetings gives one a chance to influence the shape of the organization.

Yet another reason for looking inwards is that this is where some of one's enemies may reside (see Chapter 4, Dealing and double-dealing). In highly competitive, aggressive organizations the line between friend and foe is sometimes very fine, and allegiances can shift fast and unexpectedly. Jealousy over another's position, rewards or power can be a breeding ground for warfare. As the aphorism reminds us: 'The opposition is out there. The real enemy is within – the one with the knife.'

Finally, there is a sense in most organizations that inside is where 'real work' takes place. There, one is sufficiently visible and present to be counted, to 'belong'. A person who looks outwards can be seen as rather dangerous, not quite 'one of us'. The salesperson out on the road a lot of the time is open to negative

stereotyping. He or she may be assumed to be 'living it up', 'fiddling the expenses', even 'trading with the enemy'. Occasionally a row erupts about the use of 'sweeteners' or 'slush funds' for buying contracts, and central establishment figures of the company bemoan the **ethics** of salespeople (see Chapter 5, Morals). The people who look outward from a company can be left to do a lot of the dirty work of the people at the centre.

LOOKING OUTWARD

In his novel *Truckers*, Terry Pratchett creates a world of gnomes who live between the floors and the ceilings in a department store. Their community has been there for a long time, and they do not believe in the existence of a world outside the store. Another small group of gnomes come in from the outside world, seeking an easier way of life. The existing gnomes either do not see the newcomers (because they cannot exist) or dismiss as nonsense their stories of a place called 'outside'. But the newcomers discover that the store is shortly to be knocked down for re-development. This was, in fact, known to the leaders of the community, but they had been keeping it secret from their followers. They did not think they would be able to cope with the idea.

One of the functions fulfilled by those who spend time on the boundaries of an organization is to see the things which the long-term inhabitants cannot, or will not, see. But, like the visiting gnomes, they may find themselves disbelieved or ignored. Those who feel secure with their inward-looking life can receive the outer-worlder with polite curiosity – and then get back to normal work. Less easy to ignore are outsiders who (a) have the backing of top management, or other influential insiders, and (b) have a strong reputation as experts in their field. This is one reason why companies employ external **consultants**. In these circumstances outside information is routed more acceptably into the internal **culture** of the organization.

What do organizations gain from looking outward, at their **environment**? Like the gnomes, organizations may learn about *threats* looming out there. Equally, they may realize that there are *opportunities* which can be tapped. Threats and opportunities come in different forms, but here are five common ones:

- markets
- networks and information
- technology
- local communities
- national and international developments.

Developing an intuitive feel for 'the market'

How do people in a company know what the demand is for their products? One common way is to delegate the looking-outward to independent market research agencies. But they can only investigate well-formed questions. They will not be aware of what new products may be developed by a company, because they lack the intimate understanding of the company and its potential.

A new market opportunity very often involves a re-evaluation and re-thinking of what an organization stands for. The best ideas come from insiders who can also act as outsiders, combining a sharp eye for an opportunity 'out there', with the understanding of how their organization can actually grasp it. Akio Morita, founder of Sony Corporation, did not get the idea for the extraordinarily successful Sony Walkman by hiring market researchers. Instead he combined two types of insight. As an outsider, he sensed the need of individuals to enjoy high-quality musical reproduction, without being a nuissance to others. As an insider, he sensed that it was technologically and organizationally possible to produce such an object. He put two and two together. Result: the Sony Walkman.

Arguably, the most important questions about markets can be asked only by insiders; but insiders who are prepared to cross the invisible line separating inside from outside. For example, one of the authors of this book was working with a motoring magazine during an oil crisis. The editor and his management team were doing some important thinking about what the reduction in oil supplies might mean for their magazine. Would motoring become utilitarian, such that people would probably not want to read magazines about it? Or would public transport play an increasing role in getting people to and from work, with motoring becoming more of a leisure activity? In which case people may be even enthusiastic to read motoring magazines.

To answer these questions the team spent a lot of time at trade fairs, wandering around talking to car manufacturers, economists specializing in their industry, other journalists and so on. An observer would have seen a number of smartly dressed men apparently relaxing over wine and canapés. But investigating the views of others outside their company (who in some cases might have been investigating similar questions) was an essential part of looking outwards. This type of **networking** is something that can be done only by an insider, who has **information** to trade for other information.

In many businesses there is much quiet trading of mutually beneficial information. Looking outward becomes a continuous process. Purchasers, suppliers and manufacturers who are linked in commercial agreements will **communicate** with those who are not – in conferences, on golf courses, at parties. Presents will be exchanged. Even direct competitors will sometimes seek a rapprochement if that helps their separate causes. Special relationships can smack of corruption (see Chapter 5, Morals); however, they can also assist organizations determine the shape of the stage on which they wish to play.

Looking outwards does not mean that organizations take what they see as fixed. Nor do they only react passively, by adapting to **changes** in their markets. They also seek to influence and **control** these markets. A tobacco company which perceives threats from government's anti-smoking campaigns may respond by producing low-tar cigarettes or by diversifying into 'clean' products. Alternatively, it may seek to counter anti-smoking campaigns by its own advertising. This could link its products with healthy outdoors activities, sport and glamour.

Advertising is one of the main ways in which organizations seek to control their **environments**. It can be highly effective but unpredictable. Lobbying of politicians, the offer of directorships, the recruitment of effective opinion-shapers, are other ways in which organizations may seek to control their environments and create favourable markets for their products.

Developing a network . . .

In Chapter 4, Dealing and double-dealing, we discuss the way in which **competition** and co-operation can go hand in hand. There sometimes develops a kind of affection between competitors. Although such intimacy does not decrease their intention to fight each other, it does reduce the likelihood of all-out war. Many organizations will value the existence of competitors, and will hope that competitors will try out ideas and make mistakes on their behalf. In many industries, the total market size is by no means fixed. If one company advertises, this can increase the market for their competitors' products too. Advertisements for bottled water by a few firms have increased the overall consumption of bottled water, including the products of those firms which did not advertise.

In some industries, there are **informal networks** of people who keep in touch with one another. This applies particularly in relatively small **professional** fields, where the most significant audience for an individual's actions may be fellow-professionals in competitor organizations. For example, in some branches of electronic engineering, people feel a closer attachment to their fellow engineers in competitor companies (whom they know from student days, conferences, or trade conventions) than they do to the accountants in their own company. This meeting of like minds often leads to an informal trade in technical advice between high technology companies, of the sort: 'I'll tell you how we solved the problem with that processor, and then no doubt you will help me some time on some similar issue.'

Some of this co-operation between competitors is formalized, for example through trade federations and the trade press. The need for a common stance on training and education, on responding to government policy, or on agreeing standards, will often override the need to compete. Sony attribute the failure of their Betamax video system (which was excellent in terms of its **technology**) entirely to its inadequate co-operation with its competitors who were promoting the VHS format, now a universal standard; even Sony do not always look far enough outwards. The same mistake was not made with the compact disc system – where a number of large and highly competitive companies collaborated to establish the standard.

At the cutting edge of technology?

The world is full of the graves of companies which did not keep up with technology (see Chapter 8, Machines and mechanizing). It is tempting to believe that success comes to those early pioneers who develop new revolutionary technologies. But this is not always true. Take the watch and clock industry. Most of the companies that were early into the quartz watch market, producing digital watches with light-emitting diodes, have disappeared. Some of those which entered a bit later but learned from the mistakes of the early innovators, on the other hand, have dominated the industry. In adopting new technologies, *timing* is of the essence, judging when enough is known about a promising new technology to make it a winning commercial proposition.

A few of the old manufacturers of mechanical time-pieces survived in a different way. Instead of adopting electronic technology and competing with the aggressive newcomers, they re-evaluated their markets. Instead of producing mass products, they have survived by producing niche products of exceptional quality and snob value. In this way, they essentially re-defined themselves as well as their **environments**. Environments, then, are not just given 'out there', but are chosen, interpreted and addressed by organizational members.

In choosing, interpreting and addressing environments, people are sometimes blinded by wishful thinking. One potential problem here is 'technomania'. Unless there is sufficient interest and skill within a company to place an 'exciting technological scenario' alongside other important business considerations – finance, marketing, sales, strategy – there is a danger that the company will go to market with a state-of-the-art product that nobody wants to buy.

Compare the Sony Walkman case discussed earlier with the 'C5', the brainchild of UK inventor/entrepreneur Clive Sinclair. This was a cross between a car and a bicycle, not only a technically innovative product, but also in tune with current environmental concerns. Yet, it bankrupted the company. While 'society' may have needed it, individuals had little use for a product which they saw as cumbersome, dangerous and vaguely ridiculous. Unlike Morita, it seems that Sinclair failed to put himself in the position of the 'outsider', the man in the street, who has little trouble in recognizing a dead duck when he sees one.

Community awareness . . .

There are organizations which function with little regard for the interests of their local community. However, outward-looking enterprises would regard such a policy as a short-sighted one – which, ultimately, could work against the organization's interests. For example, environmental concern has risen on the political agenda, so that companies seen as polluting their local environment invite deep local unpopularity, and possibly legal sanctions.

Most organizations employ a local workforce and wish to attract some of the best skills from the community; this is easier if the organization's image is a positive one, enhanced by its involvement in, and support for, local causes. The local community also comprises government agencies and planning authorities from whom permission is required for things such as new buildings, extensions and rights of access. Being seen as a good employer and a good citizen will affect what elected members and public officials feel about the organization, and how it ought to be treated.

So, if for no other reason than pragmatic self-interest, looking out to the community can reap its rewards. Like market awareness, community awareness means more than just *adapting* to **changes** in the environment. It may equally mean *initiating* changes, and seeking actively to influence the environment; not only being *reactive*, but equally being *pro-active*. This may take various shapes and forms: donations to charitable events; sponsoring sports meetings, exhibitions and concerts; gifts to local schools; supporting safety campaigns; and so forth.

Sometimes phrases such as 'putting something back into the community' invite the cynical comment that they amount to nothing but 'backdoor advertising'. This is particularly evident when there is a **culture** clash between sponsor and event – such as a young person's sporting event (symbolizing health, fun and fitness) sponsored by a tobacco company. Or, as recently experienced by one the authors of this book, a jazz concert attended by a youthful, non-establishment audience, sponsored by a major bank. As the curtain went up a giant image of the bank's logo was projected onto a screen – to sustained boos and hisses from the audience. The offence seemed to be (a) the intrusion of the sponsor, and (b) a sponsor who was ideologically incorrect for the audience and event.

Such tales illustrate that the cultures of communities vary, and that companies cannot assume that their forays into the community, however well-intentioned, will always be kindly interpreted. This is most evident when a national company tries to implement a single formula of liaison in different parts of a country (and perhaps cross-nationally). What is right for the good people of Godalming may fall flat in Farnham. Without anticipating how a community will receive such gestures and what **meaning** they will read into them, companies risk doing more damage than good to themselves. But this danger is, of course, equally present in all mass advertising.

World changes . . .

Sometimes, looking outwards also means looking past the local community to national and international movements which could affect the organization. In 1991, many companies failed to anticipate the consequences of the end of the cold war between East and West. As governments cut back on defence expenditure, business which depended on it collapsed.

A few, though, had anticipated what was going to happen and were moving into other markets where they could adapt their technology and expertise. They had 'got out there', persuading banks, exploring opportunities in countries which were now open for investment and trade, adapting their technologies. They 'enacted' their **environments**, actively shaping opportunities and re-defining themselves. They ceased seeing themselves as armaments manufacturers, re-defining themselves, both to their own members and to outsiders, as software, electronics or telecommunications firms.

TOO MUCH AWARENESS?

There is a classic visual illusion: a picture which switches in form depending on whether you focus attention on its foreground or background. The maddening thing about it is that, after a while, you can get stuck with just one of the images no matter how hard you try to see the other. In other words, as we get more familiar with one perception of the world, other interpretations can elude us.

All the environmental areas we have mentioned (markets, networks, technology and so on) carry dangers for those who concentrate too closely on them. For example, organizations which seek to grasp every market opportunity may spread themselves so thinly that they end up as conglomerates lacking purpose or identity. 'Stick to the knitting', do what you are best at, is the kind of advice frequently offered to organizations in this situation.[28]

Developing a **network** can also have drawbacks. In some industries, competitors watch each other so closely that they do not notice that a great gap has opened up in the market, leaving room for a serious challenger to come in. Knowing what technology is available sounds like a thoroughly good idea, but it can lead to technomania, where new technology is employed for the excitement of doing so without regard to other factors.

Even involvement in the community can backfire dramatically when a company decides, for 'operational reasons', that it has to make workers redundant. Sponsoring worthy community causes while sacking your own employees may justifiably be seen as hypocritical.

IN CONCLUSION

Individuals in organizations have good reasons for looking inwards. This is where careers and reputations are made or broken, where important decisions affecting them are taken, where much of the dealing and double-dealing in organizations takes place. Yet, few organizations can afford to keep their eyes fixed in an inward direction. Doing so, they will fail to notice threats as well as opportunities lurking in their environments.

In this chapter we singled out some critical dimensions of organizational environments, markets, networks, technological developments, local communities as well as the national and international context. We saw how organizations may adapt to changes in their environments by adopting new technologies, launching new products or seeking to change their 'public image'. We also indicated how they may seek to actively change their environment, through lobbying politicians or advertising.

Most important, perhaps, this chapter tried to show that the boundaries between organizations and their environments are not fixed. 'In' and 'out' are not given. People describe specific matters as 'internal', 'external' or 'irrelevant' to the organization.

But in doing so, they make assumptions about what the organization and its business is or ought to be about.

What is and what is not 'our business' is argued and negotiated almost constantly. Some of the best ideas as well as some of the worst blunders result from this shifting of boundaries, from deciding that what was not 'our business' yesterday, becomes 'our business' today.

In the last resort, we have argued that the successful organizations are not so much those which are constantly 'looking outward', but those which are most skilful at defining themselves and their business in relation to what is going on around them.

- An organization's environment is not 'given', but is to an extent chosen or defined by those inside the organization itself.
- The way organizations define their environments is connected to the way they define themselves.
- Whether to look 'outward' or 'inward' is experienced as a choice in organizations, even if it is acknowledged that 'in' and 'out' are defined by members.
- There are strong incentives for concentrating on looking inwards in many organizations.
- While it may be in the interests of individuals to look inwards, there are many reasons why organizations need to have some of their members focusing outwards.
- 'Bringing the outside in' is an increasingly popular way of handling this dilemma in companies.

THESAURUS ENTRIES

change	environment
communication	ethics
competition	gossip
consultants	group
control	impression formation
culture	informal networks
decision making	information

meaning
organizations
professions
role
rules

socialization
stereotyping
talk
technology

16

CAREER-ING

Try responding 'Well, nothing', or 'I eat a lot' to inquiries at parties about what you *do*. The notion of job and career reaches deep into our childhood experiences. 'And what are you going to do to when you grow up?' is a challenge put to most children, long before paid work has any remote significance in their lives. But that soon changes. At school your parents' occupation becomes part of your own social identity, and there are pressures from friends to state your future job. Thereafter, things move fast. In our especially vocational times, subject choice at school, college and university get firmly pinned to future work. At job interviews they ask about your career plans, and 'where you expect to be in five years' time'. There is little escape for those who are uncomfortable about being job labelled.

We soon **learn** that we *ought* to have job or career ambitions (see also Chapter 17, Working and living). This point was forcefully brought home to one of the writers of this book when his nine-year-old son was enticed onto the stage of a professional theatre during a Christmas pantomime show. The little fellow was inter-rogated by an ebullient compere: 'And what's *your* name sonny?' 'Where do you live, Daniel?' 'Now, tell me what job you're going to do when you're grown up?' To the astonishment of his parents, Daniel grasped the microphone and firmly asserted, 'I'm going to be an archaeologist.' There were roars of approval from the audience. In a post-pantomime debrief, Daniel said he had no idea what archaeologists were, nor what job he would do, but he felt he ought to say something that sounded good.

Daniel's response is part of the story-telling about careers. Despite the many advice books and supportive techniques that speak strongly about *planning* one's **career**, events tend not to unfold that way. We usually have hazy ideas about the future, and rarely can we predict the way a particular job, or our life and relationships surrounding that job, will work out. Often we do not know what we want out of a job until we have tried it. And then we can be left with a sharp image about what we do *not* like, but still confused about what we want next. More often than not our **decision** 'choices' are determined by expediency and chance.

So why hang on to the notion of career? Maybe we should abandon the idea? This could be difficult. We often feel more comfortable about the future if we believe that our past was coherent and logical. This is no more strongly symbolized than in the curriculum vitae or résumé – a document in which a careful selection of academic qualifications, prizes, jobs and civic duties are assembled to show just how planned, and glorious, was our past. Career gaps are carefully camouflaged; we need to convince others, and ourselves, that we know where we are going. This may be a fiction, but it is one that dovetails with the traditional image of the organizational career: a succession of challenging steps within and across organizations. With each move there is an increase in power and status, and most rewards are reserved for those who reach the top of the pyramid and attain **leadership** positions. But does this image stand up to close examination?

CLIMBING WHAT?

Firstly, we need to appreciate that the concept of an occupational career is somewhat rarefied, even elitist. There are some 30 million people in industrialized countries where the idea of a career, or even a job, would be regarded as absurd. The majority of these people are **unemployed**. They are unskilled or semi-skilled, and seek work, any work, simply to survive. There has been a movement of these people from poorer, high-unemployment, communities looking for jobs in richer neigh-bouring countries. None of them are helped by economic recession, which has taken its toll even of those who have traditionally expected to walk into jobs – newly qualified graduates and professionals. In the recession of the early 1990s, like that of a decade before, it was not uncommon to find taxi drivers and waiters with PhDs.

Those starting their careers in the 1990s are likely to face very different types of organizations and working patterns from their parents. Once, an employee traded his or her loyalty for security and lifetime employment. Now employers tend to regard themselves as very vulnerable to international market forces, and less able to protect their workforce from recessions and takeovers. Ownership, and managership, of organizations can **change** rapidly. People get knocked off the corporate ladder in this process, which can be catastrophic for those whose career and identity has been wrapped up in a company for many years. A 56-year-old chief engineer describes what it feels like:

> I *never* considered I'd be out of work. I was really shocked when I learned I'd have to go. The more people sympathized with me the worse it got. I was there fourteen years, and most of this period I enjoyed the job. I've been trying virtually everything to recover my self-respect and status – but people just walk over me. Yes, I'm feeling bitterly disappointed.

A works director, also in his mid-50s, is even sharper in his summing up:

> After 28 years in an enjoyable job, what on earth can replace it? A damn big part of your life, just gone.

These sentiments are consistent with studies which reveal the anchoring effects of employment in our lives.[29] Apart from providing us with a livelihood, employment gives us something to get up for in the morning (the unemployed soon find themselves disoriented in time). It offers us people to be with, beyond friends and family. It confers social **status** (try approaching a bank manager, finance house or new employer when jobless). Most of all, perhaps, it gives us regular activity (the unemployed soon run out of ideas about how to pass the time). Employment is woven deep into our social and psychological life, and is part of our self-**perception**. But the old formula of a job for life, or a career practising one particular kind of expertise, no longer applies. Indeed, **skills** can date fast so that people who start climbing the corporate ladder can soon find that their ladder rests against the wrong wall – other skills are being rewarded, not theirs. The trick now is to become sufficiently qualified and flexible to be *employable*, rather than just being *employed*.

CHANGING SCENES

How does one become employable, and for what? To answer these questions we must pull together a variety of technological,

cultural, and societal changes, and see how they are affecting the organization and availability of work. One British city, Birmingham, serves as an excellent illustrative case.

In the 1970s the famous engineering factories of Birmingham were booming, and the region's unemployment was amongst the lowest in the country. By the mid-1980s unemployment soared to 20 per cent, some communities having up to 90 per cent of people without work. The huge factories which provided their, and often their fathers', livelihoods lay silent and derelict. Famous names in Birmingham, such as Lucas, Leyland and Land Rover were struggling to survive a combination of recession and fierce international competition. As we write, in the 1990s, the scene looks very different. New warehouses have replaced many of the factories, places equipped to automatically store and retrieve goods. Few people are needed to work them. The surviving manufacturers have become ultra-modern, with computerized **technology** at virtually every stage. The time to change the design of a product has been reduced dramatically – from years to months or even weeks. More is being produced by far fewer people, and managers now talk openly in terms of 'quality' and 'customer service'. There is very little room now for people wishing to sell their muscle and labour; technical skills are all-important. Those unable to adapt to the new requirements are unemployed.

Walking into Birmingham's city centre it is hard to miss the proliferation of banks, building societies and fast food outlets – amongst the first institutions to grab prime city space as it has become available. Many small high street shops have closed, unable to compete with the supermarkets and superstores. Family-owned greengrocers, butchers, tailors and clothes shops have given way to country-wide chains run by professional managers and owned by huge financial institutions. Checkout tills hint at the massive investment in information technology. They automatically provide an instant flow of information direct to local and national managers – on what is selling and what needs re-stocking. The managers then can issue appropriate instructions on their own VDU screens taking charge directly of stock control, once a labour-intensive task.

The Birmingham phenomenon is observable across Britain and, to varying extents, across the industrialized world. As machines take over the manual work, flatter, leaner organizations require people with specific complex skills and knowledge. Labour-intensive work still survives, but mainly in countries or regions where labour is cheap. The new factories are not greasy; they employ people who wear suits or white coats, such as computer experts, systems engineers, accountants, professional managers, sales and marketing executives, designers and researchers. In Britain the revolution in manufacturing has made what remains of this sector of our economy more 'efficient' – and with far fewer jobs. In contrast, jobs in the services have expanded, especially in banking, accountancy, insurance, management, security, health professions and fast food. Some analysts contend that service jobs which process **information** – by pen, keyboard, microphone, or camera – are those of the future. This would include data processing, computer software, research, the media and teaching.

Some of the staff in these re-structured organizations work together in project teams and task forces and are concerned about the intrinsic rewards – the direct satisfaction from the work itself – as much as, if not more than, climbing up what is left of the organizational hierarchy. Loyalty to the company, once the fulcrum of the organizational career, takes on a different complexion. Allegiance is more to the project of the moment and the work team; but that can dissolve when the project is completed. Where there is a **matrix** organization different work teams can come together for different purposes at different times. In such enterprises self-management is emphasized, as there is unlikely to be a **structure** of many layers of managers to refer to for help. Some of these organizations have been termed '**learning organizations**' because of (a) the large amount of training and learning support they offer to their employees, and (b) their flexibility in changing their working practices to meet shifts in business circumstances.

. . . FROM A DISTANCE, WITH BUTTONS

We have, so far, spoken almost exclusively of organizations to which people *go* to make their careers and deploy their specialist skills. But changes in the technology of handling and conveying information have also created a new kind of work opportunity – **teleworking**. This involves working partly or wholly from home, offering a service which can be transmitted to a client through computer and telecommunications technology. It is the **technology** which makes this new, not the principle. Working from home has a long history, reaching back to before the Industrial Revolution when the weaver produced cloth at home, to be collected by the wool master.

The most glamorous, and most publicized, teleworkers are highly skilled professional programmers, software engineers and systems designers. But teleworking is also used for word processing services, travel reservations and ticketing, market research, and fault-advisory services for computer users. Given that physical distance is no barrier to telecommunicating, it can provide some unusual, if not bizarre, opportunities – such as the consortium of medical practitioners in the USA who get their medical notes collated and word processed by workers in Indonesia. They find it cheaper and quicker that way.

Teleworking needs only a room, or a bit of a room, with space to plug in a computer, telephone and fax machine. This has been attractive to companies such as IBM and Rank Xerox who wish to save on city centre overhead costs (offices, travel, pensions, insurance) but retain essential support services. It is also attractive to workers who do not want to, or cannot, physically commute to work. It has offered employment opportunities for single parents, part-time workers and the disabled. It also offers opportunities for appropriately skilled people who fail to get 'normal' employment because of their age or the stigma of redundancy.

Tales from teleworkers, and from others who are employed to work from home, reveal that the opportunities and freedom provided by their kind of work can be exploited by big companies – some regarding them as cheap labour. Some home workers, for example, will do sewing and knitting for minimal pay; they have little choice. As part-timers, in the UK, they have poor legal protection concerning their conditions of work. Telework favours those who have good childminding facilities and some private workspace at home. A proportion of teleworkers find it impossible to get the conditions and balance right, especially if they cannot afford to hire a minder for their pre-school children. Teleworking, by its very nature, is socially isolating. There are no work colleagues with whom to share problems or gossip. The daily time structure of organizational life is missing, which means that considerable self-discipline is required about when, and when not, to work. The common complaint is about overwork – there is always something important do 'just upstairs'. There are now a few telecottages. These are local centres packed with information technology equipment where the teleworkers can meet and experience some of the social and time routines of more conventional employment.

STRESSES

As microchip technology penetrates more deeply into our careers and lives, we can see the first signs of 'technostress': people who feel lost without their computers. Their constant interaction with computers shows in their emotional flatness and low tolerance for other people's uncertainties. Logical thinking, like their computer, is valued highly. If we couple this with the veritable explosion of information that swamps these, and other, professionals we can detect the prototype of a new, skilled technology worker: he or she has a brilliant, but short, work life – rather like a firework.

The strong influence of technology on careers means that many people have to contend with a work environment which is progressively shifting in emphasis away from people to machines – so there are likely to be fewer jobs to go round. Careers are beginning to be shaped around periods *out* of direct employment – when re-training or new learning takes place. Also emerging are careers which include significant sabbatical breaks, part-time employment, job shares, and earlier retirement. At first glance this looks like providing a more interesting mix of career opportunities. In practice, though, it can also bring its insecurities – such as an irregular income flow, not knowing when the next employment will occur, difficulties in filling time, status problems and poor support for family care.

TRICKS AND TRAPS

Teleworking, small organizations and self-employment offer significant work opportunities. However, 'orthodox' employment is still mainly the province of large private and public corporations. To get on in such enterprises is often more complex than it seems, each organization having its own particular career logic, or logics. One writer has suggested that it is a bit like facing a climbing frame, the shape of which varies from company to company.[30]

The frame determines the possible path of careers; it is up to you, however, to make the path an actuality.

Career climbing frames are not apparent to the unattuned eye. They are not to be found neatly illustrated in company brochures, nor will they match the organization chart. They are to be found in the reward, **power** and **political** arrangements of the organization. People soon get a feeling as to whether they are at the centre of things, or peripheral to their department's affairs. They also know how high up, or low down, they are in the organization. But moving within or across the organization's invisible lines requires an especially keen sense of the unwritten climbing-frame rules. For example:

'It's not what you know here, it's who you know.'

Personal expertise is essential to organizational functioning, but does not necessarily get you promoted – if that is what you desire. It can often help to have a powerful friend or **mentor** in the organization who can speak well of you – to other powerful people who make promotion decisions. Winning friends and influencing people has a long tradition in public and corporate politics. It can be a remarkably effective way of getting on – while being equally effective at putting the wrong person in the wrong job. Most of us can spot people who are progressing rapidly in organizations, yet who seem to display extraordinary incompetence. The *realpolitik* of organizational life has, it seems, little to do with natural justice. Mentoring can backfire. High-profile mentors can use their protégés to mask their own shortcomings. They get all the good publicity while their adjutants get little or none.

'You've got to be seen, really noticed, to get on here.'

People who perform well may not progress because their job has low visibility; they are not noticed. A key administrative **role** can require much hard work and dedication, but because it is in the back-room the results are not seen; they are taken for granted. Other roles are more visible – such as those associated with company rescues or product launches. If successful, the person is remembered: a recognizable face in the crowd. We see here, once again, that appearances seem to matter a lot. As in the theatre, pulling off a good performance in front of important critics can make one's career. The stars are remembered; the walk-on parts are forgotten (see Chapter 15, Looking outward).

'If you're a woman here, watch out for the glass ceiling.'

It is relatively rare for women to reach top management posts. The authors of this book teach in a university which espouses liberal values – but there are no female heads of department. Organizations offer a host of reasons for this, such as: they do not apply for top posts; they do not have suitable qualifications; they are not likely to want the pressures of senior positions; they are more likely to leave because of family commitments . . . and so forth. None of these survive close scrutiny, suggesting that **prejudice** and **stereotypes** are often at the root of such judgements (not unlike those applied to different ethnic groups). The frustration for an ambitious woman is that there are no visible barriers preventing her progress, but she certainly knows when she is being blocked: she hits an invisible ceiling. To break through it usually requires exceptional courage, ability and political skill. If we look at the informal power networks of men – their clubs, golf courses, lunches, locker rooms and mentors – it is soon apparent what women are missing. They are not connected to the 'helpful' networks of influence, and they are excluded from entry. There is also a more primitive **gender** prejudice, of the sort: 'Would you really like to work with, or be bossed around by, a woman?' The 33-year-old male general manager of an expanding company of 500 employees put it as follows:

> Working with men is cosy. You can eff and blind, and if they don't like it, tough. Men are like that. One of the things that would make me uncomfortable about having a woman on the team is that if somebody picked on her, I'd feel it was bad form.

This manager did have one woman in his department who, he acknowledged, was 'indisputably better' than a man of similar status. But the manager could not bring himself to promote the woman over the man: 'I owe him a lot. If he hadn't been working with me, I probably wouldn't have been able to move on. He would take great exception to working for her and I feel I would be letting him down enormously.'

'You've got to move fast, early on, if you're going to get to the top.'

In some Eastern parts of the globe an employee with wisdom accumulated from many years of experience is much valued. People in their 50s and 60s upwards are regarded as key personnel. In the West there is a reverse ageism. Some professions, such as advertising, marketing and publishing, are known for their 'if you haven't made it by 30 . . .' ethos. It is rare indeed to spot an advertisement for a senior industrial position aimed at the over-40s. Those on the fast track get there at an early age. Not, it seems, because they have planned things that way, but more by recognizing and capitalizing on opportunities, with a sense of timing on when to move and when to stick. Like good poker players, their game improves fast with practice. Most make a number of rapid job changes in early career, maximizing their visibility and network of contacts. Because of this they are more likely to be 'head-hunted' – approached by another company, or by a consultant employed to find talented executives for client organizations.

Things are changing – slightly. Demographic shifts have meant fewer youngsters entering the workforce, while some occupations have become less popular than they once were. Employers, therefore, have had to look elsewhere for now scarcer skills. This is most noticeable in banking and teaching where employers have offered financial and child-care inducements for trained, older people to return to their professions on a part-time or full-time basis.

CAREER INTERFACES

Career-ing is intimately interconnected with what happens in the rest of one's life (see Chapter 17, Working and living). Where our careers take us, and our feelings about them, are not totally determined by the organization. We are, for example, more able to move job locations when we have no specific ties to family or community. If we have children at school and a home in a neighbourhood we enjoy, the psychological and social costs of moving to a new job at another locality can be considerable – a point often underestimated by companies who assume 'total mobility' of their employees. People who have felt forced to move (the alternative being unemployment) have pointed to their difficult period of adaptation, and sometimes the long resentment of their children who have had to uproot mature friendships.

A compromise solution is long-distance commuting. Many early-morning and evening trains (as well as planes and cars) are packed with commuters making expensive journeys to and from their place of work. Some choose to avoid the hassle of the longest journeys by setting up a weekday home near their place of work. Other commuters with families will claim that their lifestyle allows them to spend more quality time with their partners and children, as well as use the travel time to do work. At best this is possible. But the reality for most commuters is often very different. Apart from being a financial strain, long hours of often unreliable commuting can be exhausting, leaving little capacity to devote to important relationships in the evenings and weekends. The internationalization of business has accentuated this issue. The glamorous image of the jet-travelling, multi-lingual, 'briefcase' executive should be set against the stresses of global travel, the executive's much reduced opportunities for developing stable personal relationships – and a single place to call home. Such difficulties are compounded in **dual career** relationships, where both partners are trying to balance career demands with those of their own relationship and family pressures.

Highly career-oriented people find it difficult to manage their jobs and family in parallel – they spill emotionally into one another. In traditional marriages the woman at home has supported the breadwinning male – absorbing his work anxieties and managing the household and children. There has been some shift away from this structure, with a significant growth in two-career families – either from the outset of a partnership, or when a woman returns to work after a career break to raise children. The balance varies – from two full-time careers to combinations of part-time and full-time. This new equilibrium in work roles has had far-reaching consequences for the organization of careers.

Domestically, it has left a question mark over who is going to manage the household and children. Traditional beliefs about male and female roles overshadow the new liberalization of work arrangements. Many women find themselves returning home from work to then take on most of the domestic chores and child managing: in effect, they are working an extra shift.[31] Even in 'new man' families (he does the shopping, vacuums the floor, and cooks some of the meals) the woman still finds herself shouldering the responsibility for planning these events, while constantly having to anticipate the needs of her children. If they can afford it, some dual career families will buy in help for household and child management. In some countries this employs people (usually women) who, ironically, have to leave their own children unattended: it is the only kind of work they can obtain.

Organizations, in the face of an increase in dual careers, have had to reflect on their employment policies. People are more reluctant to re-locate, and desire greater flexibility to accommodate the needs of children – maternity/paternity leave, creches, child minders, time off for sickness, school holidays and emergencies. Furthermore, the heightened profile of women in the workforce adds to pressure for career compatibility with men. There has, however, been no rush by companies to adapt to changing career needs, and the United Kingdom lags noticeably behind many of its European counterparts. Most working women work part-time. They are a more malleable, and vulnerable, work population than their full-time counterparts.

'WHAT WAS ONCE IMPORTANT ISN'T SO IMPORTANT NOW.'

Finally, we should stress that career-ing ebbs and flows as the events of life unfold. What seems important at 21 feels less so at 41, and perhaps quite irrelevant at 51. People's career **motivation** rarely maintains an even course or force. There are peaks and plateaux. The **mid-career** plateau, or crisis, is much discussed – so much so that people who do not experience it can feel guilty or embarrassed. The 35–45-year-old, goes the argument, is having to come to terms with what she or he has achieved, and what has been missed. Or, perhaps, now they have made it, 'it' does not seem nearly as interesting or rewarding as it once did. What new challenges are there? Do I have the energy or ability to do something new? And if I do not do something, might I get stuck for the rest of my working life?

The most serious form of plateauing is *burnout*, where high initial expectations of what can be achieved at work are gradually thwarted – to the extent that one gives up, withdraws, or offers just about the minimum to get by. Some jobs are more prone to burnout than others. Helping professions, such as nursing, social work, medicine and school teaching, have more than their fair share of burnout. The jobs all deal with human problems. They often have limited resources and are emotionally demanding. The professionals who work in them can face big and difficult failures along with their successes. After a time all this takes its toll, leaving them exhausted and disillusioned.

The end of an organizational career opens what have been termed 'third age' opportunities. For example, further paid work is possible for some professional or skilled people whose expertise is still in demand – such as offering consultancy services to a network of personal contacts built up over the years. Formal learning and re-training can continue through special courses which are aimed at the retired population. But this optimistic image of post-career activity is not the typical one. Not everyone has skills to sell or the inclination to pick up formal education. Without special preparation and contingency plans the organizational careerist can find retirement a shock. The switch from organizational routines to domestic ones can be confusing, especially if the person's status and identity were shored up by his or her position and earnings in the organization. Outside the context of regular work, holidays, do-it-yourself activities and gardening can lack lustre. A lifetime's career, or sequence of jobs, leaves a legacy of habits, routines and social expectations which do not disappear suddenly after the final farewell to one's work colleagues, at 65 years of age (see Chapter 2, Entering and leaving).

- A career, or job, becomes part of our self-image at an early age.
- There are many people for whom a career or job seems unattainable because of age, sex, ethnicity, infirmity, lack of skill or chronic unemployment.
- Career patterns are changing; a job for life is now rare; employability is more important.
- Matrix and flat organizations are replacing traditional hierarchies.
- Politics, personal connections and private networks influence many career paths.

- Women are less likely to be part of the informal (male) power networks and they can hit a 'glass ceiling', blocking their career progress.
- New technologies are producing new styles of working – such as teleworking. They have significant drawbacks along with some benefits.
- Work and non-work inter-relate and can produce highly conflicting demands.
- Career motivation fluctuates considerably over a lifetime.

THESAURUS ENTRIES

burnout	motivation
career	perception
change	politics
culture	power
decision making	prejudice
dual career	role
gender	skills
information	status
leadership	stereotyping
learn	structure
learning organization	technology
matrix structure	teleworking
mentor	unemployment
mid-career crisis	

17

WORKING AND LIVING

'I come here and work my shift; I don't trouble them, they don't trouble me. People do sometimes get into trouble; I haven't got into trouble yet. I come here to do my job. I don't need much help. My private life is my private life.' These are the words of Mrs Vickers, a hospital cleaner. No-one has difficulty understanding what 'My private life is my private life' means. It separates the world of work and organizations, the public sphere, from the world of the family and the home. The division between work and home has become second nature to most of us, although it makes less sense to people like farmers, self-employed shopkeepers, sailors or soldiers, who either work 'from home' or whose organization *is* their home.

'Work is a four-letter word,' says a poster. 'Thank God it's Friday,' says another. The 'Monday morning feeling' is not one of excitement and joy at the prospect of the start of a new week. In the world of work, our time is generally someone else's time, the tools and machines we use are someone else's, the premises we occupy someone else's, our **actions** determined by someone else's **decisions** and directions.

In the private world, the world of the family and the home, we do not feel accountable to an employer, our time is our own, our business is our own. Mrs Vickers was not just expressing what most of us take as a fact. She was also erecting a fence: 'You may ask me questions about my work. My boss gave you permission to do that. You may *not* ask me questions about my life outside this hospital. What I do there is my own business and does not concern you.'

The separation between public and private lives has the cast iron appearance of a 'fact'. Yet, it does not take much probing to make the distinction disintegrate. **Work** does not take place exclusively in the public sphere, nor does play only take place in the private. Looking after a young child is work, whether you are doing it in your own home and the child is your own, or at a nursery and the child is someone else's. Some people play golf or drive fast cars for a living, while others mop floors, change nappies and cook lunches for little more than gratitude, if that. What separates the work we do in the public sphere from that of the private is neither its quantity nor its quality. It is whether we get paid for it or not.

There is no denying that the two types of **work**, paid and unpaid, enjoy vastly different **status** in our **culture**. Looking after your infirm grandmother who lives with you requires effort, skill and application, but ironically is not seen as 'proper work', the way that looking after other people's grandmothers in an old people's home is. Washing up at home hardly makes you anybody; washing up in a restaurant makes you an 'employed person'.

Some people have found it helpful to distinguish between work, the activity involving physical and mental effort, and employment, the means whereby the majority earn a wage or salary. The public world can then be seen as the time which we spend in 'gainful employment', in contrast to private life, essentially the rest of our time. Organizational theory, since Weber's pioneering theory of **bureaucracy**, has drawn a sharp line between private and public. On the one side of the line lies the clean, predictable and orderly realm of organizations, of **rationality**, efficiency and **impersonality**. On the other side of the line is the messy and unpredictable world of emotions, of personal and family life. Organizational theory has concentrated on the former, leaving people's private lives alone. The leading British and most American textbooks on organizations say not one word about people's home lives or 'leisure' activities. They disregard the fact that people have other **roles**, apart from those assigned to them by organizations. But as we all know, people eat, sleep, go to the movies, join amateur dramatic societies, have children, become interested in macramé, look after sick relatives, suffer from neurotic attacks and so on. Have these things no bearing on our behaviour in organizations?

One of the central assumptions of this book is that the private and the public are inextricably linked. We take our work back home and, conversely, we take our home out to work. **Attitudes** and **values** formed within the family, the school or the wider

culture remain part of us when we cross the boundary of an organization, as do our **sexuality**, sense of humour and **emotions**. Equally our experiences inside organizations inevitably colour our personal and family lives. Our lives outside organizations and our lives in them cannot be studied apart from each other, even though some of us like to keep different parts of our lives in rigid compartments, while others manage to integrate them. Very few can develop totally split **personae**, one for work and one for home.

NIGEL'S STORY: WHEN HOME DISRUPTS WORK

Nigel prides himself on being a 'good' father. Ever since Emily and Alex were born, he has taken an active interest, spending as much time with them as his busy job as a senior advertising executive will allow him. Nigel loves the long summer evenings, when he can spend time playing with the children in the garden. The children are both at school now, and Anne, Nigel's wife, has decided to resume her own career, as a hospital administrator.

Monday 27 May was an important day for Nigel. It was the day of two crucial events, a presentation to a key customer and a meeting with the Customs and Excise over a disputed VAT return. It was also a significant day for another reason. This had been the first weekend that Nigel had spent alone with the children; Anne was on a three-day residential course, due to end that day.

The weekend had been a terrific success. Safari park on Saturday, splashing around the garden Sunday, the kids had loved it and Nigel was happy. Nigel had some apprehensions about Monday morning. Taking both children to school, then dashing off to the office for the 10.15 presentation was going to be tight. But it could be done and it would be done.

Monday morning. Nigel wakes up and cheerfully calls the children. No answer. He goes to their room, where they seem to be sleeping soundly. 'Alex, Emily, quick, time to get up,' he shouts, but his voice has no effect. It takes some more calls (his voice now has developed an edge) before Nigel realizes that the children's bright red cheeks, the bleary eyes, the sullen expressions tell their own story. Both children are running a fever.

Now Nigel is nothing if not a man who loves a challenge. 'Problems don't exist, only challenges' is a favourite motto of his. For once, however, Nigel has a problem. He quickly appraises the options. The children must clearly be seen by a doctor, someone has to be found to take them and look after them during the day. But who? Anne perhaps; she could come back early from her residential; oh God, she will be so disappointed. What is more, Anne couldn't be back in time for him to make it to work on time.

The children are now awake; they need care, they need reassurance, they need affection. And Nigel needs someone to give them all this and to take them to the doctor. The minutes are ticking away and Nigel is no nearer to meeting his challenge. He looks out of the window into the street. All these women inside all these houses, all with masses of free time, and yet he cannot think of one, not one, he could turn to. Nigel is getting desperate and what's more, he is getting furious with himself for getting desperate. He, the champion of dozens of bruising campaigns, the winner of apparently lost causes, the master problem solver, is coming apart with the simple task of having two sick children looked after for say eight, ten hours at most.

He feels angry. He knows it; he should never have let Anne go to her wretched residential. Look at the mess she has left him with. Besides, what the hell did she need the residential for? Isn't it just an excuse for drinking, anyway? The children are now crying but Nigel can only think of his own chagrin, his own problem. Strange thoughts come into his head. Perhaps one of the girls from the office could come and spend the day with the children. Or, perhaps he can stuff them solid with medicine, take them to school, let the school sort it out . . . good God, what a thought. If only his parents lived a bit nearer! If only . . . Nigel thinks of the client, all the top brass, getting ready at that very moment for a decisive day. He is covered in cold sweat.

Then Nigel thinks the unthinkable, he thinks a thought that makes all other taboos seem like kids' play. *He* is the 'someone' who will have to take the children to the doctor, *he* will have to look after them, to comfort them and soothe them. They are still *his* children, just as they were his children yesterday, when they were playing happily in the garden. He is still their father. His mind is made up at once. A quick nagging question – how will he present his absence to the office? Surely, he can't say that he is staying at home to look after his sick children. What will they think of him? To hell with it, *he* is a man, *he* is not a child, *he* needs no excuses.

He picks up the phone. Good old Shirley, she is already there to answer the phone, a good twenty minutes before the office opens. 'Oh, Nigel, glad you phoned,' says Shirley as soon as she hears his voice, 'Mr Wilmott called just a minute ago, from United Cereal, to say that they can't make it to the presentation today, any chance of re-scheduling it for next Monday?' Nigel feels a surge of elation. Had Shirley been in front of him, he would have kissed her.

For an instant, Nigel thinks he might squeeze out of his resolution to devote the day to his children. Take the kids to the doctor, call Anne, make sure she's back in time for him to meet those Customs and Excise clowns, the thought crosses his mind like a flash. But no, Nigel has understood something and there is no going back.

'Thanks, Shirley', he says. 'That's funny, because something has cropped up here, and I was phoning to say that I can't make it to the office today.'

'I hope it's nothing serious,' said Shirley.

'No, no, it's just . . . I need to take my children to the doctor,' says Nigel. He feels vulnerable, saying this, exposed. 'Would you please phone the Customs and Excise and ask to re-arrange our meeting, for another time.'

'Yes, of course, Nigel, don't worry at all about it, I'll sort it all out,' says Shirley.

She too is aware that an important barrier has been crossed, and is pleased to be reassuring and business-like. 'What's going on in Nigel's life,' she wonders. 'I should try and find out discreetly.'

Nigel's story is a true story. If you see nothing exceptional in the incident, you are quite right. Most working women would regard his 'problem' as boringly familiar, accustomed as they are to juggling work and family commitments, to being in two places thinking of four things at once. 'Who's picking up Liz from school?' 'When can I nip to the shop to get James' scout uniform?' 'Ought to phone Janet quickly to see if she could pick up the dry cleaning.' These are ordinary thoughts, the likes of which are rarely far below the consciousness of a large section of the population, and yet rarely trouble the minds of people like Nigel, who have been sheltered from the painful **conflict** between the demands of work and the demands of the family and home.

What makes Nigel's story interesting, is that an ordinary experience should have an extraordinary effect. Nigel is neither an insensitive nor an inconsiderate person, as a father or as a husband. Yet, his work had until that Monday morning been 'sacrosanct', untouchable. Nothing could be made to interfere with his important appointments. What his children's sickness forced him to confront were the double standards he had always employed in evaluating man work and woman work. It forced him to confront his own responsibilities as a father and to re-assess his own priorities. It also forced him to question one of his assumptions about his own colleagues and subordinates at work – the assumption that people should leave their homes behind them when they go to work, and should devote themselves wholeheartedly to their work and their organization. Finally, it forced him to question what he had always taken for granted: that people should not grumble when asked to work late, or to take a bit of work home over the weekend.

Nigel, being not an unintelligent man, realized that to the extent that some men are able to devote themselves, spirit and body, to their work, it is because of an army of women, supporting them and their children, nurturing them and working for them. By assuming the **gender role** of 'main family bread-winner', they have abdicated from the responsibilities created by other roles, leaving the painful conflicts, the messy compromises and the juggling to their wives. And yet, at the same time, they have been the first to criticize women for lack of commitment to the organization. Nigel himself had not been above the odd dig at Shirley for 'abandoning him' in the office to sort it all out, long after all other secretaries had left for home.

ORIENTATIONS TO WORK AND WORK ETHICS

Many working mothers would find Nigel's story unexceptional. Yet, many workers would find it difficult to appreciate the leap of imagination that it took for Nigel to decide that he would not go to work. What is the big deal about taking a day off work, when whole industries run on four-day weeks? An American car worker was asked why he only turned up to work four days each week and his answer is legendary: 'Because I can't earn enough to make a living on three days a week.' His attitude is a universe apart from Nigel's, who thought that the world would grind to a halt if he missed a single day in the office.

Attitudes towards work vary widely. In the Bible, work is God's punishment for disobedience; it must be endured with good grace. The ancient Greeks, on the other hand, thought that work is a base activity suitable for slaves, unworthy of cultured free men. The free Spartans did *no work at all*, occupying themselves with things martial, while the free Athenians preferred intellectual and aesthetic pursuits. The Trobriand islanders of the South Pacific, by contrast, worked hard on their gardens and harvested many times the amount needed to sustain them; the quantity and quality of their product was seen as a sign of their worth as members of their community.

The attitudes which we bring to the workplace are partly shaped by the wider **culture** of which we are part. In trying to understand the development of capitalism in the West, it has been suggested that a crucial role was played by the 'Protestant **work ethic**'. This was an orientation towards work which grew out of the emergence of Protestant religion and, especially, Calvinism. Hard work was seen as a sign of godliness. Wealth and profit, far from being derided, were seen as signs of God's favour. Saving money, living frugally, refraining from the pleasures of the flesh and sheer hard work are the key ingredients in this type of the Protestant ethic. [32]

Views on the Protestant ethic differ. Most people would agree, however, that, nowadays, its meaning has been stripped of its religious association. It has come to mean 'a sense of duty to work hard', and it is by no means restricted to Protestants. A friend told one of us about his Chinese Buddhist father:

> He used to keep his shop open until 10.30 every night. No-one came in after 8.30, but it is part of the Confucian culture that you should keep your shop open whether anybody wants it or not, because they always *might* want it. And even if they don't, you have to do your best for everybody.

Much has been written about the weakening of the Protestant ethic as a source of economic decline in the west. Conversely, it seems that the Japanese have raised the Protestant ethic to new heights, voluntarily cancelling their holidays and working over-time on assembly lines for no extra pay. Yet, arguments which equate the wealth of nations to hard work hardly stand any close scrutiny. Individuals and nations may work terribly hard and enjoy little economic prosperity, if they lack technology or organization, or if they each work hard at undoing the other's work.

The Protestant ethic hardly explains the prosperity of nations; it does, nevertheless, describe a distinct set of work **attitudes** and work **motivation**, like Nigel's. In the 1980s, it became common to brand as 'workaholic' people whose commitment to work creates a dependence, similar to that of an alcoholic or drug addict. The adjective seems to add little other than to underline the fact that Nigel's orientation to work is not shared by everyone else, such as the car worker quoted earlier.

Alternative work attitudes

An important study conducted in the 1960s, called *The Affluent Worker* [33] found that a majority of industrial workers saw work purely as a means of earning a living. Many had given up more interesting jobs, to take better paid employment. They did not expect satisfaction and fulfilment from work, nor did they see hard work as a moral duty. *Leisure* was seen as the sphere of enjoyment and fulfilment. The Protestant ethic certainly had no grip on these workers, whose orientation to work is described as **instrumental**, that is, work is a means to material well-being. By contrast, people who prize the interest and variety of their work above all else have an intrinsic orientation. Those who value workmates and the social aspects of work are described as having a social or solidaristic orientation. Such orientations distinguish between different groups of employees, affecting the **meaning** which they attribute to it and the way their work becomes part of their **identity**.

Even within a group of students taking the same university course there are variations in work orientations. Some will choose a more interesting job over a better paid one; some will choose one which gives an opportunity to socialize; some are attracted by jobs which 'look good on paper'. These orientations have been shaped by earlier experiences, role models, parental influences, careers advisers; they act as a powerful link between work and the rest of life.

Work and class

In spite of such individual variations, work attitudes, like many other types of attitudes in Britain, are linked to social *class*. The same study which established the instrumental orientation of manual workers, found that clerical workers were more concerned with the work itself, its **status**, and chances of **career** advancement. White collar or clerical workers have traditionally been seen as having middle-class lifestyles and attitudes, emphasizing style, status and individual effort. They speak with middle-class accents and have middle-class tastes.

Class divisions in society account for a wide range of attitudinal differences, a fact well-known to opinion pollsters, who divide the population into five categories: A ('high professions' and senior management), B ('low professions' and management), C1 (clerical) and C2 (skilled manual), D (semi-skilled) and E (unskilled), based on occupational status. Our consumption patterns, voting behaviour and opinions on a wide range of social matters display a degree of correlation with these categories. More generally, our class background affects ways we think and talk, our attitudes to work and leisure, our understanding of 'success', our views on society, crime, education, and so forth.

Class and work often reinforce each other. Middle-class people manage, control and command working-class people. Many of the misunderstandings, breakdowns of communication or trust and conflicts at the workplace which seem bizarre or irrational to an outside observer become understandable when the class barriers which divide people are taken into account. A comment which might have gone unnoticed in most cases can make a person feel deeply hurt if it is interpreted as a class insult, just as a **joke** can go very badly wrong if it is seen as a sexist or racist jibe.

Alternative work and non-work ethics

Work ethics change. They change with changes in the class structure of society, they change with technological innovations as well as with broader economic and cultural developments.

There are some who argue that the Protestant work ethic is disintegrating under the massive changes currently affecting our societies. Instead of work, individuals turn elsewhere in their search for **meaning** and **identity**; they turn to family life, hobbies, 'style' and material possessions.

Some young people with limited hopes of permanent work and even fewer opportunities for **careers**, it is argued, espouse a 'welfare ethic', content to live off the state and refusing to feel degraded or shamed by unemployment. The southern coast of England has acted as a magnet for young unemployed people, doing casual work in the summer and living on state benefits for the rest of the year. The tabloid press have nicknamed it 'Costa del Dole'!

The rich and the upwardly mobile are rediscovering a different type of ethic, a 'wealth ethic'. Wealth, according to this view, is to be attained not through hard work but through clever deals or inheritance, and is to be enjoyed rather than copiously saved and invested. The wealth ethic merges with a 'hedonistic' or 'leisure' ethic which places great emphasis on pleasure, and paradoxically unites the 'idle rich' and those 'on the dole'. Enjoying life becomes more important than having a good job. **Success** is to be measured not through achievement, but through happiness.[34]

Arguably, neither the rich nor large sections of the working class, at least in Great Britain, have ever been ruled by the Protestant work ethic. What is more surprising is the decline of this ethic among the achievement-**motivated** middle class. One of our friends was recently headhunted for a job which carried with it a very smart 'compensation package', as the financial terms were euphemistically referred to. He was flattered and excited to be offered the job. However, as he thought about it, he decided that the phrase 'compensation package' was all too apt. In terms of how much of his identity he was expected to hand over, and how many weekends he was expected to work, 'compensation' was exactly what he would need. He did not wish to give precious hours out of his life to something which was going to require compensation. He already had a satisfactory job. He turned down the offer.

As the Protestant work ethic is waning, it has been suggested that the middle class are moving to different ethics. These include the 'narcissistic ethic' centred on self-admiration, the 'body ethic' based on lavish care for the physical body, and the 'spirit ethic' focused on self-development and self-actualization. What unites all these ethics is the shift away from *hard work* as a source of

value and **meaning**. Yet, the importance of work as a dimension of **identity** is unlikely to be supplanted in the near future. The time has still to come when people introduce themselves as avid readers of Proust, as owners of a Golf GTI, as 'being in analysis', or as proud fathers of two delightful children, rather than by referring to the work that they do.

Instead of disappearing completely, the Protestant work ethic may be about to undergo yet another radical transformation, just as it earlier shed its religious connections. And so long as work provides our main means of livelihood, most of us will have to reconcile the demands which it makes with demands made by our homes, our families and friends, as well as our own desires.

CONCLUSION

The separation between home and work serves **organizations** well enough. The conflicts and worries of people's personal lives are not *their* problem or responsibility, but private concerns of the individuals involved. This separation, as Nigel discovered in our illustration, profoundly disadvantages working women and enables men to disregard their responsibilities at home. It creates a set of double standards, justifying or even encouraging **discrimination** against women. It fosters the curious stance that employees should, for the duration of the working day, cut themselves off from emotional and moral attachments to their families and friends and commit themselves wholly to their organization.

Several chapters of this book take the view that this separation, though generally taken for granted, does not stand close scrutiny. The line between work and home is fictional, it is part of the fiction of *order* perpetuated by organizations and their gurus. Our lives in organizations cannot and should not be studied in isolation from the rest of our existence. Organization itself, as we study it in the pages of this book, is not a separate, distinct universe of human activities, isolated and cushioned from the forces of disorganization and chaos. On the contrary, disorganization and chaos, as Nigel discovered in the course of a very ordinary incident on a Monday morning, constantly threaten the best laid plans.

- 'Home' and 'work' constantly interact.
- Work as well as play take place both inside and outside the home.
- Our attitudes and values, shaped within the family, the school or the wider culture, influence our actions at the workplace, as do our family and other commitments.
- People's orientations to work vary enormously, across individuals and cultures.
- The Protestant work ethic is a set of attitudes towards work which stresses self-reliance, hard work and frugality.
- There is some evidence that the Protestant work ethic is in decline in the West, though the work that people do is an important dimension of their identity.
- Work orientations (for example, whether work should be a means towards an end or whether it should be enjoyable in itself) differ across the social classes.
- Traditionally working-class attitudes towards work were instrumental.
- Middle-class and clerical attitudes, by contrast, have emphasized other aspects, such as status, career or self-actualization.
- The separation of work from home severely disadvantages women, whose responsibilities are still predominantly seen as lying within the family, and whose careers are hampered as a result.
- Men's undivided commitment and loyalty to their organizations frequently rests on the sacrifice of women's career prospects and their confinement to the home.

THESAURUS ENTRIES

actions	decision making
attitude	discrimination
behaviour	emotion
bureaucracy	gender
career	identity
conflict	impersonality
culture	instrumental orientation

jokes
meaning
motivation
organization
persona
rationality
role

sexuality
status
success
values
work
work ethic

18

PARTING THOUGHTS

What do you do next after reading this book? One well-known writer on organizations concludes by telling his readers that, if they want to understand more, they should go and write a book on the subject. Admirable advice, if a little unrealistic. Another writer ends his book with a chapter which consists entirely of blank pages. The point is the same; the next step for readers is probably not the study of more detailed texts, but rather to engage in *inquiry*, active *sense making* and *action*. There is no need to wait for a more suitable moment, or until the end of your course of study, to do this. All readers are constantly involved with organizing and organizations in some form or another.

We hope that, as you went through the pages of this book, you made connexions with your own experiences of organizing or of being organized. Some of these experiences will have provided support and illustrations for our arguments, others may have qualified, modified or even contradicted what we have been saying. We have stressed throughout that **meaning** and making sense of things are personal as well as corporate. What makes sense to one person does not always make sense to another. It is not just that different people would wish to say different things about organizing; the aspects of organizing about which they think it is worth saying something are different too.

BEING IN THE DRIVING SEAT: ACTING WITH SENSE

In the early days of space exploration, monkeys and dogs were propelled into space in 'capsules'. Later, however, as human space travel became possible, space capsules were renamed space*ships*. Why? One reason was that astronauts were not content to play the part that animals had played in earlier trips. Nor, if they were trapped inside 'capsules', could they be presented as *heroes* exploring a new universe. Astronauts had to be given some **control**. Unlike the dogs and monkeys of the early trips who had been just physical bodies surviving extremes of speed, acceleration and gravity, astronauts were given buttons to push, instruments to read and levers to pull. This made them captains of ships whose fates seemed to be in their own hands.

Of course, astronauts had limited choices. They could hardly decide to go out for a walk, change direction and fly off to Mars, or like Icarus, try and reach the sun. They could, however, manoeuvre their spaceships and actively participate in their missions.

We are hoping that this book will enable readers to accomplish a similar change in their journeys through organizations. We are hoping that they will understand more about their missions and the ways in which their organizations function, with better chances of being pilots of their ships rather than passive passengers. It would be absurd to suggest that reading the book will take you to the top of your organization or that it will free you from all organizational pressures and constraints. We do, however, hope that the book will help you better understand what is going on around you and better appreciate the choices you *do* have and the demands you *can* make.

A word sometimes used to describe this relation between an individual and an organization is **stakeholder**. A stakeholder is someone who has a claim on the way an organization is run, its goal and directions; it is someone with *some* choices, *some* power and some responsibilities as opposed to a bystander or a pawn. We are hoping that our readers will emerge from this book with an understanding that enables them to decide when and how they may participate as stakeholders in their organizations and when it is desirable or inevitable to sit on the sidelines. Understanding organizing and organizations does not make a person immune from occasional powerlessness or dependency. But it does reduce the chances of their needing to resort to statements such as 'I was only obeying orders', or 'This doesn't sound right but it must be – I'm only a small cog in the machine.'

MOVING ON

We have written about the aspects of organizing, being organized, and living in organizations that seemed interesting and important to *us*. Numerous questions, themes and chapter headings, after discussions, were left out. You may emerge from this book with a whole host of different questions and themes of your own.

For those who want to explore further, a good starting point is to compare the arguments, ideas and examples which we provide with your own experiences. Thereafter, different readers will pursue different paths, crafting their own questions, addressing their own interests. Here, to conclude, are a few hints that may help:

- Criticize our ideas, qualify them, revise them, fashion them in a way that makes sense to you. How do *you* find **organizations**, **bureaucracy**, **leadership**, **emotions**, and so forth, work for you?
- Identify those gaps in our arguments or in our charting of the terrain of organizing and organizations which need filling. What fits and does not fit between the various topics? How, for example, are sexual and moral issues linked? Do machines dictate our life? How do we resist their influence?
- Focus on the paradoxical, the out-of-place, the irregular in your own experiences of organizing. Frequently one unusual observation is worth more than large volumes of uniform data. What happens during a *crisis*, such as a breakdown, resignation, personality clash or redundancy programme? Often, the organization's colours are revealed in ways in which are normally obscured.
- Mistrust jargon, clichés and the use of language in general. If you think that the answers to numerous problems lie in a single concept (such as **'motivation'**, **'leadership'**, **'organization'** etc.), test out whether that seems fair and true. Often we like to give slick and simple labels to issues which are basically complex, and can be analysed in various possible ways.
- Mistrust simple cause-and-effect explanations of human phenomena. It is unlikely to be 'all a **personality** problem', or a 'just a matter of changing the leader' to sort out the organization. Organizations are the products of many factors,

systematic and accidental; change one part and others are affected in unexpected ways.

- Try using **metaphors**, similes and models to make sense of your observations. If you see the organization as a machine, mad house, brain or battle field, does it bring some things into perspective?
- Whenever you make a generalization look at the exceptions to check it out. Do *all* students, women, lecturers, civil servants and so forth do what you think they do? If not, how useful is the generalization?

And finally, there is little to be gained by prematurely closing discussions and debates in the interest of order, certainty and organization. Some of the best ideas in organizations (and in science) have resulted from accident, misunderstanding and error. Others have emerged from doing exactly the opposite of what intuition, good sense and methodology dictated. Inquiry, understanding and action will not always be in step with one another. Do not try to be *too* organized.

THESAURUS ENTRIES

bureaucracy	**metaphor**
emotion	**motivation**
knowing	**organization**
language	**personality**
leadership	**stakeholder**
meaning	

THESAURUS

CONTENTS

INTRODUCTION

This thesaurus is not meant to provide an exhaustive treatment of each entry but to introduce some of the main academic arguments surrounding these concepts. Thesaurus entries are **bold** in the book's main text, though the match is not always perfect; for example, **ethnicity** and **real** are not as such in the Thesaurus, but **ethnic groups** and **reality** are.

You may find that a topic which you wish to examine does not have an entry in the Thesaurus at all; try to think of a related concept and see if there is a relevant entry. For example, there are no entries for 'humour' or 'objectives', but there are entries for '**jokes**' and '**goals**'.

References to books and articles in or at the end of each entry can be found in full in the bibliography. In some cases, secondary sources have been suggested because they are more readable or more easily accessible than original writings. Where books are given as references, you are encouraged to look first in the book's table of contents to see if there is a chapter matching the entry in the Thesaurus, or failing that, look in the book's Index for references to the entry topic. For example, under '**sabotage**' reference is given to Beynon's book *Working for Ford*; looking at the index of that book identifies the pages where the author deals with the issue of sabotage.

action

In contrast to behaviour, action suggests purpose and **meaning**. Unlike physical entities, like electrons, which only behave, human beings act. Placing a ring on somebody's finger is more than just a physical movement resulting from the expenditure of energy. It is meant to **communicate** something, it has a meaning. Human beings act towards each other and towards things on the basis of meanings which they attribute to the objects and to the actions. Sometimes meanings are shared and sometimes not. There are different schools of thought regarding action. Some sociologists tend to regard all action as social, stemming from relatively fixed **norms** and **values** within any particular society; symbolic interactionists, on the other hand, view the meanings behind action as precarious and unstable, constantly being negotiated among the interacting parties. One school of psychologists, known as behaviourists, tend to disregard the meanings that people attribute to their actions altogether and focus on behaviour itself. Yet another school, known as depth psychologists, question some of the meanings people claim for their actions, suspecting that these are

rationalizations or excuses; they argue that the motives of many actions are unconscious.

See also **desire, motivation**.

aggression

Aggression, as an overt physical attack on another person, is regarded as one of the most socially undesirable of behaviours in work organizations. There are normally strict sanctions (often dismissal) brought to bear on the perpetrator. However, aggression may be expressed in more culturally acceptable forms, such as through 'aggressive' bargaining, 'tough, uncompromising' **leadership**, and raw **competitive** behaviour. The *way* aggression may or may not be expressed has much to do with the **culture** and **gender** balance of the organization. So in a 'macho' production organization it is not uncommon to hear people loudly and angrily swearing at each other. In the more genteel atmosphere of white collar organizations, such as the civil service or academia, aggression can be disguised as sarcasm or sniping. The psychological basis of aggression can be frustration – from feeling cheated, underrated, exploited or blocked. Some people will channel their frustrations into indirect channels – such as through political activism, and even **sabotage**.

Deaux and Wrightsman (1984), Luthans (1985)

alienation

Alienation is an important concept in sociology, following its central position in the works of the great German philosopher and revolutionary, Karl Marx (1818–83). In his early writings, Marx used the concept of alienation to describe the condition of humanity under capitalism, a condition which is summed up in Brecht's phrase 'man can only live by forgetting that he is a human being.' The root cause of alienation for Marx is capitalist production, which separates workers from the products of their **labour**, from the activity of labour, from their fellow humans and from what Marx called man's 'species being', that is, those features that make humans a unique species. Through the sale of their labour and through the production of commodities, workers surrender their productive capacities (which is what makes them distinctly human) to alien domination. A part of themselves is separated from them, it becomes estranged from them and confronts them as an oppressor. The alienated beings can be thought of as animals separated from their essential nature, animals which have spent their entire lives in captivity. They are discontented, oppressed and unfulfilled, but, more important, are not aware of the causes of their condition; their consciousness is systematically distorted. While Marx envisaged everyone under capitalism (including the owners of capital) as alienated, he conceived of the possibility of human emancipation and freedom in a society in which the **control** of the productive process is restored to the workers. As the concept of alienation has passed into everyday use, its **meaning** has shifted and has come to mean frustration and separation. The sociologist Robert Blauner argued that alienation at the workplace comprises four emotional states, **powerlessness**, **meaninglessness**, isolation and self-estrangement. He found that increasing automation leads to increasing alienation, though very highly automated chemical plants were seen as having low alienation. His theory was that as industries move from craft to mass production alienation increases, but as they move further to fully automated process production, alienation declines. His optimistic conclusion that in the long run alienation will be resolved by the very factors which fuel it, **technology** and automation, has been criticized as reflecting the optimism of the 1950s; his arguments, however, that link **technology** to the individual's experiences at the workplace and the degree of **job satisfaction** have proved influential.

Marx (1975), Blauner (1964)

anomie

A state of collapse of social **norms** and social **controls**. The concept was developed by Durkheim (1858–1917), one of the founding fathers of sociology, who argued that the cohesion of social groups and societies is achieved through two social mechanisms, which exist over and above the individuals making up the groups and societies. (1) Social integration, the product of strong social bonds, unites groups like families, clans, military and religious groups together. (2) Social regulation **controls** the individuals' **needs** and **desires**, bringing them into line with means available for their satisfaction. In Durkheim's view social regulation is accomplished through the internalization of **norms**. Anomie occurs when such norms are weakened, especially during periods of rapid economic change or social transformation when aspirations and desires grow disproportionately. Their inevitable frustration leads to feelings of injustice, unfairness and disorientation. Durkheim argued that anomic societies display an increase in suicide rates and all kinds of manifestations of social deviance. Like **alienation**, anomie has had a long career in academic discourse and its **meaning** has lost some of the sharpness which Durkheim bestowed on it. Like alienation, it has assumed an increasingly psychological quality, indicating a state of being rather than a social phenomenon coming to signify a generalized condition of **meaninglessness**, normlessness and disintegration which affects numerous social **groups** and individuals. For example, the industrial working class as well as the 'yuppies' are seen as experiencing anomic tendencies, for very different reasons. The former have seen their expectations of a 'job for life', something they had come to regard as a right, obliterated by technological developments and the arrival of mass unemployment in the 1980s. By contrast, the young whizz-kids commanding vast salaries for speculating in the world markets saw their expectations soar out of all **control** in the 'culture of greed' of the United Kingdom and the United States in the 1980s. Both groups are seen as experiencing anomic tendencies whose results may range from fatalism and deviance to **stress** disorders.

Durkheim (1951), Howe (1986)

artificial intelligence

The use of computers to imitate human intelligence. Whether computers can imitate human **intelligence** and achieve genuine originality of thinking and problem-solving is the topic of an intense debate. What is certain is that the use of computers (and their formidable 'accomplishments' in playing chess, conducting 'conversations' or proving mathematical theorems) has forced philosophers and psychologists to re-assess their notions of 'intelligence'.

Weizenbaum (1976)

assumptions

Taking a fact, an idea or a principle for granted. Assumptions are widely used in **decision making** (where it is impossible to account for all the uncertainties affecting a particular decision), in model construction (as in Weber's ideal type **bureaucracy**) and in general argument and theorizing. Some assumptions are integral parts of **culture**, for example, 'people marry for love'. These may be shared by different individuals, enhancing their **communication**. By contrast, members of different departments in the same organization may make different assumptions about the organization's priorities or **goals**. While assumptions are an inevitable part of thinking and knowing, we are not always aware of making them; this may lead to unpredictable or even catastrophic results.

attitude

A tendency to respond to people, objects, ideas or events in particular ways. Attitudes have components to do with cognition, feelings and action tendencies. Katz and Kahn studied why people need to have attitudes, and concluded that they had four functions: they help people adapt to what is around them, they enable people to feel better than others, they are a way of expressing your values, and they help people to form some sort of order out of the world. **Prejudice** is an example of attitude, and has inspired much of the research on attitudes and attitude change. It has been found that attitude change depends on the perceived status and probity of the person communicating the change message, on whether a conclusion is drawn, on whether both sides of the argument are put and on which is put first. One of the most interesting theories of attitude change is 'cognitive dissonance' (Festinger and Carlsmith), which suggests that if you behave in a way which is inconsistent with your attitudes, you may change your attitudes to fit your **behaviour**.

See also **prejudice**.

Katz and Kahn (1978), Festinger and Carlsmith (1959)

attribution

Many events have several contributory causes. Different people will attribute causes differently, particularly when talking about complex social phenomena like those involved in organizing. If John gets angry with Jane, John may attribute his anger to Jane's unreasonable behaviour, Jane may attribute it to John's sexism, one observer may attribute it to the fact that John is always getting angry, another may attribute it to Jane winding John up, and so on. Attribution theory (Kelley) is the systematic understanding of the way in which people attribute causes to events. Many of the **political** acts in organizations centre around attribution; how do I get my colleagues to attribute the success of this action to me, and not to attribute the failure of that project to me? To what do I attribute the fall in sales – staff incompetence, poor training, or market conditions beyond our control?

Kelley (1972), Brown (1986)

authoritarianism and authoritarian personality

Some people are more prone than others to believe that those in authority positions should be obeyed unquestioningly because of their position. Others would emphasize other bases of **power**, such as expertise or charisma. Research on authoritarian personality suggests that authoritarians tend to be mild and deferential with more powerful figures, and relatively imposing and inconsiderate with subordinates. Authoritarians tend to take **structures** and **hierarchies** very seriously, they like order and predictability and tend to be rigid and intolerant. The seminal research by Adorno et al. linked the authoritarian personality with **prejudice**, notably with anti-Semitic and **racist attitudes**.

Adorno, Frenkel-Brunswick, Levinson and Sandford (1950)

authority

A concept generally identified with legitimate **power**, or an unequal relationship in which the right of the superior party to order others is recognized by the subordinate as legitimate. Weber (1864–1920) elaborated on Machiavelli's view that people obey orders either for fear or for love; he distinguished between coercion, when the superior's orders are obeyed unwillingly by the subordinate, because of fear, and authority (or domination) in which the orders are obeyed willingly. He then identified three sources of authority: charisma, tradition and a rational system of **rules**. Charismatic authority is based on the extraordinary qualities of the **leader** which command unconditional respect and loyalty. Traditional authority is based on the sanction of custom and practice; the leader is seen as the rightful heir of old lines of authority. In both of these, personal and **emotional** commitment to the leader are central to the legitimation process. Weber's third type of authority is rational-legal authority based on a system of rules which command respect because of their **rationality**. Orders are obeyed in as much as they are consistent with these rules. Unlike the previous two types, rational-legal authority is based on calculation rather than **emotion**, and is **impersonal**, that is, it does not stem from the person but from the position which the person occupies. Weber saw charismatic leadership as essentially unpredictable and turbulent and argued that there is a gradual shift towards the rational-legal type; he referred to this process as **rationalization** and identified its principal **institution** as **bureaucracy**. Most contemporary organizations involve combinations of all three types of authority as well as a variable measure of coercion and force.

Weber (1948), Mouzelis (1975)

behaviour *See* **action**.

bureaucracy

A form of administration conducted by appointed officials. The theory of bureaucracy is one of the fundamental elements of the study of **organizations** and derives from the work of the German sociologist Max Weber (1864–1920). Contrary to its pejorative colloquial meaning as equivalent to red tape, slowness and inefficiency, Weber saw bureaucracy as the epitome of administrative **rationality**. He developed a model or 'ideal type' of bureaucracy based exclusively on the **assumption** of rational-legal **authority**. This type of authority is founded on a **rational** system of **rules** and regulations and is essentially **impersonal**. The ideal type bureaucracy is a hypothetical organization, involving no other type of authority or relationship, no friendships or enmities, no informal cabals or cliques, no collegiate bodies or committees, but merely individuals giving and receiving commands underpinned by a rational system of rules. Weber identified a number of defining characteristics of this type of bureaucracy which include:

1   A strict hierarchy of offices in which superior offices control lower ones.
2   The appointment of individuals to offices on the basis of their expertise, certified by written qualifications.
3   The conduct of each office on the basis of precise rules and regulations.

4   Divorce of ownership from **control**, with **power** deriving entirely from the occupation of an office.
5   Free contractual relationship between the organization and its officials.
6   Written records of all important transactions.
7   The complete separation of official activity from the private, personal and emotional lives of the officials.
8   A system of promotion and careers based on a combination of seniority and achievement.

Weber argued that ideal type bureaucracy is a formidable tool of administration, its attributes including precision, speed, unambiguity, discretion, subordination, no friction, economy, continuity and unity. While deploring the effects of bureaucracy on humanity, which he likened to an 'iron cage', Weber felt that organizations will inevitably move in the direction of his ideal type in search of greater efficiency. 'The decisive reason for the advance of bureaucratic organization,' he argued, 'has always been its purely technical superiority over any other form of organization. The fully developed bureaucratic mechanism compares with other organizations exactly as does the machine with non-mechanical modes of production.' While Weber's bureaucracy has been criticized for a wide variety of reasons, it remains one of the foundations of organizational theory. Many of the criticisms have focused on his apparent disregard for the 'human factor' in organizational life. Weber would dismiss this and related criticisms for failing to appreciate the sheer magnitude of bureaucratic impersonality and for exaggerating the importance of the human factor. Another battery of criticisms have been directed at Weber's insistence that bureaucracy represents maximum administrative **rationality**; some of these criticisms too can be refuted by pointing out that they are directed at existing bureaucratic organizations rather than at the ideal type.

See also **authority, contingency theories, oligarchy, environment**.

Mouzelis (1975), Weber (1948), Morgan (1986)

burnout

People who have high expectations and strong ideals of what they can achieve in a job, especially if it is one where they work with people in emotionally stressful circumstances, run the risk of burnout. The burned-out worker is exhausted and disillusioned from the constant frustration of failure: the social worker whose clients relapse after many months of painstaking work; the doctor who finds he or she is unable to offer sufficient care to patients because of the unremitting workload; the new teacher whose fresh ideas are fast rejected by pupils and colleagues. Such people can soon lose **motivation**, and their inspirational spark dies. The burned-out become cynical about the very people they once cared about, and will perform in a way which is only just about sufficient to get by. Burnout can be detected in many different occupations, and can occur at any stage of **career**. Burnout can be regarded as an extreme form of **stress** reaction.

Pines and Aronson (1988), Edelwich and Brodsky (1980), Fineman (1985)

career

Career, literally, refers to a pathway through life. However, it has become commonly associated with a planned occupational progression. As one's experience and formal qualifications increase, so do status, salary and hierarchical position. Traditionally careers were mainly for the clergy, the military, civil servants, doctors, lawyers and academics. Now we talk of managerial careers, political careers and careers in occupations as various as nursing, engineering, social work, marketing and accounting. Careers are sometimes contrasted with jobs, the latter involving less long-term commitment, less accumulation of skills and knowledge, and usually less security. Many companies still offer the prospect of a career to their new employees. However, as organizations become slimmer and flatter (see **structure**), the traditional career progression in, and up, a single company is being replaced by a less predictable scenario: a number of moves across different projects in a range of organizations.

See also **professions**.

Hall (1986), Schein (1978)

change

Change, and resistance to it, are intimately connected with the social psychology of organizational life. Organization change may be necessary for the economic survival of an enterprise, and very much in the interests of its owners and managers (but note that this is deliberate, managed change, just one of many sorts of change). However, others in the organization may **perceive** change as threatening to their position, **status**, relationships, competence or security. Change within an organization may be seen to occur at two possible levels. *First-order* change (the most common) concerns small adjustments to work methods – such as having more team meetings to solve a communication problem. *Second-order* change looks more deeply at the beliefs and **assumptions** behind existing work practices – why exactly are team members failing to communicate? Second-order change is about changing the way in which future changes take place. Change is often engineered by **consultants**. Here we find a bewildering array of techniques. They range from 'quick fix' first-order methods, such as intensive **training** for top **management**, or the re-design of the organiz-ation's **structure**, to more profound second-order attempts to change the whole organization's **culture** through workshops, courses, counselling and employee feedback from questionnaires. It is now common for organizations to employ specialists in change-management, or 'organizational development', an expertise which has developed over the past twenty years from our growing appreciation of how individuals and groups operate in organizations.

Smith (1991), Goodman (1982)

cognitive

To do with thinking. One way of looking at people and their **actions** is that there are (a) cognitive aspects, which are the relatively cool, calculating parts of life, (b) affective or emotional aspects, which do not necessarily imply much weight of thought but which are full of feeling, and (c) connative, referring to the will to carry things through. In practice the separation between different aspects of the human being is more complex. We know, from theories such as that of cognitive dissonance (see **attitudes**), that **emotions** can affect subsequent cognition. If you fall in love, your cognitive opinions about the person you love may follow, as well as your cognitions about other things. Similarly, some writers have argued that there is a strong cognitive element in emotion, as emotion cannot be sustained without some thoughts to keep it going. 'She should not have said that to me' is the kind of sentence which a person repeats in their heads in order to stay angry, or sad. Even such activities as chess, which appear purely cognitive to the outsider, are described as emotional and involving by those who are really good at them.

cognitive dissonance   *See* **attitudes**.

collective bargaining

An **institution** in industrial relations. It involves a system of more or less formal negotiations between employers and employees, as well as between their respective organizations, employers' associations and **trade unions**, aimed at reaching collective agreements regarding work and conditions of employment. Collective bargaining in Britain has been famously untidy, taking place at different levels, such as workshop, plant, firm and industry, simultaneously. While not legally enforceable, collective agreements are generally seen as establishing some order in industrial relations and a sense of fair play and responsibility. Collective bargaining has long been regarded as an **institution** for containing and channelling **conflict** and preventing it from assuming mutually destructive forms, such as strikes, go-slows and work-to-rules. It is said, therefore, to institutionalize conflict. In the more recent past, with the declining power of unions and the emergence of macho management, the breadth of collective bargaining has been somewhat curtailed, with numerous employers bypassing unions and making unilateral offers directly to the individual employees.

communication

One of the core concepts of organizing, and one which is much contested. Communication may be verbal, that is, to do with the words used, or non-verbal. Some communication research has used an **information** processing model, looking at the inputs, outputs, 'noise', and numbers of channels. Leavitt looked at the effect of different communication networks on the performance of tasks, and found that a star shape, where one central person can communicate with everybody else, is most effective for simple tasks, but the central person gets overloaded if the task is complex. All-channel communication, where anyone can talk to anyone, is slow but most effective for complex technical tasks, and so on. Should communication provide both sides of an argument to be persuasive? Should it offer people an appeal for action, if it is to affect what they do? What are the merits of one-way communication, like a lecture or a book, compared with those of two-way communication, like a discussion? Hovland and Janis, among others, have been studying these questions over the years.

Leavitt (1951), Hovland, Janis and Kelley (1953), Janis (1972).

competencies

Recent moves towards establishing whether **management** development programmes were good value for money, and towards trying to develop a qualification for the **profession** of management, led to questions about what managers actually needed to be able to do. What competencies did they need to have? It seemed that in law or medicine the competencies which you would expect of the professional were clear, and the same could be expected of managers. Others have questioned the validity of trying to establish management competencies on three grounds. Firstly, management is not one activity, but is different in different organizations, for different functions in the organization, and under different economic and social conditions. All of these will make a difference to the competencies required. Secondly, it may be that the mixture of competencies, and the ability to make use of others' competencies, is more important than the manager's own competency. Thirdly, management writers have not agreed sufficiently among themselves about how to describe particular activities or the competencies required for them. The labels are not yet well enough developed; to speak of 'competencies' sounds as if we all know what 'effective communication' or some such phrase means, and this is misleading.

Mangham and Pye (1991)

competition

A form of **conflict**, in which different parties are vying for the same resources or rewards, while usually agreeing to abide by a set of **rules**. Economic competition between buyers and sellers of commodities is the principal foundation of capitalist markets. Free market advocates argue that competition ensures efficient matching of supply and demand for goods and services and acts as a stimulant for efficiency and innovation. Its critics point out that competition frequently leads to duplication of effort, disregards the wider social and environmental welfare and leads to a preoccupation with short-term profit at the expense of long-term planning. In organizational studies, competition among departments has been identified as one of the dysfunctions of **bureaucracy**. The concept has never been adequately differentiated from **conflict**, though one talks about conflict rather than competition between employers and employees. Handy suggests that argument, competition and conflict are types of *difference*: argument and competition which is perceived to be open and fair are beneficial for the organization, while closed competition and conflict are damaging. Kanter has noted that internal competition, for example between research teams researching the same product, can act as a stimulant to entrepreneurship.

Handy (1976), Kanter (1984)

competitiveness

An **attitude** that predisposes to **competition**. This concept is used both organizationally and individually. For an organization, the issue may be, how does it gain more sales, lower costs or a better reputation than other organizations who might be able to do the same job for the same people. For an individual, competitiveness may mean trying to outshine colleagues, and catch the eye of those in authority. At both levels it is often assumed to be a good thing, but this needs to be questioned. In some industries (such as engineering in the UK), the competitiveness of the different companies means that none of them generate sufficient profit to finance research, or to pay salaries to encourage people to enter their profession. Individually, competitiveness may mean that a number of tasks which require inputs from several people do not get done properly. Competition usually requires a high degree of co-operation, as can be seen in any market, or in any sports event.

conflict

This may be productive or unproductive. Lack of conflict can be both dangerous and dull. Conflict can be productive when the conflicting parties do not need to work together, and when the reward system means that one or the other will be rewarded, but not both. Otherwise, it is likely to be damaging. The last person to mobilize in a conflict is usually at a disadvantage, so many conflicts arise because people want to be sure they get their pre-emptive strike in. Schein says that during a conflict the groups that are in conflict close ranks against the enemy; members of the conflicting groups listen out for negative information about the other group; the winners tend to become fat and happy, and stop working; the losers become more tense, and either learn a lesson or turn on each other; negotiators who have had contacts with the other group become scapegoats if their group loses, and often feel guilty if their group wins. Pondy suggests five stages of conflict: latent, where the conditions for conflict exist; perceived, where the individuals or groups concerned know that there is a conflict, but nothing has been publicly declared, and indeed it may still be publicly denied; felt, where one or more parties feel tense or anxious; manifest, where there is observable behaviour designed to frustrate others' attempts to achieve their goals; and the aftermath, which is the relationship between the parties after the conflict has been resolved or suppressed.

See also **aggression**, **competition**, **politics**, **power**.

Schein (1980), Pondy (1967)

conformity

There are classic psychological experiments which powerfully demonstrate that people are prepared to disbelieve the evidence of their own eyes in order to come into line with the views or behaviour of other people. We will conform to social pressures because of the discomfort and embarrassment of looking different, or standing out from the crowd. We gain comfort and security from feeling we belong, so we will often suppress some of our individuality so that we are accepted by the group. Through this, **group norms** and **values** grow which regulate group conduct. Paradoxically, many groups will also tolerate some non-conformists, perhaps one or two people who are allowed to be eccentric, like the traditional fool or jester. The non-conformist offers an emotional release for the group's worries and uncertainties; he or she is also given licence to criticize the group. Organizational **rules**, **hierarchies**, and **bureaucracy** are features of formal, managerial, **structures** designed to bring about a measure of conformity in work behaviour. However, the more restrictive these are, the greater the likelihood of loyalty and conformity to the informal **organization** – with its particular freedoms and satisfactions.

Luthans (1985)

construct

Within Kelly's 'personal construct theory', a construct is a pair of psychologically opposite words or phrases which together describe a dimension in a person's thinking. Thus 'bright . . . stupid', 'attractive . . .

unattractive', 'like me . . . not like me', might be constructs. Kelly used **Repertory Grids**, among other methods, to discover personal constructs. The word 'personal' betokens the fact that we all have different constructs, which taken together are as personal as a fingerprint. A construct is not simply a verbal tag, according to Kelly, but goes deeper than that. In some recent use and research, however, constructs have been taken to be pairs of verbal tags, like the examples above. Constructs are personal not only in the words that describe the constructs, but also in the way those constructs are organized. Within one person's own construct system 'bright . . . stupid' might be linked with 'employable . . . would not want to employ', whereas within another's it might be linked with 'competitive . . . not a threat'. It is also possible for two people to have constructs with the same first word or phrase but different second words or phrases; one person might pair 'bright' with 'stupid', while another may pair it with 'quiet'. As Kelly put it, the second pole of a construct is a psychological opposite, not necessarily a logical opposite. That is, it is an opposite in the thinking of that particular person, whether or not it seems sensible to someone else.

Kelly (1972), Bannister and Fransella (1971)

consultant

In recent years management consultancy has grown into a major industry. A consultant is a person who is contracted to work for a client company on a specific project or activity, and usually for a specified time, as opposed to an employee whose **career** is in the company. Consultants are usually hired to do some specialized work which either requires a specific skill or expertise which is not available in the company, or requires more time than any appropriate specialist can give it. Some companies who are trying to reduce the number of full-time staff, or who do not want to risk the potential cost of making a specialist redundant later, will hire consultants as and when needed. Some organizations employ 'internal consultants' – people operating as advisers or specialists from within the organization, and sometimes acting as intermediaries for external consultants. In recent years resentment has grown towards consultants from some employees; 'they come in, borrow your watch, tell you the time, walk off with the watch, and charge you for it.' 'You know they have arrived, because their Porsches are parked in your reserved bicycle space!'

McLean, Sims, Mangham and Tuffield (1982), Eden, Jones and Sims (1983).

contingency theories

Two types of theories are referred to as contingency theories: first, theories of organizational **structure** and second, theories of **leadership**. Contingency theory grew out of an impatience with classical management approaches which seemed to prescribe universal solutions to all **management problems**, irrespective of different local circumstances. For example, Burns and Stalker argued that Weber's ideal type of bureaucracy does not represent an ideal structure for all types of real organization. A structure which may serve one organization well may turn into a recipe for disaster when forced on another. Burns and Stalker pointed out that organizational **environment** affects the type of organizational **structure** most likely to be adopted by successful organizations. Woodward argued that optimal structures were contingent on the production **technologies** employed by different companies. Yet other researchers have noted that optimal organizational structure is contingent on the size of the company. Contingency theories of **leadership** argue that no single leadership style is effective in all circumstances, but that leadership styles are contingent on the organizational and situational context. Fiedler has developed a technique aimed at assisting leaders in their diagnoses of this context and enabling them to adopt a style which is likely to prove effective.

Burns and Stalker (1961), Woodward (1965), Fiedler (1967)

control

One of the central features of organizations and one of the main functions of **management** identified by classical theory. Controlling resources and outputs, controlling processes and machinery, controlling information and the environment, are all part and parcel of organizational life. In particular, organizations control individuals, to ensure reliable, predictable and consistent performance or organizational **roles**. This involves the monitoring of performance, its assessment against some stated standards, the provision of feedback, rewards and sanctions. Examination procedures, **performance appraisal** and organizational audits are all control mechanisms, aimed at ensuring that certain standards of individual and organizational performance are achieved. Physical violence was the main control mechanism of slave-drivers. In some early capitalist factories, workers were physically chained to their benches, as a way of ensuring that they put in the required number of work hours. Later, more discreet forms of control emerged. **Rules** and regulations gradually became the foundation of **bureaucratic** control, while **Taylorism** sought to incorporate control in the technical process itself. The moving assembly line, the paperwork chain set the pace and control the activities of those who work. More recently, the importance of **culture** has been emphasized as a mechanism whereby control is internalized by the individual as self-control. The organization's **values** and **norms** help to ensure that its members will behave in a certain way, not because they are forced to, but because it has become second nature to them. Generally, lack of control, or **powerlessness**, is seen as an important dimension of **alienation**.

corporate culture

A popular concept in organizational studies since the 1980s. Organizations, like nations, it has been suggested, have cultures, composed of shared **values, norms** and **meanings**. Some organizations have cultures which enhance efficiency, productivity, innovation and service while others have cultures which stand in the way of success. A corporate culture which promotes innovation, team work and commitment is often seen as the secret behind the phenomenal success of Japanese organizations. In their highly influential bestseller *In Search of Excellence*, Thomas J. Peters and Robert H. Waterman argue that successful companies are those which have strong **cultures**, that is, strong commitment to a shared set of values and norms, which both unite and **motivate** organizational members. The forging of a strong culture, the strengthening of norms and values, the creation of meanings are all important functions of **leaders**. 'Good managers make meanings for people, as well as money,' claim Peters and Waterman (1982:29). Similar conclusions are drawn by Kanter, who believes that most Western organizations have developed **bureaucratic** cultures that thwart innovation and entrepreneurship by emphasizing adherence to rules and procedures. Deal and Kennedy suggest that, in future, successful organizations will have to generate cultures in which every employee has a sense of being a hero. Such arguments have encouraged the view that managers can virtually manipulate organizational culture at will to produce a winning cocktail, through the use of symbols, stories, myths and **metaphors**. This neglects the fact that people may not like to be manipulated and that, while they strive for **meaning**, they will not embrace *any* meaning. Within organizations, **sub-cultures** and counter-cultures may spontaneously grow and prosper which may complement or undermine the official values.

Peters and Waterman (1982), Kanter (1984), Deal and Kennedy (1982)

culture

A concept, mainly drawn from anthropology, which has acquired considerable currency in the study of organizations (*see* **corporate culture**). Culture can be thought of as the material and spiritual heritage of a community, the stock of myths and stories, artistic and craft artifacts, buildings, tools, laws, **institutions**, rituals and customs. It is frequently argued that culture is the cement which holds communities together by establishing shared **meanings** and **values** which enable them to communicate with each other, taking many things for granted. Schein (1985) refers to these things as 'basic assumptions'; for example, in many Western cultures it is taken for granted that people marry for love, a notion which would seem highly alien to numerous other cultures. Likewise many of our values and **attitudes** towards work, leisure, **authority**, **career**, happiness, success, death,

sexuality are shaped by culture. We internalize culture, it becomes part of us, influencing us without our being aware of it. It is only when we are confronted by an alien culture that we appreciate many of these internalized values and assumptions that we carry along. Harrison and Handy have argued that organizations fall into four types according to their culture: (a) *Power culture*, in which orders emanate from the organizational centre and are unquestioningly observed. Political organizations, the Mafia and many small businesses have this type of culture. (b) *Role culture*, dominated by **rules** and regulations, as in classic **bureaucracy**. This is common in the Civil Service and in large bureaucratic organizations. (c) *Task culture*, in which getting a specific job done by a strict deadline is all-important. This can be found in publishing and consultancy organizations where deadlines have to be met and, in general, in organizations in which there is a lot of project work. (d) *People* or *support culture*, in which the development of human potential and well-being is paramount; this may be found in some voluntary organizations, partnerships, religious or academic organizations.

Handy (1976), Harrison (1972), Schein (1985)

decision making

Commonly regarded as a key activity in organizational life, decision making is a deliberate, distant phrase for an activity which is often more multifaceted and untidy. There are many 'stage' models of decision making, showing how it might be done in a sequence of rational steps. This does not necessarily fit with how human beings actually make decisions. People are capable of handling complex and uncertain information or ideas, at scanning situations for things that should be taken into account, or possible answers that could be taken up opportunistically. Many decisions that people have been happy with have been made by informal means. For example, some people follow logical steps, work through the possibilities, and then see whether the answer *feels* right. If it does not, they may trust their feelings more than the rational procedures they have followed. Many techniques have been introduced to assist decision making, such as 'brainstorming', 'quality circles' (see **participation**) and 'cognitive mapping' and 'mind mapping'. Recent years have seen the development of techniques for decision support and **group** decision support.

See also **rationality,emotion.**

Harrison (1981), Eden and Radford (1990)

desire

A term used to explain human **motivation**. Unlike the concept of need it seeks to incorporate a social and a psycho-sexual dimension. One may need shoes for warmth and comfort, but one desires a pair of designer trainers because of what they stand for. Whether directed towards a physical object, a human being, an activity, or a state of being, desire is driven not merely by instinct or need, but by the **meanings** attributed to them. Desires may be fulfilled either in practice (for example, by buying the desired pair of trainers) or in **fantasy**, by imagining that the wished-for object or state has been achieved. Alternatively, desires may by frustrated, in which case they may mutate into desires for different objects, which may be easier to fulfil, or they may be repressed into the unconscious. Three broad traditions in the study of desire can be identified: Firstly, sociologists have argued that desires are culturally constituted, as individuals learn to desire those objects and states of upon which their **cultures** place special **value**. Consumer societies, for example, are said to place enormous value on material commodities and identify happiness with escalating material possessions. Secondly, depth psychologists have emphasized the connection between desire and pleasure and have argued that most desires are modified residues of earlier desires, mainly stemming from childhood; these were originally repressed and later seek fulfilment in new incarnations. For example, belief in God is traced back to the child's desire to be protected by a loving father. Thirdly, more recently, **discourse** theorists have argued that desire is an element of the discourse on sexuality, in other words the complex and interconnected ways of thinking and talking about things sexual as against things unsexual (Foucault, 1979). The very **language** and words which dominate the sexuality discourse, (**gender**, **sex**, sexual **identity**, orgasm, body and even desire itself) are historically constituted as interconnected elements, in constant interaction with other discourses, like the discourse of power and the discourse of political economy.

Foucault (1979)

deskilling

In *Labor and Monopoly Capital*, Harry Braverman argued that, contrary to commonsense notions, throughout the 20th century workers have been stripped of traditional **skills** and **competencies** by the onslaught of **Taylorism** and **technology**. Traditional skills of artisans such as printers, potters, engineers, machinists, cooks and clerks, have been eliminated, either by being absorbed into the production process itself or by being overtaken by new technological processes. The deskilled worker loses not only much of his/her bargaining power, but also **control** over his/her work, and pride and dignity in his/her work. Braverman's theory has sparked off a controversy. Especially vital has been the question of whether computerization of work processes and clerical work leads to deskilling. Empirical studies have documented strong deskilling tendencies in numerous industries, one finding that the majority of workers use more skill in getting to work than in doing their job. Nevertheless, there is also evidence of the emergence of a new range of skills in response to the demands of new technology.

Braverman (1974), Beynon (1973), Blackburn and Mann (1979)

discourse

The way in which things are discussed, the argumentation and **rhetoric** that are used to support what we say. More generally, discourse is used to describe not only what we say, but also what remains unspoken or taken for granted, such as **assumptions** and evasions. Discourse analysis has become an important research method in recent years (Potter and Wetherell). This is a method which says that, instead of taking discourse as transparent, and trying to look through it to see what the meaning behind people's words may be, it is worth studying the discourse itself. Words do not merely reflect that which is being talked about. They actually construct or even constitute what is being talked about. This may lead to a focus on the **language** used. Feminist writers, for example, point to the way that specific words, and their juxtapositions, can provide a meaing that automatically give salience to one or another social group. The words both represent, and are represented by, the **culture** to which they belong. Conversational analysis (Beattie) has had a different but closely related emphasis, with more stress on precise measurement, taking note of pauses in speech, changes of intonation and other non-verbal aspects of discourse. The uses of discourse analysis have expanded considerably lately under the influence of **post-modernist** thought. It may equally be applied to an advertisement, a poem, a conversation, a film, letters, a business letter, or a set of social rituals. Each may be considered a 'text' which represents, in its own language, features or meanings about a form of individual or social reality.

See also **desire**.

Potter and Wetherell (1987), Beattie (1983)

discrimination

Giving preferential treatment, notably with respect to employment or promotion, to an individual or a group on the basis of characteristics like **gender**, age, **ethnicity**, **race** or religion. Direct discrimination, for example the hiring of a man over a better qualified woman purely on account of his gender, is illegal in both Britain and the United States. It is, however, very difficult to prove, especially if an **interview** is used as part of the recruiting procedure. More important, there are a wide range of discriminatory mechanisms resulting in unequal opportunities. The structure of the job market itself acts as an obstacle to equality. Child-bearing and child-rearing are serious impediments to women's career chances, the location of jobs and educational prerequisites inhibit the chances of ethnic minority groups, the requirement for job experience disadvantages young people, and conversely limited training opportunities disadvantage the elderly. The way a job advertisement is phrased can dissuade particular groups from even applying; for example, specific requirements such as long hours or foreign travel, will automatically exclude many women. Gender, racial and other **stereotypes** and sheer **prejudice** can equally fuel discrimination. Finally, harassment at work can act as a discriminatory mechanism, by placing the victims on the defensive, contributing to their character assassination or forcing them out of employment.

dual career

In the past decade the growth of dual careers has been a noteworthy contrast to the traditional picture of one breadwinner (usually male) per family. In dual career relationships both partners have, usually, full-time occupations, and each occupation requires considerable commitment in time and energy. Dual career couples will give a high priority to their career satisfactions, which can conflict with any domestic and child-rearing responsibilities. This is rarely resolved without family **stress** – and a measure of guilt. Despite some marked shifts towards equality in **gender** roles in and out of work, it is often the woman who picks up the responsibility for housework and child care, in addition to managing her own career – and perhaps, ultimately, gives way to her partner's career interests. Some organizations have acknowledged the special needs of dual career couples and offer more flexible working arrangements and support. There are some variations in dual career patterns, such as two people sharing part-time careers, or a job-split – both partners sharing a single job.

See also **career**.

Hochschild (1989), Lewis and Cooper (1989)

emotion

Emotions are mainly private experiences which tell us something about the quality of our interactions and performances in the world. Some writers contrast emotional processes with thinking/problem-solving ones ('**cognitive**'), although in practice the two are closely linked. A number of emotions, such as shame and embarrassment, depend on the judgements on ourselves that we experience from others. They play a significant part in social control and moral behaviour, and their **meanings** are culturally specific. Some organizations specialize in regimes of emotional **control** for their employees (the ever smiling waitress; the air hostess who looks cool all the time; the receptionist's 'have a nice day') to the extent that employees can become very cynical, or lose touch with their private feelings. **Corporate culture** can often reflect 'rules' as to how employees should feel about their company, and some corporate **leaders** are adroit at mobilizing 'good feelings' amongst their employees. The expression of emotion is gender-linked. Women who try to move up organizations in competition with men often find they have to suppress their own feelings and adopt male **norms** of emotion display. The study of emotion involves: an appreciation of society's structures of **power** and **status** which broadly shapes emotional display; the organization's **sub-culture** which more specifically determines what employees should or should not express; and finally the individual's own **personality** which accounts for his or her particular interpretation of the world, and emotional sensitivities.

Hochschild (1983), Fineman (1993)

empowerment

Empowerment has become a popular notion in **leadership** theorizing. It is based on the idea that, given the freedom, scope and resources to achieve organizational **goals**, people will, in effect lead themselves – if it is in their interests to do so. Leaders, therefore, do not *tell* others what to do, or attempt to *sell* their ideas to them. Rather, the leader's **role** is to help others achieve their own ends creatively by helping them to discover their own potential, and clearing a pathway for them. The leader, in this way, gives **power**, to his or her followers. The leader is a facilitator of other people's **action**. Empowerment is an extension of democratization in management, and the fading of the **authoritarian** leader.

Srivastva (1986)

environment

The social, economic, political and cultural context in which organizations operate. Closed **systems** theories have focused on organizations as time-capsules or black boxes isolated from the effects of what goes on around them. While suitable for the study of a few organizations which operate in highly inert environments, such theories, which include Weber's classic theory of **bureaucracy**, have severe limitations when applied to organiz-ations where the environment is a constant source of threats and opportunities. In a pioneering study, Burns and Stalker (1961) argued that firms operating in stable environments tend to adopt *mechanistic* **struc-tures**, with rigid **hierarchies, rules** and regulations. By contrast, organiz-ations operating in changing environments tend to adopt *organic* structures enabling them to respond flexibly and rapidly to environmental threats and opportunities. This was an early example of the use of **contingency theories**. While the organizational environment has assumed pride of place in management literature, it is not an unproblematic concept. In the first place, the perception of what constitutes the organization's environment may differ across different individuals. A chemical company's environment looks very different to a public relations officer seeking to allay fears about the company's record on the environment, to a production worker threatened with redundancy, to a research scientist and to a financial expert concerned with the company's standing in the securities market. Equally, in a collective way, the environment cannot be defined unless there is a shared sense of what the organization is all about. Is Ford to be seen as a car-making company (in which case the competitors' cars are a central feature of its environment) or is it a money-making organization (in which case the competitors' cars are less important as long as Ford can find new ways of making money, such as by trading in the currency markets). This has led to the concept of the 'enacted environment'. Instead of 'given' environment 'out there', enacted environment is based on the continuous trading and juxtaposing of **meaning** and **interpretations** about the organization and its purpose.

Burns and Stalker (1961), Morgan (1986)

ethics

Ethics concerns the moral principles and **values** which govern our beliefs, **actions** and **decisions**. Ethics in organizations can be seen in three main areas. First there are the organization's social responsibilities – the harm or benefit that results from its products or services. For example, there is much debate about the ethics of producing and selling cigarettes, cars which could be safer, or using materials which deplete or damage the natural environment. The second area is the everyday decisions which affect those working in an organization: is it ethical to promote a particular friend over a more competent person? Is it ethical to fire someone without warning or good reason on 'personal grounds'? And is it ethical to exclude **ethnic** minorities from a shortlist of job applicants? The third area of ethics concerns the relationships between organizations and societies. Is it ethical to choose the cheapest Third World supplier for a product, to negotiate the lowest possible price with them, and to ignore questions about their employment policies and practices? These questions involve principles of fairness and justice and standards for judging what is right or wrong. The standards will usually derive from the religious, social or professional codes that guide our lives, although moral philosophers point to two major principles – **utilitarianism** and formalism. Utilitarianism looks for the greatest good for the greatest number of people. A good decision is one where the benefits outweigh the costs. Formalism is less pragmatic; it measures the worth of a decision by the extent to which it meets certain fundamental liberties and privileges – such as the right of employees and customers not to have their lives or safety endangered, not to be intentionally deceived, and not to have their privacy invaded.

Brady (1990), Walton (1988)

ethnic groups

Communities or collectivities usually based on a sense of shared origin, shared traditions and shared fate. Ethnic groups may be culturally, territorially or historically based. Their members have a sense of 'belonging' to the **group**, sharing many **cultural assumptions** and **values**. Ethnicity does not necessarily imply that the group concerned has a sense of superiority over other traditions, although the term 'ethnocentrism' is generally used pejoratively to signify a group's assumption that its culture and values are superior to those of others. Ethnocentrism may, therefore, fuel prejudice and discrimination against members of other ethnic groups.

See also **prejudice**, **race**.

experiential learning

Learning which is initiated through experience. Most theories of learning involve experience, but experiential learning *begins* with experience which the learner then tries to make sense of. This is in contrast to propositional learning, for example, where the learner starts with an idea and then may seek to test the idea in relation to experience. Kelly (1955) pointed out that experience does not necessarily produce learning; learning is to do with how much a person is changed by experience, not simply with the number of events they collide with. The concept of experiential learning is sometimes attacked because it is difficult to verify that learning has actually taken place; it is also difficult for the person who has learned experientially to articulate precisely what they have learned. The concept has recently been taken further in a helpful way with the notion of 'self-organized learning' (Harri-Augstein and Thomas), which argues that effective learners take responsibility for learning experientially how to become better learners; in other words they learn how to learn.

Kelly (1955), Kolb, Rubin and McIntyre (1979), Harri-Augstein and Thomas (1991)

extrinsic rewards

When used in connection with employment, this concept refers mainly to rewards unrelated to the nature of the **work** itself. Although extrinsic rewards have been used as incentives to hard work through the ages, they became a central feature of **management** philosophy deriving from **Taylorism**. According to this philosophy the worker does not and cannot expect to derive intrinsic job satisfaction, so his/her **motivation** to work hard must be spurred by the expectation of extrinsic rewards, like pay, bonuses and performance-related benefits. Goldthorpe et al, in a pioneering study in the 1960s, found that manufacturing workers working in three factories in Luton had an instrumental orientation to work; work was seen mainly as a means to an end or rather to a range of ends related to material well-being. These workers did not expect intrinsic job satisfaction and many of them had swapped more intrinsically rewarding work for more highly paid jobs. This finding has not received unanimous support. Some studies, such as Beynon's investigation of workers at Ford or Gabriel's study of catering workers, have indicated that workers may adopt instrumental **attitudes** only because they feel that intrinsic satisfaction on the job is denied to them.

See also **motivation**.

Goldthorpe et al. (1968), Beynon (1973), Gabriel (1988)

fantasy

Imagination plays an important part in our lives. People day-dream, and run events through in their minds both before and afterwards. This may be done in a distant, unemotional way, or it may be as involving and powerful as if the event were actually taking place; this latter case is what we mean by fantasy. It involves the whole person and has been shown to influence later **actions**. Some fantasies are surrogates for action, while others can act as rehearsals. Some **skills** may be practised as effectively in the fantasy as by acting them out physically – even gymnastic and sports skills. Many of the activities of organizing will be tried in the imagination before acting them out, leading to a potentially less risky way of gaining experience. By contrast, when things go wrong, people may re-run events in their imagination in order to work out what happened. If people adopt a fantasy of themselves as consistently failing in similar situations, they may end up re-creating or perpetuating a problem. Ironically, this may mean that, instead of learning from experience, they are practising how to go wrong in future. Fantasy has also been related recently to **leadership** studies. Some effective leaders convey a clear and attractive fantasy of how things might be; followers are then inspired to turn this fantasy into a reality.

See also **desire, sex, sexuality**.

Sims (1985, 1986), Bennis and Nanus (1985)

femininity

A term used to describe equally the principal components of female **sexuality** and the **role** attributes of the female **gender**. Feminist theory in the 1970s and 1980s has drawn attention to distinct features of early childhood and **socialization** which mould the **personality** development of boys and girls and prepares them to assume different gender roles. Mitchell (1974), in her trail-blazing book *Psychoanalysis and Feminism*, re-assessed the psychoanalytic theory of female sexuality and used Freud's theories to argue that boys and girls follow, not symmetrical, but fundamentally dissimilar sexual developments. The boy's **masculinity** will initially grow relatively unproblematically out of the **desire** for the mother, the first object of his love. The girl's femininity undergoes a traumatic transformation 'from the active wanting of her mother to the passive wanting to be wanted by the father' (Mitchell, 1974:108). The 'making of a lady' is then inextricably linked with a repression of active **desires** and a re-orientation towards passive ones, embodied in the shift of sexual interest from the clitoris to the vagina. Chodorow (1978), in her book *The Reproduction of Mothering*, has moved away from Freudian emphasis on **sexuality** but keeps the focus on the early mother–child relationship. The fact that the majority of both boys and girls have the same primary love object, namely the mother, leads to very different types of personality development, because mothers treat babies differently depending on their gender, projecting different **emotions** and attitudes. One significant contribution of **feminist** writings since the 1970s has been to demonstrate that patriarchal capitalist societies place greater constraints on female **sexuality** than on male, turning it against women and using it to perpetuate male privilege and domination.

See also **gender, masculinity, sexuality**.

Mitchell (1974), Chodorow (1978), Wolf (1990)

feminism

The feminist movement, which began in the 1960s, draws attention to the dominantly male **values** which have determined the shape of our political, institutional and organizational **structures**. Feminist writers have argued that there is a deep imbalance in societies which systematically undervalues women, relegating them to **stereotyped roles** in the home, family and work. The unequal distribution of **power** features prominently in this analysis. In organizations, the feminist case is supported by evidence of relatively few women in top positions, the disproportionate number of women in lower-**status** jobs, the poorer pay of women compared to men, and the inadequate support offered to women who wish to work and have children or to take career breaks. Feminist theorists must be credited for introducing into academic studies issues which had gone unnoticed earlier, notably relations between public and private lives, and between work and sexuality. The 1990s has been described as the 'post-feminist' era where many younger people have been exposed directly or indirectly to feminist thought. While some of the most rigid sex demarcations have begun to soften in the UK and America, most observers believe that there is still a long way to go. The shift also has been marked by some backlash from both men and women, disenchanted with more radical forms of feminism, for whom the simple associations of 'feminist equals good' have broken down.

See also **femininity, gender**.

Marshall (1984), Spencer and Podmore (1987), Greer (1970)

fiddling

An array of illegal operations going on in many organizations, at times with the tacit or active involvement of **management**. These include pilfering and stealing, the illicit use of company property, the tampering of records (for example, for the purpose of clocking additional overtime), the making of false expense claims and the use of company accounts for private ends. Some organizations have virtually **institutionalized** fiddles as a job benefit, whose proceeds increase the longer an employee stays and the more loyal he/she proves. Fiddling can be collective in which case it serves to bind together those involved, or individual, engaged in mainly by those who feel **powerless** or excluded. The frequency, scale and scope of fiddling vary enormously across different organizations, most of which make provisions for 'shrink-age'. People rarely regard their own fiddling as a criminal, illegal or immoral activity but see it as a **norm**-guided **behaviour**, with its own **rules, ethics** and limits.

Mars (1982), Mars and Nicod (1984), Gabriel (1988)

Fordism

A system of mass production based on standardization of products and processes pioneered by Henry Ford (1863–1947). Stretching **Taylorist** principles to their extreme, Ford initiated the production of cars on assembly lines, substantially cutting production costs and improving overall quality. 'They can have it any color they like, so long as it's black,' he said about his famous model-T, which was the first affordable car for the mass population. While paying his workers substantially more than his competitors, Ford experienced rates of labour turnover up to 400 per cent, resulting from the **deskilling** and **alienation** of his workforce. 'We expect our men to do what they are told. The organization is so highly specialized . . . that we could not for a moment consider allowing men to have their own way' (Ford 1923:11). While Fordism dominated the world of manufacturing industries for 60 years, its domination is now virtually over. New **technologies** and new manage-ment and manufacturing techniques, notably those pioneered by the Japanese, have undermined the equation of volume, standardization and efficiency. Instead flexibility, customer-centredness, **corporate culture** and concern for **quality** have assumed central significance. These new production systems are sometimes referred to as post-Fordism.

Ford (1923), Doray (1988)

games

This term is used in at least two senses in organizing. A style of individual and group training called transactional analysis was made popular by Berne in a book called *Games People Play*. The games he identifies have names like 'wooden leg' – a game in which a person seeks sympathy, and many other 'games' have been identified in which people treat each other in slightly inauthentic ways to achieve some other end. Games also refer to game theory, in which the **strategy** that a person adopts in dealing with colleagues can be understood by thinking of what they are doing as a game, with **rules**, moves, possibly a referee and so on. Radford has described a number of game approaches to organizational analysis. Allison pointed out that in organizations the players are usually involved in many different games at once, and the progress of one game will affect play in another. The game that is going on in the new products committee will affect the chief engineer and the finance director when they are both also players in the quite different game going on in the policy committee. To make matters more complicated, in organizational games you may use one of your 'turns' to try to change the rules, rather than to play within the rules. This is called a 'hypergame', and is often indicated by phrases such as 'I wonder if we could just check on how we are going about this task . . .'

Berne (1964), Radford (1986), Allison (1971)

gender

The division of humanity into men and women has since the 16th century been assigned to the term **sex**. Sex, in other words, marks the physiological differences between the genders. Gender, however, is used to distinguish between the culturally specific patterns of behaviour or **roles** attached to the sexes (Oakley, 1972). Thus while one is born a particular sex, one is socialized into one's gender. **Socialization** prepares individuals to perform roles consistent with their gender **identity**. Such roles may include sexual roles, family roles and work roles. In organizational settings, gender acts as a formidable divide, with women being concentrated in the lower echelons of organizations, in generally low-pay, low-status industries. Even in high-pay, high-status industries, women are concentrated disproportionately in low-skill grades, mainly clerical and sales. This is partly due to old structures of **prejudice** and **discrimination**, which inhibit women's progress and **career** opportunities. More subtly, gender **stereotypes** presenting men as rational, tough, aggressive and task-oriented and women as emotional, soft, caring and process-oriented have further disadvantaged women. Women's skills, notably in clerical, sales and service jobs, are often taken for granted (Crompton and Jones, 1984) and lead to neither material nor **symbolic** rewards. Nevertheless, it is becoming increasingly accepted that **femininity** offers organizations a powerful though subtle mechanism of **control**;

organizations like supermarkets, airlines, restaurants, media groups and banks find it desirable to maintain a low-level sexual 'simmer', the key to which is femininity, to promote their sales, enhance their image and lure customers.

Tancred-Sheriff (1989), Crompton and Jones (1984), Oakley (1972)

goals

Most authors include 'goals' as a defining feature of **organization**. At first, this appears unproblematic; the goal of a university is to educate people, of a hospital to treat people, of a firm to make profit. On a closer look, however, it seems that the goals of an organization will differ in the view of different organization members. A lecturer may place 'research' above 'teaching' in his/her list of goals for a university, an administrator the balancing of the books, and so on. Thus, the goals of an organization appear different from different angles. Moreover, even specific goals, like 'educating students', may **mean** different things to different people. Traditional theory, following Max Weber (1864–1920), saw organizations essentially as *tools* for the achievement of more or less fixed goals in a rational, business-like manner. Michels (1876–1936), however, pointed out in his Iron Law of **Oligarchy** that goals are constantly displaced in accordance with changes in the organization's **environment**, to ensure organizational survival. A political party dedicated to a particular cause will change its objectives, if they turn out to be unrealistic or unpopular. Much current management theory has sought to re-emphasize the concept of goals by subsuming it under concepts like mission or vision, which are forged by the **leaders** and espoused by all organizational members.

Weber (1948), Michels (1949)

gossip

The act of sharing stories with other people. Gossip is traded in most organizations; people exchange stories, usually with others who have stories to trade. Gossiping may be done for pleasure or profit. Some managers will go out of their way to be in the right place to gossip with other people, believing this to be one of the most reliable ways of gaining **information** about what is going on in their organization. The problem is that there is very little quality control on gossip. The way it is passed on means that there is no chance for the person being gossiped about to challenge the truth of the things being said about them. It is relatively easy to set a rumour going, and once you have heard a rumour, even if you do not believe it, the suspicion lingers. People will make some allowance for the source of gossip, but by the time it has been through several hands, and each person has reframed it a little to fit their interests, it may have little relationship to any physical event.

Gossip can sometimes be a virtuoso activity, for the sheer joy of spinning a good story, or to see what you can get away with. There is a related body of research, summarized by Rosnow, on rumours in organizations.

Rosnow (1980)

group

Much work is undertaken by groups in some form or another. These may be formal, such as committees, project groups, or teams; or informal, 'unofficial' relationships and cliques which influence the pace, quality and output of work. The study of formal groups has focused on the way different sizes, **structures** and compositions of groups affect productivity and satisfaction, and the kind of **roles** that people play. The dominant research in groups had been in the area of 'group dynamics' – why and how groups form and change over time. The now classic 1930s study of workers at the Hawthorne Electric Plant in the USA first revealed that it was the groups' informal allegiances, **norms**, and pressures to **conform** that could far outweigh managerial attempts to manipulate productivity. One more-recent application of this type of thinking can be seen in Volvo's attempt to replace the long car production line with autonomous working groups of assemblers. Informal groupings often emerge as a way of meeting social, emotional and security **needs** which cannot be addressed in the formal organization. Groups can be highly cohesive, to the extent that they will resist changes which disturb their pattern of relationships. Likewise, they can freeze out or eject members who break the informal codes of practice – such as on levels of productivity or time-keeping. Groups will often go through discernible stages of development, from an early 'sounding out' of members, through to a surfacing of differences and personal agendas (hidden desires, anxieties or aspirations), to ultimate consolidation or collapse. When groups are able to creatively combine the strengths of their members, 'synergy' is said to occur: the total product is greater than the sum of the individual efforts of the members of the group. On the other hand, groups can become trapped in their own cohesiveness. Studies of major decision-making teams have revealed the tendency to 'groupthink', where individuals feel invulnerable, fast dismiss opposing ideas, and take wild risks. Groupthink can be seductive – and dangerous – and has been thought to be behind some of the biggest mistakes in decision making at national and international levels – such as Britain's do-nothing policy towards Hitler prior to the Second World War, and the unpreparedness of US forces at Pearl Harbor. Janis has described groupthink as 'deterioration of mental efficiency, reality testing and moral judgment that results from in-group pressures' (1972:9). Typically, people who try to resist the group are **stereotyped** as weak, stupid – even evil.

Douglas (1983), Janis (1972), Luthans (1985), Smith (1991)

group cohesion *See* **group**.

groupthink *See* **group**.

harassment *See* **sexual harassment**.

hierarchy

A feature of organizational **structure**, usually referring to a **system** of **control**, in which higher offices control the lower ones. Weberian **bureaucracy** forms a strict hierarchy of control, essentially like a military command structure, with no horizontal lines of **communication** across levels. While most organizations have hierarchies, they deviate considerably from Weber's model by incorporating horizontal lines of communication and appointing collegiate bodies, task forces or committees which cut across the hierarchy. Organic organizations (see **environment** and **contingency theories**) permit individuals to communicate across levels of the hierarchy with scant regard for ceremonial. Classical **management** theory envisaged each officer as capable of controlling no more than about ten subordinates. The result was that large organizations tended to have numerous levels, and their structure was tall and thin. The fashion now, following Japanese practices, is to move towards short and flat hierarchies eliminating most middle levels of management.

homosexuality

A sexual orientation towards members of the same **sex**. While seen as a sin, a crime or a disease by some **cultures**, it has been condoned or even encouraged by others (like the ancient Greeks). Homosexuality is normal and natural among both men and women and has been studied in numerous different cultures and societies, where it often merges with heterosexuality in a bisexual orientation. Psychologically, there is evidence of homosexual **desires** even among heterosexuals, even though such desires may remain repressed or may be sublimated in feelings of camaraderie and friendship. In spite of the decriminalization of homosexuality in the US and Britain, homosexuality is viewed with hostility by some, whose sexual **norms** it undermines. Within organizations, many gays and lesbians prefer to conceal their **sexuality** rather than face the intolerance and bigotry of their superiors and peers. Gay and lesbian liberation movements are fighting to eliminate **prejudice** and **discrimination** and to ensure that people's opportunities and freedom are not restricted by their sexual orientation.

Hearn and Parkin (1987), Hearn, Sheppard, Tancred-Sheriff and Burrell (1989)

Human Relations

One of the early influential **management** theories. Human Relations emerged in response to **Scientific Management** in the 1920s and emphasized the importance of the social and **group** factors in explaining **motivation**. Elton Mayo (1880–1949), widely regarded as the father of this approach, argued that through work people try to fulfil social needs. They generally work harder when they feel part of cohesive groups, rather than in response to financial incentives and **extrinsic rewards**. Each individual's output is tied to a group **norm** to which people tend to conform. While the Human Relations approach dominated business schools and management theory for over 60 years, its impact on industry is arguably smaller than that of **Taylorism** and **Fordism**. As a generalization, it might be said that many managers preached Human Relations and practised **Scientific Management**.

See also **group**, **norm**.

human resources

A disturbingly distant phrase for 'people'. It is not necessarily innocent jargon: it may be that you can treat 'human resources' differently from the way you treat 'people'. If you talk about your requirement for human resources, it sounds as if a **rational** economic decision is being made, without moral or personal overtones. It may be easier for a manager to release human resources than it is to sack people. If you are the human resource in question, you will not be able to detect the difference. Human Resource Management (or HRM) is the phrase which turns this dehumanizing language into an academic subject, covering the areas previously known as personnel management and industrial relations.

humanistic perspective

A view in the behavioural sciences which says that humans are, or at least may be, different in kind from other creatures and objects, and need to be studied in a way which recognizes this. It grew out of the philosophical tradition of humanism which approached humans as free agents, capable of improving their lot through education and enlightenment. This perspective may be contrasted with the logical positivist view of Ayer (1910–89), and the behaviourist approach of Skinner (1904–90). In Skinner's work, experiments were done to find what responses can be associated with what stimuli, taking the human being from whom the response comes as a 'black box'; the behaviourists do not deny that something interesting is going on in the black box, but they say that it is in principle impossible to study it, because it cannot be seen. If you restrict yourself to what can be seen, you can be more sure that what you are studying is really happening, they argue. The humanist argument has been put by Harré and Secord, among others, when they propose an anthropomorphic model of man. By this they mean that we should study human beings as we actually know them to be, and not pretend that we know nothing of what goes on in the mind of a human. It is not appropriate to study our **actions** in the same way we study the behaviour of electrons. Humanist social researchers would argue that we should not be restricted in our studies by scientific method as it applies to the natural sciences; instead, we should adapt our methods to the matter being studied. Among the distinctly human qualities that may be worth studying is **meaning**; without a consideration of meaning, and the extent to which it is produced by individual interpretation, much of what we know about organizing would be lost. This book is an example of the humanist perspective.

Skinner (1966), Harré and Secord (1972)

identity

How a person sees him/herself. If the fact that I go wind-surfing is very important to my view of what it means to be me, then we say that it is part of my identity. It is possible, but not easy, for people to change their views of themselves. On the whole, people respond quite differently to criticism when the matter in question is part of their identity. If you mock all wind-surfers, and wind-surfing is one of my hobbies, I may not mind. But if that hobby is part of my identity I may feel personally attacked, and wish to defend myself. Identity is often connected with job position. If you ask people what they do, the answer will reveal something about where their identity lies; they may answer in terms of a profession ('I am a doctor'), an organization ('I work for IBM'), a rank ('I am a Lieutenant-Colonel'), or an activity ('I act as a sounding board for people'). Hewitt has pointed out some of the confusions surrounding identity. He distinguishes between (a) identity, a person's sense of their place relative to others; (b) social identity, which is the others' cumulative sense of that person's place; (c) situated identity, the sense of who the person is in a particular situation; and (d) situated social identity, which is the others' view of who the person is in that particular situation.

See also **alienation**.

Hewitt (1984)

impersonality

A dominant feature of modern **bureaucracies**, in which many transactions and relations are stripped of their human interpersonal content and reduced to their formal dimension. Contrast the impersonal procedure of being selected for a course in higher education on the basis of your application form by people who have never met you, with the complex interpersonal relations with your friends and relatives. Arguably, impersonality confers some advantages to organizations. It limits the time spent on irrelevant chatter, it reduces arbitrariness and inconsistency and it goes some way to ensuring equal treatment. If everyone is treated as a number, everyone will be treated equally. Being treated like a number, however, is not something that most people appreciate. Impersonality is often seen as one of the main factors contributing to **alienation, meaninglessness** and **anomie**. Within modern organizations, lamented Max Weber, 'the performance of each individual is mathematically measured, each man becomes a little cog in the machine and, aware of this, his one preoccupation is whether he can become a bigger cog' (quoted in Mayer, 1956:126–7).

Mayer (1956)

implicit personality theory

An implicit personality theory refers to the beliefs that each of us holds about the personal qualities that 'go together' when we make a judgement about another person. For example, if we see a person as aggressive we may also expect that person to be energetic, or loud; an honest person might also be expected to be kind and considerate. An experiment conducted by Kelley back in 1950 illustrates the point. He gave students brief written descriptions of a new guest lecturer shortly before the man performed. The description was the same for all students, except for one item – which portrayed the man as 'rather cold' for half the students, and 'very warm' for the other half. After the lecture the 'warm' group rated the lecturer as significantly more considerate, informed, sociable and popular than the 'cold' group. In other words these qualities were seen to go with a warm, not a cold, person. We call on our implicit personality theories to make our social judgements. They may not be accurate in an objective sense, but they are convenient and economical.

Kelley (1950), Deaux and Wrightsman (1984)

impression formation

We form our impressions of other people by using the cues available, such as dress, voice, gait, accent, setting. We then fit them together with our 'assumptive framework': what we *expect* people to be who dress like . . ., talk like . . ., are in places like . . ., to be and do. Our **implicit personality theories** are important in this process, as are our **prejudices** and **stereotypes**. Generally, these all serve to help make complex judgements manageable, regardless of their accuracy. The signs and **symbols** which facilitate impression formation are amenable to manipulation, to the extent that 'impression management' has become an academic field of interest in its own right. Like professional actors we learn what 'mask' to wear for what occasion, our aim being to create the socially desired impression. So we 'need' to look jolly at parties, and 'should' look authoritative at meetings. Impression management is exploited for commercial purposes – such as the training of sales staff, waiters, receptionists and flight attendants to appear neat, bright and positive. Some executives, like professional politicians, are coached on how to look and sound right in front of an audience or camera. Also job applicants can receive detailed instruction on how to sharpen their self-presentation skills in order to impress an interviewer.

See also **interview**.

Giacalone and Rosenfeld (1991)

impression management *See* **impression formation**.

influence

A concept related to **power**, with the proviso that while you wish to see matters move in a certain direction you may not wish to be seen as the cause of the movement. Influence is more subtle or discreet than power, relying more on persuasion or manipulation than on force or the threat of **sanctions**. Influencing **skills** have long been seen as a legitimate aspect of individual development, involving psychological skills, use of **rhetoric** and argument. There is also a difference in the time-scale. Power is usually related to a particular instance, where influence may refer to a long-term relationship. To say that 'Jenny has considerable influence with Nigel' is not specific to a situation, whereas to say that one person has power over another immediately raises questions of where, and for how long, and of what may happen if or when the tables are turned.

informal networks

Informal networks refer to the personal connexions and **communications** instigated by people within and between organizations, and maintained to serve their interests. Informal networks reflect the need for **action** or **influence** that formal channels impede or inhibit. They are based on personal friendships, family associations, or ties from shared professional, club, sect or religious interests. Studies of informal networks reveal that they can be a significant, often invisible, force influencing how resources are allocated in an organization, how staff appointments are made, and how certain jobs are done. The informal network can act well as an antidote to inflexible **bureaucracy**; on the other hand, it can reinforce power elites and **oligarchies**.

See also **group, politics**.

Tichy and Fombrun (1979)

informal organization *See* **informal networks, group**.

information

This has developed a meaning distinct from data. Information is what you know, including the interpretation you put on it. When you are driving, you pass a large number of objects, usually at high speed. Any of those objects might be taken as data on what is going on around you. You manage to pay no attention to most of them, and to focus only on the objects from which you want information, for example, traffic lights, road signs, brake lights, police cars and so on. This is information, and is selected from a large pool of possible data. There are always far more data available than can be used. It is often argued that managers suffer not from lack of data, but from chronic overload. **Decisions** which are regretted later arise more often from not **knowing** what to do with the information available than from lack of information. Being well-informed may be more a matter of having good strategies for dealing with information than of having most information. You can tell something of your own information-handling strategy from the way you read a newspaper; if you are reading everything, straight through, you are probably ploughing through data rather than absorbing information. There is research which stems from Leavitt on the effect of different **communication** networks on the transmission of information.

See also **knowing**.

Leavitt (1951)

information technology

This phrase is often used to refer to recent electronic advances in handling information, but may also be seen more widely. Computers are an important part of information technology. So too are electronic diaries, manual card indexes, typewriters, telephones and even paper and pens. In fact, all technologies concerned with storing, processing, retrieving and communicating information can be seen as information technologies. Yet, the phrase 'IT' has now come to denote exclusively electronic types of information technology. The emphasis on savings and **rationalization** accomplished through the use of IT has tended to obscure some of its effects on styles and quality of **work**. Weick has identified five types of deficiency resulting from working with computerized information systems: action deficiencies, because you get less feedback (sounds, smells etc.) from an information system than you do from, say, the factory that it is informing you about; comparison deficiencies, because you cannot walk round and look at it from the other side, as you would with a physical object; affiliation deficiencies, because you are less likely to form your opinions by talking through the output from an information system with others; deliberation deficiencies, as you struggle to see the wood for the trees (a particularly appropriate metaphor when thinking about the piles of print-out that can come from a computer); and consolidation deficiencies, as you may assume that the hard work of thinking through the conclusions has already been done (because it all looks so final when it comes from the computer).

Weick (1985)

institution

A set of practices, a **system** of relations or an **organization** which is infused with **value** and recognized as part of the way of doing things. The monarchy in Britain, a regular television soap opera, the Superbowl, Harvard University, Rolls-Royce and marriage are all institutions. Institutions sometimes acquire venerability with time as they become invested with special **meaning** and as they prove their staying power by becoming traditions. In *Leadership and Administration*, Philip Selznik argued that the task of **leader** is to infuse **organizations** with **meaning**, thus turning inert **bureaucracies** into institutions. Institutions have a sense of permanence, consistency and clear **rules**, and are objectified. Selznik's argument has re-surfaced in recent literature of **corporate culture**, in which a primary function of leaders is the **management** of an organization's **values** and **meanings**. In industrial relations, **collective bargaining** is seen as an institution, that is, not just a set of practices and procedures, but the right, sensible and decent way of dealing with **conflicts** of interest between employers and employees. It is for this reason that collective bargaining is said to have institutionalized industrial conflict, by preventing it from assuming violent uncontrolled proportions, with outcomes unlikely to please all parties.

Selznik (1957), Peters and Waterman (1982), Hyman (1989)

institutionalization

The process of (a) becoming dependent on an institution (in the case of patients, for instance), (b) becoming contained by an institution (say, political or industrial **conflict**), and (c) turning into an institution (such as, eating turkey at Christmas). The second and third meanings of the term are explained under **institution**, so we restrict our comments here to the first. People who have worked or lived in an organization for a long time may find life outside frightening and confusing. This is a well-documented effect for people who have spent a long time in 'total institutions', like prisons, secure psychiatric hospitals, ships or military organizations. Such organizations control large areas of the lives of their members or inmates, eliminating choices about what time to get up in the morning, what to wear, where to go and so on. Life outside gradually becomes difficult to imagine and the person becomes unable to function independently. Similar processes occur among long-serving employees of some organizations, for whom working for another company becomes unimaginable. Such employees may find the transition to retirement especially taxing.

Goffman (1961)

instrumental orientation *See* **extrinsic rewards**.

intelligence

Intelligence is a controversial concept with definitions varying from 'whatever an intelligence test measures', to a 'profile of a range of mental abilities'. The latter includes deductive reasoning, memory, number facility, and verbal comprehension. Measured intelligence is often expressed as a numerical score, an 'intelligence quotient' (IQ) in relation to the population group to which the person belongs, such as men, women, adults, children, adolescents. Some psychologists argue that intelligence is so important that, if we measure it early enough in a child's school career, his or her educational achievement can be predicted and planned. Others see intelligence as susceptible to many of life's influences and hard to measure fairly given people's differences in culture and socio-economic background. In response, so-called 'culture fair' paper-and-pencil tests have been devised which rely less, or not at all, on conventional language facility. These, however, often fail to account for people who have a strong practical intelligence – they show their ability through doing things. An argument has raged for years as to what proportion of measured intelligence is due to social environmental (nurture) factors, and what proportion we are born with (nature). On balance, one can conclude that both play a part, but often a stimulating learning environment will significantly boost intelligence scores.

Vernon (1979)

interpersonal attraction

The topics of sexual attraction and love have probably been treated as effectively and convincingly in novels and plays as in formal research studies. The mechanical view of attraction found in some cheap romantic fiction ('Darling – this thing is bigger than both of us – we have to give in to it . . .') is unconvincing to most of us, whereas the more complicated accounts of attraction produced by great novelists and dramatists have been tested out by readers over time, and are probably more thoroughly tested than most theories. Going more widely into attraction, Kleinke has reviewed the studies of who attracts whom. Landfield has shown that pairs with similar **cognitive** styles (as measured by their **Repertory Grids**) are more likely to work well together, but are less likely to produce creative ideas. It may be that attraction and revulsion are related, and that the opposite of them both is indifference. People often find themselves moving from attraction to revulsion or vice versa in their feelings towards another, but indifference seems to be more stable.

Kleinke (1986), Landfield (1971), Duck (1982)

interpersonal skills

Interpersonal skills refer to the particular **competencies** we have in relating to one another, face-to-face. Just as someone might be skilled at painting, lathe-turning, brick laying or word processing, so we may be skilled in the way we socially interact. Typical interpersonal skills include listening, communicating, diagnosing, negotiating, talking and assertiveness. We can become more proficient in these skills with training and practice. Consequently, there are training programmes available (within and outside companies) where interpersonal skills can be learned. In some occupations, such as medicine, lecturing, dentistry, social work and hairdressing, interpersonal skills are intrinsic to effective performance. Ironically, though, many of these occupations do not offer interpersonal skills **training** for new recruits.

Chung and Megginson (1981)

interview

Interviews have become virtually taken for granted by employers and job candidates. They are seen to be an important way of evaluating a person's character and **competence**. Nevertheless, studies frequently show interviews to be questionable in their reliability and validity. In other words, the judgements made are often inconsistent and they poorly predict later performance on the job. The 'halo' effect is a common problem, where one quality or trait of the candidate swamps the interviewer's judgement – such as perceived attractiveness, the type of school attended, **race, ethnicity**, or age. Research indicates that many decisions are made within the first few minutes of an interview, and the interviewer often spends the remaining period seeking evidence to support that judgement. Well-prepared and skilled interviewers are able to reduce some of these difficulties. This involves a careful study of the job in question and its personal requirements, and a thorough familiarization with pre-interview material — application forms, references, psychological tests. Additionally, the interviewer will need to agree with any co-interviewers the structure of the interview, the roles to be played, and how it stands in relation to any other selection methods being used.

See also **impression formation**.

Lewis (1985)

intrinsic orientation See **extrinsic rewards**.

job satisfaction

Early theories of **management** and administration focused on ways of enhancing worker productivity, and assumed the main incentive to work was money. This assumption was challenged by series of studies from the 1930s onwards which indicated that many people will seek job satisfaction by meeting social and emotional needs at work, as well as financial ones. Influential **motivational** theorists, such as Abraham Maslow, Douglas McGregor, Frederick Herzberg and David McClelland supported this line of thought, coalescing in the 1950s and 1960s into a **Human Relations** perspective in organizational behaviour. This explored various ways in which job satisfaction can be achieved, and how opportunities for achievement, self-actualization (realizing one's potential) and control can be designed into a job. In the 1970s job satisfaction ideas were expanded in a wider Quality of Working Life movement which placed a strong accent on the importance of worker **participation** in the decisions which affect their lives. Elements of this thinking have become standard practice in 1990s **Human Resource** Management.

See also **informal networks, group, motivation**.

Steers and Porter (1975), Hellriegel, Slocum and Woodman (1992)

jokes

Like myths, stories and rituals, jokes are ingredients of organizational **culture**; they offer insights into the feelings and **desires** of organizational members. Freud argued that jokes offer a partial amnesty, allowing repressed **desire** to surface and taboo ideas to be expressed. More recently, it has been argued that jokes provide a symbolic route of escape out of the iron cage of **bureaucracy**, enabling the individual to poke fun at a system which is **impersonal** and inhuman.

Freud (1905), Davies (1988), Gabriel (1991)

knowing

A word with a considerable range of connected meanings. They range from the completely relational ('Adam knew Eve his wife') to the completely propositional ('I know the periodic table'). In between are innumerable shades of knowing, with different degrees of relationship between the knower and the known. School science training tends to emphasize the separation of the knower and the known, in the interests of **objectivity**. This means that what is known about, the object, is treated as separate from the subject, the one who knows. This is commonly regarded as a worthy goal in the interests of finding the unbiased 'truth' of the matter. However, at higher levels in the physical sciences, scientists' accounts suggest much more involvement between themselves and the objects of their knowledge. In studying people and organizations there is always likely to be some kind of relationship between the knower and the known. Indeed many writers argue that such a relationship is desirable. It enables us to use our insight into other people, something that we are all practised at using. To pretend that in the interest of objectivity we can look at our fellow human beings or our organizations as if they were electrons, without forming a relationship with them, may lead us to throw away the best-quality knowledge available to us.

See also **cognitive**.

Reason (1988)

labour

The ability of human beings to use their creative capacities in moulding nature to their **needs**. Marx argued that labour is what makes humans distinctly human, and that through labour intellectual, spiritual and technical capacities develop. Capitalist production impoverishes labour, **alienating** men and women from their products, from their creative activities, and from their fellow humans. Instead of marking the proud and joyful deployment of people's creative powers, labour comes to be equated with oppression, exploitation and dehumanization. In such labour, people become like animals, and only in leisure can they obtain a taste of freedom and fulfilment. Marx's uncompromising equation of labour with what makes people distinctly human has been criticized, or at least complemented by other uniquely human qualities, notably **symbolic** communication and **desire**. Nevertheless, Marx's contention that the organization of labour in a society has profound repercussions on the society's cultural, religious, legal and family **institutions** has found substantial support in the work of anthropologists.

See also **work**, **work ethic**.

language

'The limits of my language are the limits of my world.' Managers spend most of their time on **talk** and **discourse**, much of it in **metaphor**. As their activity is mediated by language, they need to be good at it. For visionary or charismatic leaders, language is crucial in conveying images. The images of an 'Iron Curtain' and a 'Cold War' were central in post-World War II politics. Studying the language people use in an organization can help us understand many of its processes. Types of address (first names, surnames, titles), jargon and so on can tell much about an organization's **culture** and **hierarchy**. For example, if you want to look at the style in which things are done, look at the adverbs used to talk about it: 'quickly', 'impatiently', 'sensitively' and so on. Language is of special significance in international **communication**. Important nuances may be lost in translation, or even between different versions of the same language. People whose second language is English often find it easier to understand each other, even when speaking English, than to understand Americans or British people. The study of language has assumed extraordinary importance in the human sciences in the 20th century. It is now widely accepted that language is not merely a *means* of expression but a central faculty of the human mind, directly affecting the ways we think and feel.

Beattie (1983)

leadership

Leadership theorizing has been prolific in organizational behaviour writings. Many different approaches have been taken. The most commonsense one has been to seek the personal ingredients for leader success – the **personality** characteristics which mark out leaders from followers, or successful leaders from unsuccessful ones. Despite a multitude of studies, this line of inquiry has been fairly sterile. What we do learn, though, is that 'it all depends'. In some situations some people can be effective leaders, in other situations they are not. But we need to be clear about what we mean by effective. For example, high output may be achieved, but at the cost of much **stress** and depressed morale. Consequently, work has gone into creating '**contingency theories**', mapping out the kind of personal qualities and behaviours which link with particular characteristics of situations to produce different leadership effects. The style of leader behaviour ('people' or 'task' orientation), his or her power, the structure of the task, and the particular needs of the followers, are some of the ingredients that have been put into the contingency equation. Contingency theories can be complex and difficult to translate into practice. Recent attention has moved towards a more subtle understanding of the way that followers and leaders interact, and the role of the leader's face-to-face **interpersonal skills** in moulding and directing that interaction. This can involve the leader using various

symbols – **language**, strong images, **metaphors**, physical settings – to influence the way people see their worlds; the leader 'manages their **meanings**'. Sometimes this activity is aimed at **empowering** people to direct their energy and enthusiasm to organizational **goals**; at other times it may amount to little short of emotional manipulation and devious **influence**.

See also **management, management of meaning**.

Srivastva (1986), Wright and Taylor (1984), Bryman (1986), Warr (1987)

learning

Some people argue that the only way to learn is through experience. Others have noticed that it is possible for people to be in a situation for a long time without seeming to learn very much. Have they had 25 years' experience, or one year's bad experience repeated 25 times? Kelly (1905–66) argued that experience was how much one's **constructs** were changed by the events that happened, and this is one description of learning. Kolb suggests that people leave school with passive models of learning, as symbolized by a classroom or a textbook, where jugs full of knowledge are poured into the mugs who are listening to them, perhaps not the best way of equipping people to meet the continuous learning required throughout life. Kolb proposes that learning in organizations happens as a four-stage cycle: concrete experience (something happens), leading to reflection and observation (thinking about it), leading to abstract conceptualization (coming up with an idea), leading to active experimentation (trying that idea out), leading once more to concrete experience. Different people place different emphases on the four parts of the cycle, and thus have different learning styles. Other views of learning draw from an area of psychology called 'learning theory'. Learning theory focuses on the precise way that observable **behaviour** can change – under what circumstances and to what degree. 'Classical' conditioning is one feature of learning theory, deriving from the early work of the Russian physiologist Pavlov (1849–1936). It refers to unconscious changes in our behaviour, when we automatically associate one thing with something else. A 'stimulus' elicits a 'response'. Pavlov 'conditioned' dogs to salivate at the sound of a bell (associated with seeing and eating food). The closest we get to classical conditioning in organizational life is in the shaping of consumer preferences – such as advertisements which aim to make us (condition us to) choose a particular product because of its association with a sexy image. 'Operant' conditioning, emanating from the work of B.F. Skinner, looks at our conscious learning from doing. It refers to the rewards, or punishments, that we receive when our specific actions lead to specific outcomes. It describes how such associations are strengthened, or 'reinforced', to bring about learnings. Complex schedules of reinforcement (breaks, different types of rewards, different timing of rewards) may be required to master, and sustain effort on, specific tasks.

These principles have been applied to the design of systems of pay, **motivation**, and **training** in industry. Learning theory has also been extended to 'social learning', where people are seen to learn by modelling their behaviour on what they see others do. They watch others, develop a mental picture of the behaviour and its results, and imitate. If it works for them (they achieve positive results), learning occurs. The organizational applications of learning theory are not without controversy. By its very nature, learning theory does not take heed of 'inner' psychological processes, such as people's feelings, desires and personality. Only changes in outward **behaviour** matter. More crucially, some aspects can be criticized as being manipulative – effectively bribing, or forcing, people to do things, where the conditions and controls are in someone else's (usually the managers') hands.

See also **experiential learning**.

Kelly (1972), Kolb, Rubin and McIntyre (1979), Luthans (1985)

learning organization

This is a term applied to organizations which are able regularly and naturally to monitor and reflect on the assumptions by which they operate. They are well 'in touch' with themselves and their working environment, so they are able to adapt and change as a matter of course – rather than traumatically, in a crisis. Typically, most enterprises are not learning organizations. They become defensively locked into beliefs and working patterns that they have operated with for a long time, and are unable to re-constitute them without a great upheaval.

Kanter (1989), Argyris, Putnam and Smith (1985), Torbert (1987)

management

Both a set of functions and activities and the people carrying them out. Management functions are present whenever several people work together. Yet, management as a distinct **group**, separate from the owners of businesses, requiring specialized knowledge and **training**, is a late-19th-century and 20th-century phenomenon. Classical theory of management derives from the work of Henri Fayol (1841–1925) and Frederick Taylor (1856–1915), and approaches management essentially as 'running a business'. This involves functions like (i) co-ordination, (ii) **communication**, (iii) **control**, and (iv) planning, aimed initially at profit-making. By contrast, the term *administration* was used for the Civil Service and state organizations, and while it involved similar functions, its **goals** were not market-driven. Since the 1920s and the work of the **Human Relations** School the human side of management has been highlighted; its preferred definition would be 'getting things done through people' and its main emphasis has been on employee **motivation**. In the 1980s, the **symbolic** function of management has acquired prominence in the literature, with management being seen as 'the ability to define reality for others'. Instead of looking at managers as individuals who can run **organizations** smoothly, the emphasis now is on managers as agents of **change** and renewal. This brings the concept of management very close to that of **leadership**, and a substantial debate is going on as to whether managers and leaders are the same. Henry Mintzberg has criticized many of these approaches, for focusing on what managers *should* be doing rather than on what they actually do. Based on intensive observation of actual managers, he found that much of their work involves **talking** or **communicating** and that it is conducted in short bursts of activity. Handling crises and emergencies takes a substantial part of their time; they have little time for systematic thought or planning and make most **decisions** on the basis of ad hoc information.

Mintzberg (1973)

management of meaning

The notion that **meaning** can be managed presupposes that the social world comprises individuals who strive to make sense, or meaning, out of their interactions and tasks. To some extent our meanings will reflect our own backgrounds and personal desires, so they are partly self-managed. However, they can also be influenced by the actions of those around us, so we can talk about leaders and managers as people who manage other people's meanings. This involves the manipulation of **symbols** which convey a particular message. For example, furniture is arranged informally; the boss's door is left open; staff are trusted to manage their own budgets; secretaries do not intercept telephone calls; maternity and paternity allowances are generous, and so forth. In this way, the leader is signalling how he or she would like people think of the organization (and its leader) – as open, liberal and caring. The way meaning is managed can be political in that it can be manipulated to achieve personal ends – such as power to control others, to capture scarce resources (budgets, equipment) or to gain status.

See also **culture, leadership, meaning**.

Deal and Kennedy (1982), Morgan (1986)

masculinity

A term used to describe equally the principal components of male **sexuality** and the **role** attributes of the male **gender**. The study of masculinity has lagged behind that of **femininity**, the **assumptions** being (a) that everyone knows what 'real men' are like, (b) there is no problem about men being 'real men'. Many **stereotypes** of masculine **behaviour** are currently being questioned, leading to an increase in interest in masculinity, notably in the United States. Books like Robert Bly's *Iron John: A Book about Men* and Sam Keen's *Fire in the Belly: On Being a Man* have argued that the attainment of real manhood is problematic for men, as are **stereotypes** of macho masculinity. Such books have sought to promote a new vision of masculinity at once caring and heroic, founded not on hate or contempt for women but on strong male bonding and a reappraisal of the relation between fathers and sons. Masculinity has generally been seen as unproblematic in **organizations**; those stereotypical traits associated with the male **gender**, **rationality**, assertiveness, **competitiveness** and so on have been seen as serving organizations very well. The new debate on masculinity, however, with its emphasis on a different set of male **values**, **desires** and **needs**, threatens to undermine the earlier cosy co-existence. Organizations, it is now argued, place almost as formidable constraints on masculinity as they do on **femininity**.

Bly (1990), Keen (1992)

matrix structure

Traditional organizations have divisional or functional **structures**, typically shaped like a pyramid. They have a command structure which is narrow at the top, where the chief sits, and wide at the base where the lower management and workers can be found. There is unity of command, like a military unit. A matrix organization breaks down the single command structure, and is shaped more like a flat rectangle with operating 'cells' of expertise (managers and workers) which come together in different ways at different times. The matrix organization has a dual **authority** system, and is suited to organizations that change projects or products fast, in several functional areas at once – such as in manufacturing, marketing, engineering and finance. Each of the specialist functions serves a separate project or product, which has its own manager and team. The project/product units share the specialized functional resources with other units, so preventing duplication of these resources. Matrix structures can be extremely flexible, unlike the traditional **hierarchy**. But they have their drawbacks. Without unity of command everyone has two bosses, a functional manager and a project manager, so there is potential for **conflict**, confusion in loyalties.

Hellriegel, Slocum and Woodman (1992), Mintzberg (1983)

meaning

Human beings can be seen as 'meaning-seeking' animals; words have meanings, as do stories and myths. Meaning is what one seeks to convey through the use of **language** or other forms of **communication**, like gestures and expressions. In this sense, meaning is the ultimate object of human **communication**. However, humans seek to discover meaning even in phenomena where no other human being is explicitly trying to communicate anything; since time immemorial, people have looked for the meaning of dreams, of solar eclipses, of the death of their loved ones, of the position of the stars and planets at the time of their birth, or even, as Aristotle remarked, the accidental collapse of a statue. In some of these instances, people are looking for a meaning which they think a super-human being is trying to convey to them. Meaning is linked to **symbolism**, since meaning is what the symbol stands for. Discovering the meaning of anything, like a joke, a poem or an action, requires a process of *interpretation*. Sociologists, especially those known as symbolic interactionists, argue that meaning is the product of human interaction, with people trading interpretations and inferring contrasting meanings. Depth psychologists on the other hand emphasize that the meanings of mental phenomena, like dreams, accidents, obsessive acts, slips of tongue or pen (the famous 'Freudian slips') and so on are linked to repressed **desires**. Existential psychologists argue that men and women strive to create meaning through decisive acts of will, because without them life is unbearable. These views are not incompatible but illustrate some of the diversity of **discourses** surrounding the concept. As far as work is concerned, all three approaches have a significant contribution to make. Sociologists have argued that the meaning of work differs across different cultures, each of which has a distinct **work ethic**. Depth psychology emphasizes that many incidents of organizational life are invested with meanings which derive from unconscious desires and wishes. Existential psychology stresses that meaningless work is unbearable work, and engages in a critique of production techniques, like **Taylorism**, which deny work its meaning and purpose.

Becker (1962), Blauner (1964), Schwartz (1987)

meaninglessness

Meaninglessness is often seen as a malaise or a disease of our civilization. Trapped in Weber's 'iron cage of **bureaucracy**' and reduced to a cog by **deskilling technologies**, the individual experiences feelings of emptiness, hollowness and purposelessness. Work, instead of adding meaning to most people's lives becomes an endurance course (see **survival**), adding little to people's sense of **identity** and self. Blauner argued that meaninglessness is one of the four dimensions of **alienation**, brought about by mass production techniques, which contrasts with the pride and self-esteem experienced by craft workers, whose work is a source of meaning in their lives. Other social trends which have been linked to meaninglessness are the decline of religion, the growing cynicism with politics and politicians and the rampant growth of consumerism. This last links **meaning** to the ownership of commodities, like cars, clothes and so on but ultimately enhances meaninglessness. As soon as the **desired** item has been purchased its magic and its mystique disappear, and the desire for a new commodity has taken its place.

Blauner (1964)

mentor

New members of organizations often find themselves 'adopted' by existing members who become their mentors. More generally, weaker members rely on their mentors for counselling, help, protection and career development. The relationship between mentors and their protégés has a political dimension, as an alliance. It may also have a psychological dimension, the mentor adopting a fatherly or motherly **role** and expecting in return total loyalty and devotion. Kanter has noted that one of the barriers to women's careers is their difficulties in establishing mentor relationships with men without fuelling sexual innuendo and gossip.

Morgan (1986), Kanter (1977)

metaphors

People talk in metaphors continually, and we also do much of our thinking in metaphors. These metaphors affect the actions that are taken. For example, if people use military metaphors (we won the battle but we still have to win the war) in their organizational conversation, they are likely to behave in a military way (possibly permitting no surrender, and taking no prisoners). Such metaphors mean that approaches which could lead to good outcomes for both parties are not likely to be explored. When we use metaphors, we are mapping one area of life on to another, and 'the map is not the territory'. But maps do have a way of becoming the territory, and people get carried away by their own metaphors. When someone is trying to bring about change in the organization they may try to do this by working on the metaphors that are in use. If people start talking of buddy groups instead of chiefs and indians, their behaviour may start to change accordingly.

Morgan (1986)

mid-career crisis

The sense of shifting aspirations and unfulfilled expectations that many people report in the middle years of their career. Some writers argue that the crisis is a part of a wider life shift where increasing age and family commitments combine with existential questions of the sort: 'Where am I *really* going; what should I do next with my life'? The response from those who experience a mid-career crisis varies. Some will embark on a dramatic change of direction 'before it's too late' – such as a new job, a complete switch in career, or back to full-time education. Others will try to re-model what they already have – at home and/or at work – so that the coming years offer new stimulation. Still others will consider themselves too entrenched in the organization to risk a move. The security benefits of some career posts can act as a strong disincentive to change (see **institutionalization**) – when change would probably ultimately benefit both the organization and the individual.

See also **career, burnout**.

Cooper and Torrington (1981), Levinson (1979)

motivation

Motivation refers to forces acting on or within an individual which initiate and direct behaviour. Motivational theories attempt to explain the source, strength and form of those forces. There are different types of theory. For example, need–deficiency theories examine the effects of unmet 'needs'. Just as hunger will direct our behaviour towards seeking food, so will our psychological hungers require satisfying, such as for self-esteem, security and achievement. An influential, and controversial, theory by Maslow (1943) suggests that our needs are arranged in a hierarchy, starting with basic physical ones, progressing through safety and social needs, ego needs, to peak with the need to fulfil oneself – 'self-actualization'. Maslow argues that one need-level has to be relatively satisfied before we are able move on to the next. Other need theorists, such as McClelland (1961), have focused on specific needs which seem particularly relevant to business activity, such as achievement, affiliation and power. Another form of theory is represented by the work of Herzberg et al. (1959). Herzberg examined the content of jobs that motivate people. His research suggests that people will receive positive *satisfaction* from certain factors intrinsic to the job, such as its scope for achievement, recognition and responsibility. Extrinsic factors, though, such as pay and working conditions, simply staved off *dissatisfaction*. Some motivational theories attempt systematically to model, and measure, the specific attractiveness or otherwise of a particular **action**, and predict the motivational effort that will ensue. These have been termed *expectancy theories*. They are a close relation to *equity theories*, which examine the importance for motivation of how fairly people feel they are being treated and rewarded, compared with others. Finally, there are motivational theories which look deeply into inner psychological processes. These *psycho-dynamic* approaches, many rooted in the work of Freud (1856–1939), show how our particular **desires**, conflicts, anxieties and aspirations result from our relationship with family members, and our adjustment to stages of development from childhood to adult. The sources of our motivation will often be unconscious, but will still significantly influence our work conduct and preferences.

Maslow (1943), McClelland (1961), Herzberg, Mausner and Snyderman (1959), Steers and Porter (1987), Luthans (1985)

myth

This term is commonly used predominantly to signify 'popular untruths', as in 'Ten myths about slimming'. As an ingredient of organizational **culture**, myths are usually based on embellished accounts of events in an organization's history, such as the overcoming of obstacles, major crises or disasters and embarrassing or amusing incidents. Myths have **meanings**; if different people all read the same meaning in a particular myth, it can have a galvanizing effect on morale and strengthen **group** cohesion. Often, however, people may read very different meanings into the same stories. While myths are not necessarily accurate narratives of events, their grip over individuals stems from the powerful **needs** which they fulfil. For this reason, the preferred types of myths within an organization reveal some of the underlying emotional factors. In some cases, myths degenerate into self-deceptions by clouding judgement and thought, leading to delusions of invulnerability and grandeur: 'groupthink' (see **group**). Some organizations have failed because of the inability of their members to detach themselves from such myths. Schwartz, for example, has argued that some major failures, such as the disaster of the American space shuttle Challenger (1986), occur when mythologies and **fantasies** get in the way of technical and scientific calculations.

Schwartz (1988), Gabriel (1991)

needs *See* motivation, desire.

networks *See* informal networks, communication.

non-verbal communication

This book is a verbal communication. We have little control over its lay-out, or the circumstances in which you read it, or the picture that you have of us. In conversation the communication is usually multichannelled; the verbal and the non-verbal go together. There is strong evidence that the non-verbal is very important. When people first meet, they focus on the non-verbal almost to the exclusion of the verbal. Non-verbal communication includes body language, but also includes intonation, clothes, the way you arrange your office and so on. If the non-verbal communication does not seem to fit with the verbal, then this is at least disconcerting. Some people smile when they give you bad news. This is probably embarrassment, but it can lead to distrust, because the non-verbal smile and the verbal news do not seem to fit together. It is often said that it is impossible not to communicate. Sitting silently can often be a powerful non-verbal communication.

Argyle (1975)

norm

Norms are standards of behaviour which result from the close interaction between people, over time. They are social inventions which help the group to control and regulate its activities, and to express its identity and values. In work organizations norms arise as complementary, and/or in opposition, to the company **rules** and regulations. Some norms may be divulged openly to new group members: 'Now you've joined us what you need to do is . . .'. Others will be inferred from the characteristic **behaviour** of established members. In practice, norms can determine dress code, where people sit and eat, time-keeping, productivity levels (maybe different from management expectations), appropriate **language**, and the **sanctions** for those who deviate. In short, norms often influence and control our behaviour in subtle ways by becoming part of us – by being internalized.

See also **group**, **socialization**, **culture**, **informal networks**.

Deaux and Wrightsman (1984)

objectivity

Viewing objects or events without bias, dispassionately. It is possible to come closer to objectivity when considering people and events about which we do not care and in which we have no interest. But even under these circumstances, objectivity is elusive. What people may mean when they say 'objective' is that they have been rigorous and critical in making their subjective judgement; they did not take their first impressions as perfect. It is possible to take steps to check on the quality of our subjective judgements. For example, if you think a particular manager is good, you can check your judgement by discussing it with other people, looking at the financial performance of her department, asking her about what she is doing and so on. But the judgement remains essentially subjective – a well-tested subjective judgement. When a number of people come to a similar judgement, this is sometimes referred to as 'intersubjectivity'. To be objective, one would need to be able to stand outside the situation being considered, neither affecting it nor being affected by it. This is possible in talking about measurable characteristics ('she is 1.75 metres tall'; 'he has hepatitis'), because these qualities are not affected by the judger. My presence, absence or consciousness has no impact on her height or his hepatitis. Such 'standing outside the situation' is not possible when talking about personal **meanings** and social judgements.

oligarchy

The rule of the few over the many. Based on a study of the German Social Democratic Party in the early part of the century, Robert Michels (1876–1936) argued that all organizations are subject to an Iron Law of Oligarchy. Arguing against his mentor, Max Weber, Michels claimed that **organizations** are not **rational** instruments for the accomplishment of administrative goals; instead, he saw political systems through which small elites control the masses. Organizational survival takes precedence over the achievement of any goals, since without it the **power** and privileges of the **leaders** disappear. To this end, **goals** become displaced, **values** and doctrines are constantly compromised and organization becomes an end in itself. Michels argued that leaders have formidable mechanisms for overcoming any internal threats. They **control** information and appointments, they can reward those loyal to them and marginalize those against them. They can divide the opposition or accuse it of 'rocking the boat'. Finally, and most important, they build their strength on the *apathy* of the organizational members, who have not the time, the expertise or the inclination to challenge the leaders' **decisions**. Michels' view approaches organizations as natural **systems** or biological organisms, preoccupied with survival, rather than as rational systems or tools, after the Weberian tradition. He draws attention to the organizational **environment** which was left outside Weber's ideal type **bureaucracy**. His view of bureaucracy has more in common with the common pejorative sense of self-perpetuating and unaccountable official-dom than does Max Weber's view. In spite of its power, Michels' rather cynical view has attracted criticism. Gouldner has argued that there is an Iron Law of Democracy opposing the oligarchic tendencies identified by Michels and uses as examples the numerous cases of tyrants who were eventually overthrown through popular mobilization.

Michels (1949), Gouldner (1961)

organization

A notoriously difficult concept to define precisely. Most formal definitions are unclear as to which human associations should be thought of as organizations (say, large corporations, armies, universities, trade unions) and which should not (say, football crowds, theatre audiences, nuclear families, tribes, gangs). They are in even less agreement on a set of criteria which will sharply distinguish organizations from other things. Instead of proffering yet another definition of organizations, we propose a set of criteria which define the general space occupied by organizations, though not all organizations need fulfil all of these criteria:

1   Organizations are associations of several people, who are aware of being members, and who are generally willing to co-operate.
2   Organizations are mainly long-term, and survive changes of personnel.
3   Organizations profess some objectives which they pursue in a methodical, no-nonsense manner.
4   Organizations involve a certain division of labour, with different people assigned to different tasks. This may amount to a **hierarchy**, a **matrix**, or some other **structure**.
5   Organizations involve a certain degree of formality and **impersonality**.

Strictly, it makes little sense to say that organizations have **goals**, that they **act**, that they **control** individuals' behaviour. Nevertheless, these are convenient ways of describing behaviours and actions of large numbers of people associated with each other, and people talk and behave as if organizations act. In the same way, when we say that the nation elected one particular party in a general election, or (more strangely) that it opted for a hung parliament, we are describing an aggregate outcome of collective **actions** and complex processes. In a strict way, organizations can be thought of as the aggregates of **actions** of numerous individuals. Nevertheless, these actions are not arbitrary; the way people behave in organizations is distinct from the way they behave at home, with friends and so on. So even if, in the last resort, organizations are nothing but people acting, they can be thought of as more than just the sum total of all the people.

participation

A general principle in politics that people should participate in the making of political **decisions** which will affect them, either through an opportunity to openly express their views or through electing representatives to the bodies which make the decisions. Yet, participation in organizations sometimes tends to degenerate into an empty slogan behind which **oligarchy** reigns. Within organizational literature, participation is discussed in connection with **leadership** (seen as a feature of democratic or participatory styles) and decision making. It is often argued that successful implementation of organizational **change** requires the participation of those affected by it in the decision-making process. Various techniques of participation have been tried ranging from consultation, suggestion boxes, quality circles (regular meetings by groups of employees on company time to discuss improvements in working practices and resolve organizational problems), some of which have attracted criticism as attempts to manipulate workers. In Britain workers have been reluctant to participate in **decisions** which can be seen as compromising them or incorporating them in the process of **management**. In Germany, however, since 1952 workers' representatives have participated in the boards of directors in companies above a certain size.

Socialists have frequently scoffed at participation, seeing it as an extension of **management control**, and have advocated instead 'workers' control' – the management of the organization by the workers themselves. Different forms of workers' control have been devised, including elected managers, works councils and workers' cooperatives, the latter emerging in the 19th century, inspired by the ideas of Robert Owen in Britain and Charles Fourier in France. Workers' co-operatives can boast a number of successes, but with some notable exceptions (like the Mondragon co-operatives in Spain) they have not been able to challenge capitalist firms, nor have they matched the success of consumers' or farmers' co-operatives.

perception

Perception refers to the processes by which we create subjective **meaning** from the stimuli received by our senses. Our perceptions are our personal interpretations of the world; the shaping of experiences and events into some coherent whole. Some philosophers and psychologists argue that it is only through perception that we can know anything, so we can never know of an **objective** world beyond our perceptions. The notion of perception in organizational behaviour leads us to anticipate that people's perceived worlds may differ and that difference can explain, at least in part, what they think and do. There are factors which influence the shape and content of perceptions. We often 'see' what we want to see: our needs, **motivations** and **emotions** will, unconsciously, start the perceptual-shaping process. For example we will more readily perceive negative characteristics in people with whom we are in conflict. Or conversely, love is blind to faults. Ideological stance, **stereotypes** and **prejudices** will also play their part. It is often in the interests of trade union members to perceive managers as exploitative of labour; while, in turn, managers may 'want' to perceive their workers as preoccupied with minimizing their efforts and maximizing their pay.

See also **meaning, construct**.

Luthans (1985), Hellriegel, Slocum and Woodman (1992)

performance

An ambiguous word in the literature on organizing. Performance can be used to refer to a fairly mechanistic notion of how well someone is doing, rather like talking about the performance of a car. So in some of the literature on appraisal, you will hear references to gauging a person's performance, and in some companies managers will take on performance targets. Performance is also used in the sense of 'putting on a performance', or acting. There is a 'dramaturgical' way of looking at organizations, which sees them as being stages for a performance (Mangham). This can be traced back through Shakespeare ('all the world's a stage') and beyond. Recent work by Snyder has offered a measure of 'self-monitoring', which is the extent to which people are able to take the stance of an audience watching their own performance. High self-monitors are continuously aware of the performance they are putting on and of the impact it is having on others. Low self-monitors are not aware of performing, tend to come over as more centred and 'all of a piece', and may see high self-monitors as slippery. High self-monitors meanwhile wonder why low self-monitors are not putting more energy into their performance, and may see this as a lack of commitment.

Mangham (1986), Snyder (1987)

performance appraisal

Many organizations use systems of performance appraisal to evaluate their employees' work progress. Performance appraisals are used to make decisions on salary, promotions, retention or termination. They can also provide an opportunity for feedback to an employee to identify strengths, weaknesses and training needs. The format of appraisal can vary from the highly structured, using pencil-and-paper rating scales, to an open-ended counselling session. The effectiveness of performance appraisal depends on how well prepared both parties are, how serious they are about the event (is it 'for real' or an empty ritual), the skills of the appraiser, the reliability and validity of the rating scales, its regularity, and the extent to which decisions or agreements from the appraisal are honoured.

See also **performance**.

Cummings and Schwab (1973), Chung and Megginson (1981)

persona

A persona is the appearance or character an individual presents to an audience. We may adopt a range of personae, according to the different situations we are in. At work we may adopt a 'hard-working, harassed' persona; in the bar we change to appear 'lively and sociable', while at home with our children we are the 'attentive, good parent'. This view leaves us with difficult questions about whether there can be a real self which is more than simply one persona among many.

See also **personality, impression formation**.

Goffman (1959), Argyle (1975)

personality

Personality is a concept which refers to the totality of a person's individuality. Personality theories, of which there are many, attempt to explain how our individuality forms, develops, changes, and is structured. 'Developmental' theories look at the influence of genetically inherited characteristics compared with those which are shaped or created by key learnings, especially in our infancy and childhood. 'Structural' theories aim to locate ways of dividing-up our personality into key ingredients. For example, some believe we are best described as a bundle of traits – such as friendly, warm, cold, secure, insecure, gloomy, bright, and so forth. Others argue that we can reduce the almost endless list of possible traits to a small number of broad factors with which any person can be described and distinguished. These may be 'types' such as extrovert or introvert; neurotic or stable. Sigmund Freud is credited with one of the most influential, and controversial, personality theories, which examines the effects of early psychosexual periods of development on individuality, and how unconscious, primitive 'id' forces will seek expression through the control of 'ego' and 'superego' layers of personality. **Psychological tests** of personality are used in personnel selection and appraisal situations to help match people to jobs, or to spot potential. They form a central element of vocational guidance. They can be easily misinterpreted or misused, therefore their availability is usually restricted to psychologists or other specially trained users.

Hilgard, Atkinson and Atkinson (1980), Deaux and Wrightsman (1984)

politics

In organizations, power and influence are traded in a complex and exciting game known as organizational politics. The members of an organization form alliances, do deals with each other, plot the downfall or the promotion of colleagues, or mobilize coalitions continually. The military and combat-based words used in the last two sentences may suggest that this is an undesirable and destructive activity, but it is just as true to say that it is a universal activity, and most people engage in organizational politics for what they see as the good of the organization. Organizations with strong ethical systems, such as hospitals and churches, are notorious for the robustness of their organizational politics. Bailey says that the more people believe that what they are doing is for the good of others, the dirtier the tricks they are prepared to resort to get their way.

See also **power**, **oligarchy**.

Bailey (1977), Hickson (1990)

post-modernism

A movement in many artistic and intellectual fields, including the study of organizations. Post-modernism is an approach to understanding which goes against the 'modernist' view that the essentials of life can be discovered through reason, careful observation, and the straightforward application of language. Post-modernism takes a view of the world in which there are no absolute standards. Words and their meanings cannot be taken for granted; they are but fleeting realities themselves, not representations of a 'reality'. Style becomes substance, decoration becomes essence. Post-modernism in the arts has often implied a colourful, playful approach which incorporates several different styles at once, without demanding consistency or coherence. In organizing, a post-modern approach would be one that acknowledges several different ways of understanding things without trying to establish one of those as superior to the others, and without expecting to be able to make firm logical links between them. Post-modern theories of organizations emphasize the negotiation of social order and leadership, the symbolism inherent in cultural systems and the irrationality/emotionality of individual and group action. They recognize no objective **structure** underpinning organizations, still less an 'environment' in which organizations operate. Permanence and solidity are only as strong as the **rhetoric**, language and **discourse** which define things as permanent and solid. Such theories of organization focus intensely on organizational 'texts', including conversations, letters, memos, logos and publicity materials, office signs and corporate achitecture.

Cooper and Burrell (1988), Reed and Hughes (1992)

power

'Power is the medium through which conflicts of interest are ultimately resolved. Power influences who gets what, when and how' (Morgan, 1986:158). Early work on organizations took a *unitary* view, which meant that it would be possible to discover common organizational **goals**, and for all members of the organization to work together for those goals. Anything which prevented such a common view should be dealt with, so that unity and organizational health could prevail once again. Within this view, power does not figure very significantly. For many recent thinkers about organizations, however, power is a key concept. They may adopt a *pluralist* perspective, in which there are many different powerful individuals and **groups** in the organization, seeking to achieve their ends through **conflict** and **politics**, drawing on a variety of sources of power as they do so. French and Raven, for example, suggest five types of power depending on their source: *reward* (being able to reward behaviour that you like with promotions, money, praise and so on); *coercive* (being able to punish behaviour that you do not like with reprimands, dismissal, sarcasm or threats); *legitimate* (being seen as having the right to a particular kind of power); *referent* (being liked, and therefore influential); and *expert* (being seen as knowing best). Other thinkers on organizations have adopted a *radical* view. As in the pluralist view, organizations are seen as made up of different groups and individuals with different interests, but without a level playing field. Some groups and individuals are seen as very disadvantaged on the basis of their class, **race** or **gender**, and power is very unequally distributed. Lukes proposed a three-dimensional model of power, associated with the three perspectives. In the first dimension, you have power over someone else if you can force them to do something which they would not otherwise do. In the second dimension, you have power over someone if you can manage the situation so that there is no open discussion of anything which can damage you. For example, in a telephone call with your parents, you may be able to keep the conversation to safe topics! In the third dimension, you have power over someone if you can affect their view of what is in their own interests. Social and organizational factors may mean that some individuals and groups are left without power (see **powerlessness**) but may still be persuaded to work hard for organizations which dominate them through **rhetoric**, **propaganda** or manipulation. Those who take a radical or pluralist view see power in almost everything that goes on in organizations. People in organizations often assume that power lies elsewhere, usually at a more senior level. Some senior managers are surprised, however, to find how constrained their **actions** seem to be. Recently the concept of **empowerment** has come to prominence.

See also **authority, influence, leadership, politics**.

Morgan (1986), Burrell and Morgan (1979), French and Raven (1959), Lukes (1975) Pfeffer (1981)

powerlessness

A condition of lack of **control**. It is widely used to describe individuals' feelings within **organizations** and, coupled with **meaninglessness**, it is generally seen as a dimension of **alienation**. Some of the same factors which account for meaninglessness, such as **Taylorism, deskilling, bureaucracy**, and the vast scale of some organizations, also account for powerlessness. Many lowly-placed members of the organization are seen as unable to control what they do, how fast they work, what they produce or a whole range of decisions which affect their lives. These are made in distant boardrooms, by people they have never met and who may have little regard for their happiness or well-being. Powerlessness may lead to fatalism and resignation which translate into absenteeism from work or poor **performance**; it may, alternatively, lead to organization, trade unionism and resistance. When the collective voicing of discontents is continuously blocked, powerlessness may lead to devious attempts at revenge through **sabotage, fiddles**, rumours and character assassinations.

prejudice

A form of **attitude**, literally a pre-judgement that a person is prepared to make of another. Allport has noted that prejudgement is a normal human response; human **groups** tend to separate from each other, and to look for characteristics of the other group that can be used to justify that separation. Sherif's studies showed that dividing a group of boys arbitrarily into two groups, and giving each group a name, was enough to generate prejudice between them. Studies of neighbours have shown that prejudice is worst when there is proximity without contact. If people of different **races** live in adjoining flats, and the doors to the flats point in opposite directions so that those people do not meet, they are likely to form negative prejudices about each other's race. If the doors are so arranged that they do meet, there is much less prejudice. **Gender**, sexual preference, race, age and class are common areas of prejudice in organizations.

See also **ethnicity, race, sexism, stereotypes, authoritarianism**.

Allport (1958), Sherif (1966)

problems

'What most people spend most of their time talking about in most organizations.' They occur when something is not as someone would like it to be, and the person is not sure what to do about it. They have the twin characteristics of something needing to be done or thought, and a degree of anxiety about whether the person can in fact deal with the problem. Puzzles are related to problems, but they tend to be tidier and with a more clearly defined solution. To set up a spreadsheet in unfamiliar software may be a puzzle, because it may take some time and thought to get it working. However, there is little doubt that it will work, and the person trying to do it will know when they have got it working. Problems are usually less well defined than this. Much time in organizations is spent trying to persuade other people to see problems the same way that you do: 'The real problem is . . .' is one way of introducing such an attempt at influence. The definition of problems in organizations is one of the main topics dealt with in the process of organizational **politics**.

Eden, Jones and Sims (1983), Bryant (1989)

professions

Traditionally, those occupations which, like medicine and law, fulfil a number of criteria, like the following: (i) a systematic body of knowledge and monopoly powers over its applications, (ii) a self-regulating code of ethics, emphasizing **values** such as respect for the confidentiality of the client, (iii) the sanction of the community at large, (iv) **control** over the profession's own qualification and entry procedures, and (v) an altruistic orientation, stressing the value of the profession's service to the community over strictly monetary rewards for the professionals. Professionals enjoy a unique source of **power** within **organizations**, which is rooted in their technical expertise. Nevertheless, doubts about the altruism and lofty motives of professionals have persisted, summed up in Bernard Shaw's mischievous definition of a profession as 'a conspiracy at the expense of laity'. This more cynical view sees professions as labour cartels, which control entry into an occupation through the erection of a variety of barriers, such as over-lengthy traineeships and examinations or the use of incomprehensible jargon to mystify and confuse the non-professionals.

propaganda

An important mechanism for influencing others through the careful manipulation and presentation of **information**. This can involve a selective presentation of facts (being 'economical' with the truth), presenting facts out of context so as deliberately to create a false impression, using emotive **language** (like 'fatherland', 'treason' and so on), powerful **symbols** (like flags and anthems) or **metaphors** (like 'iron curtain'). The Nazis officially recognized propaganda as a function of the state meriting a ministry to itself, headed by the notorious Dr Josef Goebbels. Successful propaganda shares many ingredients with successful **leadership**, notably an ability psychologically to 'read' the **needs** of those who will receive the message, to time and fine-tune the message exactly for the occasion and to build cumulatively on the effect of each message. The line between devious and callous manipulation, on the one hand, and good leadership, through legitimate **influence**, **motivation** and **information** is often a thin one; sometimes it is only a matter of different perspectives. Within **organizations**, propaganda is usually referred to through polite terms like public relations and advertising.

See also **rhetoric**.

psychological contract

The notion of psychological contract refers to the unwritten set of expectations that exist between people in an organization, and is closely related to the concepts of **norm** and **role**. A psychological contract usually goes beyond the letter of the legal contract. It implies that co-workers meet certain mutual expectations and obligations arising from the simple fact that they share the same organizational space and activities. These may include basic courtesies, respecting each other's dignity and worth, working to the spirit rather than letter of the formal work contract, constructive feedback, and providing work which is not demeaning. The nature of the psychological contract sets the spirit and tone of an enterprise, and its development can be crucial to the organization's success and individual well-being.

Schein (1980)

psychological testing

Psychological testing has become a common feature of employee selection and appraisal processes, and vocational guidance. Psychological testing is based on the assumption that key features of our personality can be inferred from our performance on specially devised exercises or questionnaires. The most respectable tests have been carefully structured and tried out on a lot of people in advance, and have extensive 'norms' – population scores against which to compare individual scores. They provide relative measurement, and are restricted in availability to qualified users. Psychologists will judge a test by its published reliability and validity; that is, how consistent it is and how well it predicts behaviour or performance. Tests used in industry may be behavioural simulations – such as measuring performance on a set of 'real' decision-making tasks, under time pressure. Also used are standardized pencil-and-paper questionnaires which tap areas such as interests, specific aptitudes and abilities, and personality qualities.

See also **intelligence, personality**.

Anastasi (1982), Hilgard, Atkinson and Atkinson (1980)

race and racism

Race is a difficult and politically sensitive concept to define. Unlike **ethnic groups**, races are usually thought of as involving some inherited physical characteristics, most notably colour. Yet, physical differences between human groups tend to be far less significant in terms of biology than in terms of the political and symbolic **meanings** attached to them. Nazis tried to develop biological 'theories' of race, mainly as a justification of racist and genocidal practices. Some psychologists have tried to link **intelligence** to race, arguing that this accounts, at least in part, for educational and social inequalities between races. Such arguments approach both race and intelligence as 'scientific concepts', obscuring the extent to which they are both socially defined **constructs**. Race acts as a common basis for negative **stereotyping**, as well as for **prejudice** and **discrimination**. Many organizations seek to overcome these injustices through equal opportunities policies, explicitly denouncing colour, gender and so on as factors in hiring or promoting staff. In the United States and Canada, affirmative action programmes go considerably further by seeking actively to encourage the hiring and promotion of members of disadvantaged groups. This is sometimes achieved through the setting of quotas or the relaxation of qualifications and standards for entry into the organization. Such programmes are at times criticized as undermining the 'best man [sic] for the job' principle. Yet, without active encouragement, past inequalities tend to reproduce themselves. Disadvantaged groups find it difficult to break out of a vicious circle of **powerlessness, prejudice** and **discrimination.** Disadvantages in housing reinforce disadvantages in education, which, in turn, reinforce disadvantages in employment opportunities.

rationality

Rationality is generally thought of as the unique property of human beings to make **decisions** on the basis of careful assessment of **information.** Economists incorporate assumptions of rationality in their theories of economic behaviour, employing a model sometimes referred to as *'rational economic man'*; consumers, for example, will try to get best value for money when faced with a purchasing decision. Max Weber distinguished between two kinds of rationality. Rationality of means implies that, given a certain set of goals, one adopts the optimum means for its achievement, on the basis of careful search, calculation and evaluation of the alternatives. The system of **rules** underpinning **bureaucracy** is rational in as much as it is carefully devised so as to enhance the achievement of organizational **goals.** This type of rationality is based on expert **knowledge** of the alternative courses of **action** available. It is the foundation of technical efficiency, even though it may be applied to entirely evil, insane or arbitrary goals. For example, one can go about very rationally burning down one's own house. The rationality of the ends is the second type of rationality, identified by Weber, though his view is that science is of little help here. Modern economists have argued that the classical criteria for rational action are too strict; if the consumer was intent on buying carrots at the lowest price, he/she would end up spending his/her entire life comparing the prices in different shops. The same goes for organizations. Instead of **decisions** based on absolute rationality, Simon has suggested that they are based on 'bounded rationality'; one makes a decision as soon as one has found a solution which is 'good enough', or 'satisficing'. Rational models of human behaviour, like those favoured by economists and Taylorist management, tend to disregard people's impulsive, **emotional, desiring** and irrational qualities. These are of central importance to certain schools of thought in social psychology (like the **Human Relations** School), and depth psychology.

Weber (1948), Simon (1947), March and Simon (1958)

rationalization

A term used to signify three different things: firstly, increasing the efficiency of an organization by eliminating redundant or non-profitable elements (including departments, operations and people); secondly, the provision of credible or plausible motives for one's **actions** which conceal the real motives – this includes the finding of convenient excuses; and thirdly, the tendency of organizations and societies to shed their traditional, emotional, supernatural, aesthetic and moral qualities in favour of ever increasing concern with economic efficiency.

See also **rationality**.

reality

Berger and Luckmann argue that reality is **socially constructed**. Within a society, there will be a view about what is real, and this will be different in another society. Magic is real within some societies and not others. In some societies, smiling is a sign of aggression. If a visitor thinks that the locals are 'really' being friendly, his/her failure to understand their reality could prove fatal! Kelly and others say that reality is also *personally* constructed. I may live in the same society as you, but still have quite a different view of what is real. I know that my department is the real core of this organization, but you may well think the same of your department. We may share a common social framework, but make different judgements about whether hard work is 'really' worthwhile, or whether there is a God. While reality may be socially and personally constructed, there also seems to be some common reality that we share; if this were not so, would we take the trouble to talk to each other, and to read books written by someone else? Thomas and Thomas, in 1928, said, 'If men define situations as real, they are real in their consequences.' Whether or not I agree with your view of reality, you really will behave as if your view was correct.

See also **objectivity**.

Berger and Luckmann (1967), Kelly (1972), Thomas and Thomas (1928)

Repertory Grid

A device introduced by George Kelly (1905–66) to identify personal constructs. In the original Repertory Grid, a person was presented with three elements – for example three different people, and asked in what way any two of them were similar and different from the third. 'Two of them are . . . whereas the other one is . . . .' The answers to these questions are the two opposite poles of one of that person's constructs. Some have argued that Kelly's genius was as a mathematician, to produce something as neat and effective as the Repertory Grid to provide a clear measurement of personal constructs. Kelly, however, told one of his younger colleagues that he wished he had never invented the Repertory Grid. Apparently this was because of the extent to which Repertory Grid research had proceeded as an easily mechanized and possibly misleading form of psychological research, rather than as a means for discovering personal constructs. The extent to which Repertory Grids are mechanized and appear **objective** has been abused by some researchers and consultants. Instead of discovering the richness of a personal construct system, they have used the Repertory

Grid as just another way of collecting manageable but not necessarily meaningful data.

Kelly (1955), Adams-Webber (1978), Bannister and Fransella (1971)

rhetoric

Rhetoric is the art of persuasion, and is inherent in our use of **language** – conversational and written. The skilled rhetorician learns to shape phrases and select words and **metaphors** in ways which enhance their attractiveness, or accentuate a given message or **meaning**. Politicians are often marked apart by how well they form their rhetoric. Rhetoric is often seen in pejorative terms; it deals with surface appearances and lies. While such interpretations have validity, some academics – who study rhetoric as a discipline – argue that, to a greater or lesser extent, all **reality** is shaped by rhetoric; it is a fundamental part of human **communication**.

See also **influence, propaganda, management of meaning**.

Simons (1989), Billig (1987)

rite of passage

Rites of passage were first documented by anthropologists to describe the way people ritualize and celebrate key social transitions in their communities – such as birth, coming of age, marriage and death. We see, for example, the importance of the barmitzvah in the Jewish tradition where the thirteen-year-old boy becomes a man after reading a specifically prepared piece of the Old Testament within a carefully orchestrated **ritual** in the synagogue. Rites of passage in organizations also mark a change of personal status. They can be informal and/or formal occasions. For example, a craft apprentice can earn full craftsman status by passing formal tests and exams. However, colleagues can also create their own tests – such as by abuse or humiliation. This latter type of rite of passage can be meted out to new recruits in the military, or to new prisoners by their cell mates. In each case the initiate is having to earn his or her new or changed place in the organization by 'passing' or **surviving** the tests. More gently, there is the rite of passage out of the organization after a successful career. The leaver is expected to receive gifts and praise at a ceremony, give thanks, celebrate – and leave.

Kuper (1977), Trice and Beyer (1984)

ritual

A formal **action**, normally repeated in a standardized way. While religion has traditionally been a rich source of rituals, like the Eucharist, organizations too generate rituals. Some of the rituals, like the singing of the company anthem in Japanese corporations, are formal, while others, like the purchasing of a new Rolls-Royce by each incoming Chairman of ICI, are informal. In both cases, the essence of ritual is its **meaning** and **symbolism**. Rituals are generally thought of as having a strong bonding effect, though their compulsive repetitive quality gives them a similarity to certain neurotic traits, like the compulsive washing of hands (itself a form of ritual in several religions). Trice and Beyer have identified six different types of rituals in organizations, including **rites of passage**, rites of degradation and rites of renewal.

Trice and Beyer (1984)

role

A central unit of analysis in sociology and social psychology. It refers to the duties, obligations and expectations which accompany a particular position. We can visualize ourselves as a member of a 'role set', a number of significant people who influence how we should behave – they are our 'role senders'. A married man could have his wife, children, best friend, boss, mother, and clergyman all setting different role expectations for him, which may conflict with, or complement each other – or some mix of the two. At work we may experience role conflict – such as expectations on us to increase productivity without sacrificing quality – two seemingly incompatible demands. Or there is ambiguity of role – unclear or confusing messages about what is expected of us. Reconciling various role demands can be a significant source of **stress**. Students, for example, will often report the enormous pressures they feel in trying to satisfy the academic demands of their different lecturers, while also meeting social obligations that are regarded as an essential part of being a student.

Kahn, Wolfe, Quinn, Snoek and Rosenthal (1964), Brown (1986)

rules

Most organizations have formal rules, governing working hours, safety practices and so on. These rules will often go unchallenged, although on occasions an organizational rule will be challenged as being in conflict with social or national laws; for example, rules about retirement age in some organizations have been challenged as they have come into conflict with laws banning sex discrimination. There are also informal rules; few large companies lay down what their managers should wear. But without being told, the managers do not turn up on Monday morning in the jeans and sweaters they have been wearing over the weekend. Such informal rules operate like **norms**, and those who infringe them are likely to be ridiculed or ignored rather than openly punished. There are also the rules of the **game** of organizational life; in some organizations you are allowed to advertise your individual success, in some you are allowed to boast of having tricked a competitor, whereas in other organizations the same behaviour would not be legitimate.

See also **bureaucracy, rationality**.

Berne (1964)

sabotage

Although infrequently discussed in textbooks, sabotage is reported in numerous empirical studies. Sabotage is the deliberate destruction of the employers' property (including machinery) or more generally the hindering of the work process. In its simplest form, sabotage can be an individual act of defiance, the throwing of the proverbial spanner in the works. However, sabotage is frequently an organized activity aimed at slowing the pace of work or even at re-asserting some **control** over the productive process, especially as a last resort for the **powerless** and disenfranchised.

Beynon (1973), Hyman (1989)

sanctions

More or less coercive measures taken by **groups** and **organizations** to ensure **conformity** with their **norms** and rules. They include formal sanctions (like written warnings, demotion or dismissal) and informal sanctions (like mockery, **jokes** or withdrawal of affection).

scapegoating

In Biblical times, the sins of the Jewish people would be collectively re-assigned to a goat who would then be allowed to wander off into the wild, **symbolically** taking their sins away. From this procedure has come the term 'scapegoating', which usually means blaming one member of a group, or one group within an organization, for everything that goes wrong. It is often used as a means of not confronting what is going wrong. It can be particularly potent and toxic when combined with **stereotyping** and **prejudice**, as some person or group finds themselves blamed for everything simply because they are of a type or race that is currently an object of blame.

Scientific Management

This school of **management** is associated with Frederick Taylor (1856–1915), an American mechanical engineer working at the turn of the century. Taylor, struck by what he regarded as the inefficiency of many production systems, argued that there was one best way to perform any particular task, and that way could be discovered 'scientifically'. Human-machine operations should, therefore, be precisely tracked and measured using time-and-motion studies, standardized tools, individual financial incentives, and close supervision. The handling of pig iron, after having been exposed to the rigours of Taylor's analysis, was re-designed to increase output and decrease waste. The vestiges of Scientific Management can be seen in many of today's mass production and service operations – from cars to hamburgers. Taylor's work partly mirrored the times – high unemployment and cheap, poorly organized, labour – and Taylor himself, an engineer. But he spectacularly failed to recognize the importance of social **needs** at work, non-financial incentives, informal work practices and non-directive supervision.

Rose (1988)

self-presentation

We present our selves differently to different audiences, partly because of the various **roles** we play in life. In other words, we assume the face, mannerism, dress, language and posture that is expected of us. This might mean disguising how we feel or how we want to be. Like the stage actor, we take on the characteristics required of the role. A 'dramaturgical' view of organizational behaviour suggests that much of social life can be regarded as us working, consciously and unconsciously, at our self-presentations, and making them acceptable for various situations and audiences in which we find ourselves. **Problems** occur if (a) we do not know what image is required, (b) we are insufficiently skilled to present the desired image, and/or (c) the required image is uncomfortably different from how we feel.

See also **persona, impression formation**.

Goffman (1959), Giacalone and Rosenfeld (1991)

sex

If it is not identified with sexual intercourse, or used to distinguish between males and females, sex is a rather difficult concept to define. Sex is a quality of whatever arouses **desire**, especially physical desire. It can be sparked by a poster, an image, a person, an item of clothing, a sound, a smell, a word (consider words with instant sexual connotations). Different **cultures** have very different ideas about which things are meant to generate sexual feelings and which not as well as different ideals of physical attractiveness (*see* **interpersonal attraction**). What is certain is that we can learn to respond sexually to a diverse range of stimuli, something which has not escaped the attention of advertisers and marketers. For this reason Germaine Greer has described it as the 'lubricant of consumer society' adding that 'in order to fulfil that function the very character of human **sexuality** itself must undergo special conditioning' (1984:198). The range of consumer items whose appeal is linked to sex is bewildering – from cars to clothes, and from airlines to computer software. The sexualization of everyday objects underlines two important features of **sexuality**. First, activities, objects and states of being that appear to have little sexual content may be symbolic expressions of sexual **desires** and attempts to fulfil these desires in **fantasy**; for example, the desire to appear masculine and virile is expressed in driving a fast car. The car has come to stand for virility, it has become its **symbol**. Second, in Western cultures, fantasy, rather than passion, love or obsession, has emerged as the chief representation of sexuality. It is a shared complex of fantasies rather than as anything else that sex stakes its public terrain.

Freud (1905/1977), Packard (1957), Greer (1984)

sexism

A negative **attitude** or **prejudice** about a person on the basis of their sex. This has been considered mostly in the prejudice that men have about women, where many jobs have been kept as a male preserve. There is little evidence that this has improved significantly; in many professions, women face a 'glass ceiling' – an invisible barrier to how high they can go in their jobs. They are excluded from the informal friendship which is crucial in organizational **politics** and they are often assumed to be less concerned about their work than men, and to be willing to subordinate their careers to the career of their male partner. Underlying this may be the male ego – the enormous need of many men for approval and admiration, and their fear of women who are independent enough not to choose to give them such approval and admiration. Sexism is also found in the prejudice against homosexuals. (For equal opportunities and affirmative action programmes, see **race**.)

Marshall (1984)

sexual harassment

A concept dating from the early 1970s, describing the experience of unwanted attention – physical, or verbal, direct or by innuendo – of a sexual nature. Harassment can range from offensive **language** and **sexist jokes**, the use of exaggerated compliments and negative **stereotypes**, to the use of moral blackmail to extort sexual favours. The victim of sexual harassment is likely to feel anxious and oppressed by what is happening. Most, although not all, reported cases are of men harassing women, and here the issue interacts with the **power** structure of organizations and society – which tends to favour men. A number of studies suggest that harassment is more commonly directed towards those women who are perceived by men as threats. This supports feminist arguments that sexual harassment is not exceptional, nor just an individual's problem, but rather a wider symptom of **power** relations between the **genders**. Sexual harassment is difficult to manage institutionally because of its sensitive and personal nature, fear on behalf of the woman that her complaint will not be taken seriously and may even be ridiculed, and the likelihood of the accusation being contested by the harasser. **Perceptions** may well differ about what was 'only a bit of fun', and there are cultural and sub-cultural differences on what is regarded as acceptable sexual attention in the workplace.

Gutek (1985), DiTomaso (1989)

sexuality

Is the complex of physical bodily **desires** and their expressions. The expressions of sexuality may be physical, emotional, verbal or, even, artistic, but in a direct or indirect way these desires aim at *pleasure*. While the sexuality of most individuals may seem consistent and stable (most desires, for example, directed towards pleasure through heterosexual intercourse), social and psychological research indicates that sexuality is highly complex and variable. In contrast to animal sexuality, which is mechanically linked to instinctual **behaviour**, human sexuality is mediated by desires, a large part of which are either learned or **symbolically** constituted. Sociologists and anthropologists have observed wide variations of sexual behaviour across different cultures and societies. Malinowsky, for example, studied the highly promiscuous sexual behaviour of the Trobrianders, which contrasted sharply with the rigidly controlled behaviour of some of their neighbours. Western **cultures**, it is argued, spotlight one feature of sexuality, **fantasy**, as it is uniquely suitable to the demands of both consumer society and modern organization (see **sex** and **gender**); they also create an obsessive preoccupation with penetrative sex and orgasm as the aim of all sexual activity, at the expense of other forms of pleasurable behaviour. Psychologists have made two important observations regarding human sexuality. Firstly, it is dynamic – it develops through early childhood, going through a number of important stages, where different complications may arise. Freud (1856–1939), in particular, observed four stages of development: (1) the oral, in which most desires focus around the area of the mouth; (2) the anal, when most desires revolve around the control of the bowel movement; (3) the phallic, when the penis and the clitoris come into the centre of sexual feeling; and (4) the genital, which represents the usual terminus of adult sexual development, but incorporates features of the earlier stages. Secondly, it is complex, involving numerous desires, many of which may conflict, and most of which are unconscious. No line between 'normal' and 'perverse' behaviour can be drawn, since the sexuality of 'normal' people invariably contains repressed desires that could be classified as perverse.

Freud (1905/1977), Mitchell (1974)

significant others

We pay more attention to some people than to others. We care strongly about how some people see us, and those people are our significant others. When we are talking in a group of, say, ten people, we are likely to be aware of the reactions of two or at the most three of those people, and the rest are almost like cardboard cut-outs. Some of these people are fairly predictable (if the boss is present, he or she is likely to be a significant other). At other times our choice of who to regard as significant tells us something about our **attitudes** and **values**. If you regard yourself as an egalitarian, but always treat your superiors as significant others, we may wonder how deep your values go. Similarly, men who would be appalled to be described as **sexist** may be surprised by how often the women in a group are not their significant others.

skill

A word that has been taken from activities such as carpentry or playing a musical instrument, to life in organizations. The skills of organizing are less agreed, however. There are social and interpersonal skills involved, as well as political and organizational skills. There are also technical skills in organizations, for example in computer programming or in engineering. One of the ironies of skill is that those who have most of it are often the worst at talking about it. Perhaps this is not surprising; high levels of skill operate at a subconscious level. Those who have more difficulty with exercising a particular skill may have to think about it more, and will thus be more able to talk about it. To work on skill improvement is usually deskilling in the short term. This is because attention is being taken from the situation to the skill in question, and the person is thus distracted from what they are doing. Improvement in the performance comes when the new skill has become natural, that is, sub-conscious. High levels of skill, in sport, martial arts, and probably organizations, may depend on being able to practise and develop the skill in **fantasy**.

See also **deskilling, competencies**.

Strati (1985)

social construction

We speak of organizations as if they were solid, physical realities. However, what we experience, apart from the objects and buildings, are people doing, interacting, talking, meeting, writing, telephoning, and so forth. People create **structures**, plans, objectives, products, changes, committees, departments, status levels, redundancy plans and vacation timetables. All this activity speaks of a socially constructed world comprising much interpersonal work and personal performances. Social constructionism is a philosophy in its own right, and one which puts individuals at the centre of their own universe as architects, more or less, of their own world views and **meaning systems**. The socially constructed organization, however, cannot be understood without an appreciation of how personal realities are subject to the influence of **power, status**, coalitions which protect particular interests, and the **skills** people have in managing interpersonal relations.

Berger and Luckman (1967)

socialization

Socialization is the process by which people become part of a social unit. It is the taking on of the beliefs, **values** and mores of the society or organization to which they belong. Key agents of socialization are parents, teachers, peers and possibly religious officials. Competing hard with these traditional sources are the mass media and entertainment – magazines, television, film, pop stars. From these various sources we learn our national cultural ways, including what is appropriate behaviour for our sex, social class and educational background. Organizational socialization is a microcosm of these processes. Companies seek to mould employees to their way of thinking and doing things. They do this by stressing their values at recruitment stage. These are then reinforced by the joining **rituals, rites of passage**, training, promotional criteria, and various forms of organizational literature. Some companies are known for their heavy-handedness in such efforts, reflecting the desire to create a 'strong' organizational **culture** (for example, IBM, McDonald's, Xerox). Others achieve their aims more subtly: a 'hands off' socialization.

See also **institutionalization**.

Brown (1986), Schein (1978)

stakeholder

A group or individual seen as having some claim on the outcome of a situation. Stakeholders in organizations may be drawn more or less widely, and the decision about who to regard as stakeholders says a lot about an organization's style and **values**. Mason and Mitroff (1981) suggest that a comprehensive list of stakeholders must include those who may react to or express discontent about what is going on; those with relevant responsibilities; those who are regarded as 'important' actors by others; those who are involved in activities related to the situation; those who influence opinions about the issues involved; demographic groups affected by the issue; and people with defined **roles** in the situation. The systematic use of stakeholder analysis has been used as a way of people widening the scope of interested parties whom they consider in a situation.

Mason and Mitroff (1981)

status

Like **role**, status signifies a social position. Yet status goes beyond **role**, as it embodies an evaluation of merit, prestige or honour. Age, gender, birth, education, acquaintances and lifestyles are all important sources of status, though how they affect an individual's status may differ across different **cultures**. A person's job or occupation is an extremely important source of status in our cultures, frequently referred to as 'socio-economic status'. Within organizations, **professionals** and clerical workers usually enjoy superior status to manual workers; they are also more concerned about the social status of their job than manual workers. Status **symbols** are visible signs establishing an individual's or a group's status. A Porsche as well as a Volkswagen Beetle can be status symbols, as are the size of an executive's office, a fashionable pair of trainers, a title such as Sir or Dr, an address in a fashionable part of town, or a badge on a piece of clothing.

stereotyping

This term was introduced by the journalist Walter Lippman in 1922; he described stereotypes as 'pictures in our heads'. Stereotypes have been described by Wilson and Rosenfeld as 'clusters of preconceived notions'. Stereotyping means assuming that all the objects in some category will be similar in ways other than the one used to categorize them. Thus all students do have something in common – they are all studying. Stereotyping would go on from there to assume that all students will have other features in common too, such as all being prone to getting up late, drinking too much and not doing much work. Stereotypes can be positive too; for example, the expectation that all doctors will be intelligent and caring is a positive stereotype. Stereotyping is one of the ways in which **prejudice** operates. People may fall victim to their own stereotypes; managers who are men may start to behave in peculiarly unaware, macho ways because they have absorbed a stereotype that this is how a real manager should behave.

See also **prejudice, attitude, scapegoating**.

Wilson and Rosenfeld (1990)

strategy

Strategies are major courses of action that an organization plans to take in order to meet objectives. At its simplest, and in its military origin, it means looking several steps ahead and considering what to do over a longer term, rather than looking only to the immediate term ('tactics'). Most often, strategies are formulated by the top management team – as an expression of their interests, inclinations and views about the purpose of the business. The process of strategic planning has become central to the operation of many organizations. It involves decisions on the organization's mission in the light of opportunities and threats, and on the long-term outlook for the business. Strategic planning will also include the allocation of resources – money, personnel, plant, land and equipment. Within the overall strategic plan, tactical planning will take place – short-term decisions, such as how a particular department will spend its own budget and achieve its production targets. Much recent research in organizations has been devoted to the process of strategy-making, and to the types of strategy which seem to pay off. The word 'strategy' has become debased in recent years, as the fashion has grown for describing oneself as 'thinking strategically' or working at a 'strategic level'. Those new to reading about organizations should be warned that a number of old ideas have been repackaged and had the label 'strategy' stuck on them, and are now being offered as if they were new.

Baden-Fuller and Stopford (1992), Pennings (1985), Pearce and Robinson (1991)

stress

Stress normally refers to specific unpleasant feelings and/or physical responses that people experience when they are working beyond their capacities and levels of tolerance. The signs and symptoms of stress include anxiety, irritability, fear, skin ailments, high blood pressure, gastric complaints and heart disease. Certain work situations are likely to be potentially more stressful than others, such as where there are high levels of noise, poorly designed equipment, conflicting **role** demands, very high workload, poor support and supervision, and unpredictable changes. One approach to stress management, therefore, lies in improving the design and supervision of work. But the mechanisms of stress are also very individual. It depends on a person's **perception** of how threatening a particular **problem** or situation is, and his or her capacities to cope. Long periods of unresolved stress can lead to **burnout**, even death. In recent years it has become a more acceptable to talk openly about stress problems. Some companies run stress management training programmes and offer counselling support. Yet, a difficulty arises when stress becomes the only permissible way of talking critically about one's job or employer or a catch-all term for all the afflictions caused by modern organizations.

See also **burnout**.

Luthans (1985), Cooper and Marshall (1978), Smith   (1991), Matteson and Ivancevich (1987)

structure

A concept which derives from engineering, where it is used to describe bridges, buildings, towers or other constructions made up of different interconnected components. Structure has come to signify the patterned relations of components which make up any **system**. You can think of the structure as a framework on which different interconnected components are attached; it is not generally easy to alter one component without affecting the others. Organizations have different types of structure; in formal terms some are structured in geographical or product divisions, others in functional areas (such as marketing, finance, personnel and so on) and yet others form **matrix structures**. In more substantial terms, some have rigid mechanical structures dominated by formal **roles**, **rules** and regulations, while others have more informal and flexible structures in which people collaborate and communicate in a less highly **controlled** manner. Some organizations operating in particularly turbulent and uncertain **environments** tend to adopt an extremely fluid task-oriented structure known as adhocracy.

See also **bureaucracy, contingency theories, matrix structure, hierarchy.**

sub-culture

The concept of **culture** originates with societies, as in 'European culture' or 'Amazonian culture'. It was then applied to organizations, where 'organizational culture' meant those distinctive features of one organization which make life in it so different from other organizations. Within organizations you may find quite different sub-cultures. For example, staff in a computer department often follow a different, more relaxed dress code than staff in other departments. The sub-culture of different groups of students within a university, such as engineers and business students, may also be very different, with different **norms** of dress and behaviour. People often become aware of different sub-cultures only when they are with friends from two different sub-cultures at the same time. For example, they are in the company sports club with a friend from a different department, and meet a colleague from their own department. They may then find themselves unsure as to which sub-cultural norms to adopt.

success

An integral part of the Protestant **Work Ethic**, success in the form of material prosperity, fame and honour was regarded as a sign of God's favour and a reward for hard work. Protestantism, according to Max Weber (1864–1920), encouraged a methodical and calculating attitude in the pursuit of wealth, which provided capitalism with the work ethic required for its early growth in the 16th century. Nowadays, success has lost its religious and moral underpinning; it is no longer seen by everybody as the product of hard work, nor is it seen as generating a set of responsibilities and duties towards the community. Instead, some people would regard success as the result of successful planning, clever deals or good luck. Maccoby has argued that the successful businessman of today is essentially one who is good at **games**. Instead of hard **work** or ruthless ambition, cunning and risk-taking are seen as the requirements for success. Although different people may see success differently, it remains a powerful feature of middle-class cultures in the West as well as in the East, as part of a system of **values** which includes self-reliance, individualism, and material well-being but also entrepreneurship and risk. Some individuals may gauge success in terms of visible signs and **symbols** while others may tend to assess it through personal indicators, such as contentment, happiness or love.

Furnham (1990), Maccoby (1976)

survival

In many organizations, people's psychological well-being cannot be taken for granted. Constantly bombarded with **information**, overwhelmed by different demands and requests, worried about the future, surrounded by people whom they hardly know or like, people can find working in large organizations like surviving an assault course. Other more subtle pressures threaten people's identity, integrity or self-respect. In order to survive within an organization, people employ a variety of coping mechanisms. **Jokes, gossip** and griping are safety valves for frustration. Practical jokes and **games** break the monotony of work. Some people distance themselves from the organization, adopting a cynical attitude and seeking to protect their 'patch' or wallowing in nostalgia for a golden past. Others try to survive by identifying fully with the organization, its **goals** and **values**. These people occasionally become very disillusioned and experience profound feelings of disappointment or **burnout**.

See also **stress**.

Hochschild (1983), Schwartz (1987)

symbolism

A symbol is something that 'stands for', or signifies something beyond the literal properties of the symbol itself. So a national flag can symbolize (stand for) a nation, its freedom and independence. A small lapel badge can symbolize membership of an exclusive club or sect. Consumer products are often designed to be attractive for what they stand for as much as, if not more than, for what they actually do. To own a car of a particular make, colour and shape can give others a recognizable sign that you are the sort of person who has 'made it'. Similarly, wearing specific clothes can symbolize one's wealth, youth, status or occupation. The words, deeds and products of organizational managers can be a crucial source of symbolic influence on those whom they manage. The symbols may be very obvious ones, such as the frequency of managers' actual presence and availability; the size, shape and furnishing of their rooms; the style of their memos and announcements; the way they conduct meetings; their **language** and **rhetoric**, the kind of cars they drive; and the salaries they take and award. All these can be taken as symbols of their own values, style and degree of concern for others. Less obvious symbols relate to areas such as trust and reliability – subtle features of the **psychological contract.** Do managers deliver what they promise? Are confidences respected? Is promotion seen to be fair? Inconsistency in managerial symbols can soon undermine people's confidence and enthusiasm. Such as, for example, when bank staff are told they need to live up to the company's public slogan of 'the listening, caring bank', yet these same staff receive little attention or care from their own managers.

See also **meaning, status.**

Czarniawska-Joerges (1992), Turner (1990), Gagliardi (1990)

system

Organizations are often studied as systems. Systems are separated from their **environment** by a boundary which is crossed by inputs and outputs. For example, an organization's inputs from the environment may include raw materials, expertise, and money, while its outputs may include products, services and waste. Systems themselves are seen as made up of components in orderly relationship, each component having specific functions of benefit to the system as a whole. These relations make up the system's **structure.** Biological systems, like animals or plants, are often seen as having sub-systems, such as respiratory or nervous. Generally systems are seen as responding to changes in their **environment**, either by adapting or by seeking to change and **control** their environment. While the concept of a system has been used extensively to describe phenomena as diverse as the solar system, the transport and educational systems of a country, the global ecosystem or an information system, it has been criticized for obscuring **conflict** and disorder, and presenting too tidy and rational an image of the world. This book highlights organizations as terrains in which people make **decisions,** create **meanings,** face choices and experience **emotions;** these are all features which are generally underplayed by systems theory, which in the last resort tends to look at organizations either as machines or as biological organisms.

Keys (1991)

talk

A large part of most people's lives, and in particular, the main part of what managers do. Studies of managerial life by people like Mintzberg and Stewart show that the greater part of managerial activity is conducted through talk. Managers talk for their living as much as teachers or actors do. Relatively little time is spent by managers on their own, and little is done by solitary managers. Talk has been studied as a form of **behaviour** (Beattie), in a process called 'conversational analysis'. In a less behaviourist fashion, recent research has focused on **language** and **rhetoric** (Billig) and **discourse**. Talk is not always serious. People talk and **gossip** for pleasure as well as through necessity; such conversations may be conducted in the spirit of idle chatter, but can still have a considerable impact on later events, when the **information** that was passed on reaches someone who wishes to make use of it. The role of talk and gossip has been grossly understated in most management theorizing, which has seen it as a transparent medium by which messages are conveyed from one person to another. The richness and joy of talk, the **influence** that can be wielded by an effective talker, the activities of the virtuoso talker (who will deliberately offer a brilliant display for the joy of showing that it can be done), the significance of telling stories well, and the role of gossip in keeping informed about what is happening in your organization, are all underemphasized if talk is viewed as simply a functional way of conveying intended **meaning**.

See also **language, gossip**.

Mintzberg (1973), Stewart (1967), Beattie (1983), Billig (1987)

Taylorism *See* **Scientific Management**.

team work

Organizations are full of teams, and many of these spend time considering their team work. Teams are better than individuals on complex tasks which require either more work than one person can give, or more knowledge or **information** than one person will have. They are also important where a task calls for different **roles** or **skills** to be brought into play. But teams can also be arenas for **conflict** which may be of more interest to the members than their task. Since the 1970s, there has been extensive team development work in many organizations, usually with the intention of producing more closely knit teams, and enabling team members to be more open with each other. However, well-developed teams manifest some difficulties. They are prone to 'risky shift' – taking more risky decisions than the members would individually. They are also at risk of '**groupthink**' (Janis), of going along with the opinions of their team mates, whatever their personal doubts. Some practitioners have argued that too much work is done in teams, stifling individualism; they have then offered team destruction as an alternative package to team building.

Janis (1972), Schein (1980)

technology

Ways of mechanizing complex processes to enable them to be done in a more certain way. A list of things you must remember to do would come within this definition of technology, as would a diary, or an **information system**. Technology may relieve you of the **stress** and potential overload of trying to do a task unaided. For a typical example of the double-edged character of technology, a person may be more relaxed when they have offloaded the things they are trying to remember to their action list. At the same time, they are relinquishing some **control** over their life. There would be no point in their having an action list if they did not sometimes look at it and let it have some influence over what they did. Word processors limit where you may sit, and affect your view of the document you are working on. Technology also carries with it a risk of system failure; action lists get lost, central locking on cars fails to function, and computers become infected with viruses. The more technology seems able to help its users, the more likely they are to let it **control** them, and the more they feel lost when systems fail.

See also **contingency theories, information technology, deskilling, alienation**.

Rose (1988)

teleworking

Teleworking is a term applied to people who work at a considerable distance from their customer, client, colleagues or headquarters, but bridge the physical distance by telecommunications technology. Traditionally, the telephone has provided the necessary link, but now sophisticated additions are portable telephones, fax lines, electronic mail and video conferencing. Teleworking offers flexibility over one's place of work, which can range from the corner of a kitchen to the car. Using computer links, people can instantly transmit and edit documents over huge distances, so obviating many face-to-face meetings – and much travel and commuting (hence the phrase 'telecommuter'). The advantages of teleworking can be considerable to those who live in isolated communities, or who wish to avoid congested towns or cities. Large companies can save on expensive overheads by encouraging teleworking. On the other hand some teleworkers feel too tied to the technology, lonely working without colleagues, cramped or stressed at home, and less secure about their work status. Teleworking is suited to some jobs more than others – such as computer software services, journalism, publishing, sales, and some types of consultancy.

See also **information technology**.

Kinsman (1987)

t-group

The t-group ('t' stands for 'training') is a technique used to increase individuals' awareness of their own, and others', motivations and behaviour patterns. In organizations, t-groups are designed to improve the inter-personal effectiveness of people who work in managerial or team situations. The technique has its roots in psychotherapy where individuals are encouraged to confront their feelings, and seek ways of removing the emotional barriers to personal growth and effectiveness. T-groups have no set agenda. Some operate over a long period, helped along by a trainer. The trainer assists the group to examine its own functioning, but offers no hard and fast directions. The ambiguity is very high, and anxiety rises as some members of the group try to impose structure on the others. Interactions can be very confronting, and lay bare people's assumptions, fears and foibles. Research on the effects of t-groups has focused on whether, and what, people are able to learn in such circumstances, and how any **learning** translates to work **performance**. Some people become very disturbed; the groups do have the potential for psychological harm. Others report difficulty in relating their learning to job performance, especially in an organization which is emotionally closed. On balance, t-groups can cause behavioural change, but the picture is confused about whether that change is for good or for ill. However, they are unrivalled in helping people to understand their own feelings and approaches to **authority**.

Smith (1991), Huse and Cummings (1985)

trade unions

Organizations formed by employees to promote their common interests. Trade unions emerged in the early part of the 19th century out of the **powerlessness** of the individual worker when confronted by the **power** of the employer. They grew out of the realization that by forming an association workers could offer mutual protection and improve their conditions of work. Most early unions were craft associations, seeking to limit the supply of labour in skilled trades, thus raising the market value of these **skills**. Gradually, however, industrial unionism shifted the emphasis towards uniform conditions of work and rates of pay through industrial action, like strikes, and **collective bargaining** with the employers. In this way, unions have sought to limit the powers of employers to hire and fire at will, unilaterally to impose conditions of work on a take it or leave it basis, and to guarantee only minimal standards of protection and welfare as part of the terms of employment. In most industrial countries, following periods of acute conflict and confrontation, employers accepted unions as legitimate expressions of their employees' collective interests and recognized the legitimacy of **collective bargaining** as an **institution** for settling **conflicts** of interest. In recent years, however, unions have been on the defensive in Britain and the United States, as a result of (i) economic downturn which has curbed their bargaining **power**, (ii) new **technologies** which have wiped out traditional strongholds of unions in the skilled trades, and (iii) new **management** philosophies which have placed heavy emphasis on the individual employee as a bargaining agent or as a member of a corporate **culture**.

Hyman (1989)

training

Bringing people to high levels of **skill** or new **competencies**. The concepts of training and education are sometimes used interchangeably, but they can have useful distinct meanings. Training is bringing about specific **learnings**, with the expectation that the person who gains them will be able to use them at work more or less straight away. Education implies more personal development: a change in the understanding that the person has of their place in the world. Training is what brings you to competence in a specific technique; you should be able to go out and do something immediately with the results of your training. Education would enable you to respond more actively, to evaluate new techniques in which you are offered training, and to be able to decide when to apply the techniques you have been trained in.

unemployment

The study of unemployment can reveal much about employment, especially the social and psychological features of work that people take for granted. Paid employment has become a central feature of all industrialized societies, and provides a major source of **meaning** for those who work – even in jobs which are dreary and **alienating**. The unemployed often report a loss of time-structure to the day, difficulties with their status and personal identity, a lack of 'place' at home, and more generally a sense of purposelessness and **meaninglessness** in their lives. Poverty, or being less credit-worthy, adds considerably to these difficulties: paid work is one of the few ways of acquiring money to purchase the various commodities which have become essential to survival in modern societies. Often the loss of work can be traumatic, particularly to people who are unable easily to re-enter the workforce because of their age, out-of-date skills, or infirmity. In high-unemployment communities we find school leavers expecting not to work, and pools of long-term unemployed men and women. For some, unemployment can become a way of life, so widely shared in their community that it does not feel a stigma. However, the unemployed can rarely participate in the wealth, opportunity and consumption enjoyed by those who do work, therefore high levels of unemployment can be socially divisive – and have been linked to social unrest and crime.

See also **meaning, work ethic**.

Fineman (1983, 1987)

utilitarianism

Utilitarianism is a system of **ethical** thought associated particularly with the British social philosopher, Jeremy Bentham (1748–1832). Bentham is credited with the 'greatest happiness principle'. This principle, he argued, should govern how we should choose a course of social **action**. We should seek the greatest good for the greatest number of people. So a company should pursue not just its own benefit, but the welfare of all people affected by the company's **decisions**. This could include future generations which might be affected by the company's actions. At the time that Bentham wrote, utilitarianism was a radical view; social legislation had, up until then, tended to favour blatantly a well-heeled minority of citizens. In practice, utilitarian 'good' is usually inferred indirectly through political or economic criteria – such as the number of votes cast for a specific proposal or a price-fall in a product. It is often opposed to the notion of individual 'rights', where certain possibilities should be guaranteed to all individuals, even if this militates against the greatest good of the greatest number.

See also **ethics**.

Bentham (1897), Brady (1990)

values

In the end, what do you care about? What do you think is ultimately important? These are your values. If you ask yourself why you are doing something, take your answer, and keep asking the same question, you end up with a value. Why are you reading this book? To pass the exam. Why do you want to pass the exam? To get a better job. Why do you want a better job? To get more money. Why do you want more money? To feel secure. Why do you want to feel secure? I don't know, I just do. In this case, feeling secure is probably a value. Much of the research on values stems from Rokeach, who said that a value is 'an enduring belief that a specific mode of conduct or end state of existence is personally and socially preferable to alternative modes of conduct or end states of existence' (1973: 159). Some recent debate has questioned whether the noun 'value' can ever be more than a trivial simplification of the activity of human beings caring about what they are doing. The concept of individual values has also been questioned; what people care about is both formed and sustained in a community.

See also **meaning, culture, norm, attitude**.

Rokeach (1973)

work

Unlike **labour**, which is a concept drawn from political economy, work is in the main a sociological and a psychological concept. It incorporates a wide range of cultural **assumptions** regarding what constitutes work, what is the purpose and **meaning** of work, and what its values and rewards are. 'What work do you do?' for example, is a question which cannot be answered without understanding the meaning which a **culture** attributes to work, the expectation of receiving payment or the **status** and prestige of different kinds of work. Different cultures have assigned widely diverging meanings to work and its corollary, leisure. Some have approached it as a primeval curse afflicting humanity, some as the true road to holiness and **success**, and some, like the Ancient Greeks, as a lower form of occupation unworthy of free individuals. Clusters of meanings around work, especially those regarding the relations between work and the good life, are often said to constitute **work ethics**.

work ethic

The notion of 'work ethic' implies a moral driving force in individuals to work; it suggests that people ought personally to labour, producing goods or services. There is debate about the strength and direction of the work ethic in different populations; especially whether it has declined amongst young people. The 'ought' implied in the work ethic is associated with the 17th century rise in Protestantism in Europe where working was regarded as a religious imperative: a prime route to spiritual salvation. The link between Protestantism and business activity was explored extensively by Max Weber (1864–1920) in his influential book *The Protestant Ethic and the Spirit of Capitalism*. The religious roots of the work ethic are today diffused with the broader influences of national and community cultures. We can see significant competing 'ethics' in people's lives, such as leisure and various forms of self-development. Those who lament the apparent decline in the work ethic point to a 'welfare ethic' – people who are now keen to live off the social provisions of the state. Inevitably, however, discussions about the work ethic become intermingled with the availability of jobs, and the extent to which non-workers are personally blamed for their predicament.

See also **success**.

Weber (1958), Furnham (1990)

NOTES

1 See G. Morgan (1986). *Images of Organization*. London: Sage.

2 E. Berne (1964). *Games People Play*. New York: Grove Press.

3 Adapted from D.T. Hall, D.D. Bowen, R.J. Lewicki and F.S. Hall (1978). *Experiences in Manaagement and Organizational Behavior*. Chicago: St Clair Press.

4 S. Milgram (1974). *Obedience to Authority*. New York: Harper and Row.

5 G. Mars (1982). *Cheats at Work: An Anthropology of Workplace Crime*. London: Allen and Unwin.

6 R. Jackall (1988). *Moral Mazes*. New York: Oxford University Press. pp.105–11.

7 R. Jackall (1988). *Moral Mazes*. New York: Oxford University Press. p.109.

8 S.L. Cook (1982). *The Writings of Steve Cook*. ed. K. Bowen, A. Cook and M. Luck. Birmingham: The Operational Research Society.

9 For further details of how this works, see M. Belbin (1981). *Management Teams: Why They Succeed or Fail*. London: Heinemann.

10 B. Russell (1946). *The Philosophy of Bertrand Russell*. ed. P.A. Schilpp. Evanston, IL: Library of Living Philosophers.

11 M. Polanyi (1964). *Personal Knowledge*. New York: Harper and Row.

12 D.A. Kolb, I.M. Rubin and J.M. McIntyre (1979). *Organizational Psychology: An Experiential Approach*. 3rd ed. Englewood Cliffs, NJ: Prentice-Hall.

13 L. Mumford (1934). *Technics and Civilization*. New York: Harcourt, Brace and World.

14 'Artificial intelligence' is the use of computers to imitate and, it is hoped, assist human intelligence. See J. Weizenbaum (1976). *Computer Power and Human Reason: From Judgement to Calculation*. New York: Freeman.

15 K.E. Weick (1985). 'Cosmos vs. chaos: sense and nonsense in electronic contexts', *Organizational Dynamics*, Autumn: 50–64.

16 L. Iacocca (1984). *Iacocca*. London: Bantam Books. p.103.

17 C.I. Barnard (1938). *The Functions of the Executive*. Cambridge, MA: Harvard University Press.

18 R.D. Arvey and J. Campion (1982). 'The employment interview: a summary and review of recent literature', *Personnel Psychology*, 35: 281–322.

19 J. Carlzon (1987). *Moments of Truth*. New York: Harper and Row. p.11.

20 L. Iacocca (1984). *Iacocca*. London: Bantam Books. p.58.

21 M. Argyle (1975). *Bodily Communication*. London: Methuen.

22 A. Hochschild (1983). *The Managed Heart*. Berkeley: University of California Press.

23 H. Hopfl and S. Linstead (1991). 'Nice jumper Jim! Dissonance and emotional labour in a management development programme.' Paper presented at 5th European Congress – The Psychology of Work and Organizations, Rouen, 24–7 March: pp.5–6.

24 A. Hochschild (1983). *The Managed Heart*. Berkeley: University of California Press. p.127.

25 J. Child (1977). *Organizations: A Guide to Problems and Practice*. London: Harper and Row.

26 P. Reason and P. Hawkins (1988). 'Storytelling as inquiry', in P. Reason (ed.), *Human Inquiry in Action: Developments in New Paradigm Research*. London: Sage.

27 P. Tancred-Sheriff (1989). 'Gender, sexuality and the labour process', in J. Hearn, D.L. Sheppard, P. Tancred-Sheriff and G. Burrell (eds), *The Sexuality of Organization*. London: Sage.

28 T.J. Peters and R.H. Waterman (1982). *In Search of Excellence*. New York: Harper and Row.

29 M. Jahoda (1982). *Employment and Unemployment*. Cambridge: Cambridge University Press.

30 H. Gunz (1989). *Careers and Corporate Cultures*. Oxford: Blackwell.

31 A. Hochschild (1989). *The Second Shift*. New York: Viking.

32 M. Weber (1958). *The Protestant Ethic and the Spirit of Capitalism*. New York: Scribner.

33 J.H. Goldthorpe, D. Lockwood, F. Bechhofer and J. Pratt (1968). *The Affluent Worker: Industrial Attitudes and Behaviour*. Cambridge: Cambridge University Press.

34 A. Furnham (1990). *The Protestant Work Ethic*. London: Routledge.

BIBLIOGRAPHY

Adams-Webber, J. (1978). *Personal Construct Theory: Concepts and Applications.* New York: Wiley.

Adorno, T.W., Frenkel-Brunswick, E., Levinson, D. and Sandford, N. (1950). *The Authoritarian Personality.* New York: Harper.

Allison, G.T. (1971). *Essence of Decision: Explaining the Cuban Missile Crisis.* Waltham: Little, Brown.

Allport, G.W. (1958). *The Nature of Prejudice.* Garden City, NY: Doubleday Anchor.

Anastasi, A. (1982). *Psychological Testing.* London: Macmillan.

Argyle, M. (1975). *Bodily Communication.* London: Methuen.

Argyris, C., Putnam, R. and Smith, D. (1985). *Action Science.* San Francisco: Jossey-Bass.

Arvey, R.D. and Campion, J. (1982). 'The employment interview: a summary and review of recent literature', *Personnel Psychology*, 35: 281–322.

Baden-Fuller, C. and Stopford, J. (1992). *Rejuvenating the Mature Business: The Competitive Challenge.* London: Routledge.

Bailey, F.G. (1977). *Stratagems and Spoils.* Oxford: Blackwell.

Bannister, D. and Fransella, F. (1971). *Inquiring Man.* Harmondsworth: Penguin.

Barnard, C.I. (1938). *The Functions of the Executive.* Cambridge, MA: Harvard University Press.

Beattie, G. (1983). *Talk.* Milton Keynes: Open University Press.

Becker, E. (1962). *The Birth and Death of Meaning.* Harmondsworth: Penguin.

Belbin, M. (1981). *Management Teams: Why They Succeed or Fail.* London: Heinemann.

Bennis, W. and Nanus, B. (1985). *Leaders: Strategies for Taking Charge.* New York: Harper and Row.

Bentham, J. (1897). *An Introduction to the Principles of Morals and Legislation.* Oxford: Clarendon Press.

Berger, P.L. and Luckmann, T. (1967). *The Social Construction of Reality.* Harmondsworth: Penguin.

Berne, E. (1964). *Games People Play.* New York: Grove Press.

Beynon, H. (1973). *Working for Ford.* London: Allen Lane.

Billig, M. (1987). *Arguing and Thinking: A Rhetorical Approach to Social Psychology.* Cambridge: Cambridge University Press.

Blackburn, R.M. and Mann, M. (1979). *The Working Class in the Labour Market.* London: Macmillan.

Blauner, R. (1964). *Alienation and Freedom*. Chicago: U. of Chicago Press.

Bly, R. (1990). *Iron John: A Book about Men*. Reading, MA: Addison Wesley.

Brady, F.N. (1990). *Ethical Managing*. New York: Macmillan.

Braverman, H. (1974). *Labor and Monopoly Capital*. New York: Monthly Review Press.

Brown, R. (1986). *Social Psychology*. New York: Free Press.

Bryant, J. (1989). *Problem Management: A Guide For Producers And Players*. Chichester: Wiley.

Bryman, A. (1986). *Leadership and Organizations*. London: Routledge and Kegan Paul.

Burns, T. and Stalker, G.M. (1961). *The Management of Innovation*. London: Tavistock.

Burrell, G. and Morgan, G. (1979). *Sociological Paradigms and Organizational Analysis*. London: Heinemann.

Carlzon, J. (1987). *Moments of Truth*. New York: Harper and Row.

Child, J. (1977). *Organizations: A Guide to Problems and Practice*. London: Harper and Row.

Chodorow, N. (1978). *The Reproduction of Mothering: Psychoanalysis and the Sociology of Gender*. Berkeley: University of California Press.

Chung, K.H. and Megginson, L.C. (1981). *Organizational Behavior: Developing Managerial Skills*. New York: Harper and Row.

Cook, S.L. (1982). *The Writings of Steve Cook*. ed. K. Bowen, A. Cook and M. Luck. Birmingham: The Operational Research Society.

Cooper, C.L. and Marshall, J. (1978). *Understanding Executive Stress*. London: Macmillan.

Cooper, C.L. and Torrington, D.P. (eds) (1981). *After Forty*. Chichester: Wiley.

Cooper, R. and Burrell, G. (1988). 'Modernism, postmodernism and organizational analysis: an introduction', *Organization Studies*, 9 (1): 91–112.

Crompton, R. and Jones, B. (1984). *White Collar Proletariat*. London: Macmillan.

Cummings, L.L. and Schwab, D.P. (1973). *Performance In Organizations*. Glenview, IL: Scott Foresman.

Czarniawska-Joerges, B. (1992). *Exploring Complex Organizations*. Newbury Park, CA: Sage.

Davies, C. (1988). 'Stupidity and rationality: jokes from the iron cage', in C. Powell and G.E.C. Paton (eds), *Humour in Society*. London: Macmillan.

Deal, T.E. and Kennedy, A.A. (1982). *Corporate Cultures*. Reading, MA: Addison Wesley.

Deaux, K. and Wrightsman, L.S. (1984). *Social Psychology in the 80s*. Monterey, CA: Brooks/Cole.

DiTomaso, N. (1989). 'Sexuality in the workplace: discrimination and harassment', in J. Hearn, D.L. Sheppard, P. Tancred-Sheriff and G. Burrell (eds), *The Sexuality of Organization*. London: Sage.

Doray, B. (1988). *From Taylorism to Fordism: A Rational Madness*. London: Free Association Books.

Douglas, T. (1983). *Groups*. London: Tavistock.

Duck, S.W. (ed.) (1982). *Personal Relationships 4: Dissolving Personal Relationships*. New York: Academic Press.

Durkheim, E. (1951). *Suicide*. New York: Free Press.

Edelwich, J. and Brodsky, A. (1980). *Burn-Out*. New York: Human Sciences Press.

Eden, C., Jones, S. and Sims, D. (1983). *Messing About in Problems: An Informal Structured Approach to their Identification and Management*. Oxford: Pergamon.

Eden, C. and Radford, J. (eds) (1990). *Tackling Strategic Problems: The Role of Group Decision Support*. London: Sage.

Festinger, L. and Carlsmith, J. (1959). 'Cognitive consequences of forced compliance', *Journal of Abnormal and Social Psychology*, 58: 203–10.

Fiedler, F. (1967). *A Theory of Leadership Effectiveness*. New York: McGraw-Hill.

Fineman, S. (1983). *White Collar Unemployment*. Chichester: Wiley.

Fineman, S. (1985). *Social Work Stress and Intervention*. Aldershot: Gower.

Fineman, S. (ed.) (1987). *Unemployment: Personal and Social Consequences*. London: Tavistock.

Fineman, S. (1993). *Emotion in Organizations*. London: Sage.

Ford, H. (1923). *My Life and Work*. London: Heinemann.

Foucault, M. (1979). *The History of Sexuality*. New York: Vintage Books.

French, J.R.P. Jr and Raven, B.H. (1959). 'The bases of social power', in D. Cartwright (ed.), *Studies in Social Power*. Ann Arbor: University of Michigan Press.

Freud, S. (1905). *Jokes and their Relation to the Unconscious*. London: Hogarth Press.

Freud, S. (1905/1977). 'Three essays on the theory of sexuality', in *Freud on Sexuality*. Harmondsworth: Penguin.

Furnham, A. (1990). *The Protestant Work Ethic*. London: Routledge.

Gabriel, Y. (1988). *Working Lives In Catering*. London: Routledge.

Gabriel, Y. (1991). 'On organizational stories and myths: why it is easier to slay a dragon than to kill a myth', *International Sociology*, 6/4: 427–42.

Gagliardi, P. (ed.) (1990). *Symbols and Artifacts: Views of the Corporate Landscape*. Berlin: De Gruyter.

Giacalone, R.A. and Rosenfeld, P. (1991). *Applied Impression Management*. Newbury Park, CA: Sage.

Goffman, E. (1959). *The Presentation of Self in Everyday Life*. Garden City, NJ: Anchor.

Goffman, E. (1961). *Asylums*. Garden City, NJ: Anchor.

Goldthorpe, J.H., Lockwood, D., Bechhofer, F. and Pratt, J. (1968). *The Affluent Worker: Industrial Attitudes and Behaviour*. Cambridge: Cambridge University Press.

Goodman, P.S. (1982). *Change in Organizations*. San Francisco: Jossey-Bass.

Gouldner, A.W. (1961). 'Metaphysical pathos and the theory of bureaucracy', in S.M. Lipset and N.J. Smelser (eds), *Sociology: The Progress of a Decade*. Englewood Cliffs, NJ: Prentice-Hall.

Greer, G. (1970). *The Female Eunuch*. London: Granada.

Greer, G. (1984). *Sex and Destiny: The Politics of Human Fertility*. London: Secker and Warburg.

Gunz, H. (1989). *Careers and Corporate Cultures*. Oxford: Blackwell.

Gutek, B.A. (1985). *Sex and the Workplace: Impact of Sexual Behavior and Harassment on Women, Men and Organizations*. San Francisco: Jossey-Bass.

Hall, D.T. (1986). *Career Development in Organizations*. San Francisco: Jossey-Bass.

Hall, D.T., Bowen, D.D., Lewicki, R.J. and Hall, F.S. (1978). *Experiences in Management and Organizational Behavior*. Chicago: St Clair Press.

Handy, C.B. (1976). *Understanding Organizations*. Harmondsworth: Penguin.

Harré, R. and Secord, P.F. (1972). *The Explanation of Social Behaviour*. Oxford: Blackwell.

Harri-Augstein, S. and Thomas, L. (1991). *Learning Conversations*. London: Routledge.

Harrison, E.F. (1981). *The Managerial Decision-Making Process*. 2nd ed. Boston, MA: Houghton Mifflin.

Harrison, R. (1972). 'How to describe your organization', *Harvard Business Review*, Sept–Oct.

Harvey-Jones, J. (1988). *Making it Happen*. Glasgow: Fontana.

Hearn, J. and Parkin, P.W. (1987). *'Sex' at 'Work': The Power and Paradox of Organization Sexuality*. Brighton: Wheatsheaf.

Hearn, J., Sheppard, D.L., Tancred-Sheriff, P. and Burrell, G. (eds) (1989). *The Sexuality of Organization*. London: Sage.

Hellriegel, D., Slocum, J.W. and Woodman, R.W. (1992). *Organizational Behavior*. St Paul, MN: West.

Herzberg, F., Mausner, B. and Snyderman, B. (1959). *The Motivation to Work*. New York: Wiley.

Hewitt, J. (1984). *Self and Society: A Symbolic Interactionist Social Psychology*. 3rd ed. Boston: Allyn and Bacon.

Hickson, D.J. (1990). 'Politics permeate', in D.C. Wilson and R.H. Rosenfeld (eds), *Managing Organizations*. London: McGraw-Hill. pp. 175–81.

Hilgard, E.R., Atkinson, R.C. and Atkinson, R.L. (1980). *Introduction to Psychology*. New York: Harcourt Brace and Jovanovich.

Hochschild, A. (1983). *The Managed Heart*. Berkeley: University of California Press.

Hochschild, A. (1989). *The Second Shift*. New York: Viking.

Hopfl, H. and Linstead, S. (1991). 'Nice jumper Jim! Dissonance and emotional labour in a management development programme'. Paper presented at 5th European Congress – The Psychology of Work and Organizations, Rouen, 24–7 March.

Hovland, C., Janis, I. and Kelley, H.H. (1953). *Communication and Persuasion*. New Haven: Yale University Press.

Howe, I. (1986). 'The spirit of the times: greed, nostalgia, ideology and war', *Dissent*, 33/4: 413–25.

Huse, E.F. and Cummings, T.G. (1985). *Organization Development and Change*. St. Paul, MN: West.

Hyman, R. (1989). *Strikes*. Basingstoke: Macmillan.

Iacocca, L. (1984). *Iacocca*. London: Bantam Books.

Jackall, R. (1988). *Moral Mazes*. New York: Oxford University Press.

Jahoda, M. (1982). *Employment and Unemployment*. Cambridge: Cambridge University Press.

Janis, I. (1972). *Victims of Groupthink*. Boston, MA: Houghton Mifflin.

Kahn, R.L., Wolfe, D.M., Quinn, R.P., Snoek, J.D. and Rosenthal, R.A. (1964). *Organizational Stress: Studies in Role Conflict and Ambiguity*. New York: Wiley.

Kanter, R.M. (1977). *Men and Women of the Corporation*. New York: Basic Books.

Kanter, R.M. (1984). *The Change Masters*. London: Unwin Hyman.

Kanter, R.M. (1989). *When Giants Learn to Dance*. London: Simon and Schuster.

Katz, D. and Kahn, R.L. (1978). *The Social Psychology of Organizations*. 2nd ed. New York: Wiley.

Keen, S. (1992). *Fire in the Belly: On Being a Man*. London: Piatkus.

Kelley, H.H. (1950). 'The warm–cold variable in first impressions of persons', *Journal of Personality*, 18: 431–9.

Kelley, H.H. (1972). 'Attribution in social interaction', in E.E. Jones, D.E. Kanouse, H.H. Kelley, R.E. Nisbett, S. Valins and B. Weiner (eds), *Attribution: Perceiving the Causes of Behaviour*. Morristown, NJ: General Learning Press. pp. 1–26.

Kelly, G.A. (1955). *The Psychology of Personal Constructs. Vol. 1. A Theory of Personality*. New York: Norton.

Kelly, G.A. (1972). *A Theory of Personality*. New York: Norton.

Keys, P. (1991). *Operational Research and Systems: The Systemic Nature of Operational Research*. New York: Plenum.

Kinsman, F. (1987). *The Telecommuters*. Chichester: Wiley.

Kleinke, C.L. (1986). *Meeting and Understanding People: How to Develop Competence in Social Situations and Expand Social Skills*. New York: Freeman.

Kolb, D.A., Rubin, I.M. and McIntyre, J.M. (1979). *Organizational Psychology: An Experiential Approach*. 3rd ed. Englewood Cliffs, NJ: Prentice-Hall.

Kuper, A. (1977). *Anthropology and Anthropologists*. London: Routledge and Kegan Paul.

Landfield, A.W. (1971). *Personal Construct Systems in Psychotherapy*. Chicago: Rand McNally.

Leavitt, H.J. (1951). 'Some effects of certain communication patterns on group performance', *Journal of Abnormal and Social Psychology*, 46: 38–50.

Levinson, D. (1979). *The Seasons of Man's Life*. New York: Ballantine.

Lewis, C. (1985). *Employee Selection*. London: Hutchinson.

Lewis, S. and Cooper, C. (1989). *Career Couples*. London: Unwin.

Lukes, S. (1975). *Power: A Radical View*. London: Macmillan.

Luthans, F. (1985). *Organizational Behavior*. New York: McGraw-Hill.

Maccoby, M. (1976). *The Gamesman*. New York: Simon and Schuster.

Mangham, I.L. (1986). *Power and Performance In Organizations: An Exploration of Executive Process*. Oxford: Blackwell.

Mangham, I.L. and Pye, A.J. (1991). *The Doing of Managing*. Oxford: Blackwell.

March, J.G. and Simon, H.A. (1958). *Organizations*. New York: John Wiley.

Mars, G. (1982). *Cheats at Work: An Anthropology of Workplace Crime*. London: Allen and Unwin.

Mars, G. and Nicod, M. (1984). *The World of Waiters*. London: Allen and Unwin.

Marshall, J. (1984). *Women Managers: Travellers in a Male World*. Chichester: Wiley.

Marx, K. (1975). *Early Writings*. Harmondsworth: Penguin.

Maslow, A.H. (1943). 'A Theory of Human Motivation', *Psychological Review*, 50: 654–61.

Mason, R.O. and Mitroff, I.L. (1981). *Challenging Strategic Planning Assumptions*. New York: Wiley.

Matteson, M.T. and Ivancevich, J.M. (1987). *Controlling Work Stress*. San Francisco: Jossey Bass.

Mayer, J.P. (1956). *Max Weber and German Politics.* London: Faber.

McClelland, D.C. (1961). *The Achieving Society.* New York: Van Nostrand.

McLean, A., Sims, D., Mangham, I. and Tuffield, D. (1982). *Organization Development In Transition: Evidence of An Evolving Profession.* Chichester: Wiley.

Michels, R. (1949). *Political Parties.* New York: Free Press.

Milgram, S. (1974). *Obedience To Authority.* New York: Harper and Row.

Mintzberg, H. (1973). *The Nature of Managerial Work.* New York: Harper and Row.

Mintzberg, H. (1983). *Structure In Fives: Designing Effective Organizations.* Englewood Cliffs, NJ: Prentice-Hall.

Mitchell, J. (1974). *Psychoanalysis and Feminism.* Harmondsworth: Penguin.

Morgan, G. (1986). *Images of Organization.* London: Sage.

Morita, A. (1987). *Made In Japan.* London: Collins.

Mouzelis, N. (1975). *Organisation and Bureaucracy.* London: Routledge.

Mumford, L. (1934). *Technics and Civilization.* New York: Harcourt, Brace and World.

Oakley, A. (1972). *Sex, Gender and Society.* London: Temple Smith.

Packard, V. (1957). *The Hidden Persuaders.* Harmondsworth: Penguin.

Pearce, J.A. and Robinson, R.B. (1991). *Strategic Management.* Homewood, IL: Irwin.

Pennings, J.M. (1985). *Organizational Strategy and Change.* San Francisco: Jossey-Bass.

Peters, T.J. and Waterman, R.H. (1982). *In Search of Excellence.* New York: Harper and Row.

Pfeffer, J. (1981). *Power in Organizations.* Marshfield, MA: Pitman.

Pines, A. and Aronson, E. (1988). *Career Burnout.* New York: Free Press.

Polanyi, M. (1964). *Personal Knowledge.* New York: Harper and Row.

Pondy, L.R. (1967). 'Organizational conflict: concepts and models', *Administrative Science Quarterly*, 12: 296–320.

Potter, J. and Wetherell, M. (1987). *Discourse and Social Psychology: Beyond Attitudes and Behaviour.* London: Sage.

Radford, K.J. (1986). *Strategic and Tactical Decisions.* Toronto: Holt McTavish.

Reason, P. (1988). *Human Inquiry in Action: Developments in New Paradigm Research.* London: Sage.

Reason, P. and Hawkins, P. (1988). 'Storytelling as inquiry', in P. Reason (ed.), *Human Inquiry in Action: Developments in New Paradigm Research.* London: Sage.

Reed, M. and Hughes, M. (eds) (1992), *Rethinking Organization.* London: Sage.

Rokeach, M. (1973). *The Nature of Human Values.* New York: Free Press.

Rose, M. (1988). *Industrial Behaviour.* Harmondsworth: Penguin.

Rosnow, R.L. (1980). 'Psychology in rumor reconsidered', *Psychological Bulletin*, May: 578–91.

Russell, B. (1946). *The Philosophy of Bertrand Russell.* ed. P.A. Schilpp. Evanston, IL: Library of Living Philosophers.

Schein, E.H. (1978). *Career Dynamics.* Reading, MA: Addison-Wesley.

Schein, E.H. (1980). *Organizational Psychology.* 3rd ed. Englewood Cliffs, NJ: Prentice-Hall.

Schein, E.H. (1985). *Organizational Culture and Leadership.* San Francisco: Jossey-Bass.

Schwartz, H.S. (1987). 'Anti-social actions of committed organizational participants: an existential psychoanalytic perspective', *Organization Studies*, 8/4, 327–40.

Schwartz, H.S. (1988). 'The symbol of the space shuttle and the degeneration of the American dream', *Journal of Organizational Change Management*. 1/2: 5–20.

Selznik, P. (1957). *Leadership and Administration*. New York: Harper and Row.

Sherif, M. (1966). *In Common Predicament: Social Psychology of Intergroup Conflict and Cooperation*. Boston, MA: Houghton Mifflin.

Simon, H.A. (1947). *Administrative Behavior*. New York: Macmillan.

Simons, H.W. (1989). *Rhetoric in the Human Sciences*. London: Sage.

Sims, D. (1985). 'Fantasies and the location of skill', in A. Strati (ed.), *The Symbolics of Skill*. Trento: University of Trento Press. pp. 12–17.

Sims, D. (1986). 'Mental simulation: an effective vehicle for adult learning', *International Journal of Innovative Higher Education*, 3: 33–5.

Skinner, B.F. (1966). 'An operant analysis of problem solving', in B. Kleinmuntz (ed.), *Problem Solving: Research, Method and Theory*. New York: Wiley. pp. 225–58.

Smith, M. (ed.) (1991). *Analysing Organizational Behaviour*. London: Macmillan.

Snyder, M. (1987). *Public Appearances Private Realities: The Psychology of Self-monitoring*. New York: Freeman.

Spencer, A. and Podmore, D. (1987). *In a Man's World*. London: Tavistock.

Srivastva, S. (1986). *Executive Power*. San Francisco: Jossey-Bass.

Steers, R.M. and Porter, L.W. (eds) (1987 4th ed/1975 1st ed). *Motivation and Work Behavior*. 4th ed. New York: McGraw-Hill.

Stewart, R. (1967). *Managers and Their Jobs*. London: Macmillan.

Strati, A. (ed.) (1985). *The Symbolics of Skill*. Trento: University of Trento Press.

Tancred-Sheriff, P. (1989). 'Gender, sexuality and the labour process', in J. Hearn, D.L. Sheppard, P. Tancred-Sheriff and G. Burrell (eds), *The Sexuality of Organization*. London: Sage.

Thomas, W.I. and Thomas, D.S. (1928). *The Child in America: Behavior Problems and Programs*. New York: Knopf.

Tichy, N.M. and Fombrun, C. (1979). 'Network analysis in organizational settings', *Human Relations*, 32: 923–65.

Torbert, W. (1987). *Managing the Corporate Dream*. Homewood IL: Dow Jones-Irwin.

Trice, H.M. and Beyer, J.M. (1984). 'Studying organizational cultures through rites and ceremonials', *American Management Review*, 9: 653–69.

Turner, B. (1990). *Organizational Symbolism*. Berlin: de Gruyter

Vernon, P.E. (1979). *Intelligence: Heredity and Environment*. San Francisco: Freeman.

Walton, C.W. (1988). *The Moral Manager*. New York: Harper.

Warr, P.B. (1987). *Psychology at Work*. Harmondsworth: Penguin.

Weber, M. (1948). *From Max Weber: Essays in Sociology*. ed. H.H. Gerth and C. Wright Mills. London: Routledge.

Weber, M. (1958). *The Protestant Ethic and the Spirit of Capitalism*. New York: Scribner.

Weick, K.E. (1985). 'Cosmos vs. chaos: sense and nonsense in electronic contexts', *Organizational Dynamics*, Autumn: 50–64.

Weizenbaum, J. (1976). *Computer Power and Human Reason: From Judgement to Calculation*. New York: Freeman.

Wilson, D.C. and Rosenfeld, R.H. (1990). *Managing Organizations: Texts, Readings and Cases*. London: McGraw-Hill.

Wolf, N. (1990). *The Beauty Myth*. London: Chatto and Windus.

Woodward, J. (1965). *Industrial Organization: Theory and Practice*. Oxford: Oxford University Press.

Wright, P.L. and Taylor, D.S. (1984). *Improving Leadership Performance*. London: Prentice-Hall.

INDEX